Urban Destination Marketing in Contemporary Europe

ASPECTS OF TOURISM

Series Editors: Chris Cooper, *Oxford Brookes University, UK*, C. Michael Hall, *University of Canterbury, New Zealand* and Dallen J. Timothy, *Arizona State University, USA*

Aspects of Tourism is an innovative, multifaceted series, which comprises authoritative reference handbooks on global tourism regions, research volumes, texts and monographs. It is designed to provide readers with the latest thinking on tourism worldwide and push back the frontiers of tourism knowledge. The volumes are authoritative, readable and user-friendly, providing accessible sources for further research. Books in the series are commissioned to probe the relationship between tourism and cognate subject areas such as strategy, development, retailing, sport and environmental studies.

Full details of all the books in this series and of all our other publications can be found on http://www.channelviewpublications.com, or by writing to Channel View Publications, St Nicholas House, 31–34 High Street, Bristol BS1 2AW, UK.

ASPECTS OF TOURISM: 66

Urban Destination Marketing in Contemporary Europe

Uniting Theory and Practice

John Heeley

CHANNEL VIEW PUBLICATIONS
Bristol • Buffalo • Toronto

To Ali, Stephen, Gillian and Jennifer, with all my love

Library of Congress Cataloging in Publication Data
A catalog record for this book is available from the Library of Congress.
Heeley, John
Urban Destination Marketing in Contemporary Europe: Uniting Theory and Practice/
John Heeley.
Aspects of Tourism: 66
Includes bibliographical references and index.
1. Tourism—Europe—Marketing. 2. City promotion—Europe. I. Title.
G155.E8H46 2015
338.4'7914–dc23 2014039869

British Library Cataloguing in Publication Data
A catalogue entry for this book is available from the British Library.

ISBN-13: 978-1-84541-493-1 (hbk)
ISBN-13: 978-1-84541-492-4 (pbk)

Channel View Publications
UK: St Nicholas House, 31–34 High Street, Bristol BS1 2AW, UK.
USA: UTP, 2250 Military Road, Tonawanda, NY 14150, USA.
Canada: UTP, 5201 Dufferin Street, North York, Ontario M3H 5T8, Canada.

Website: www.channelviewpublications.com
Twitter: Channel_View
Facebook: https://www.facebook.com/channelviewpublications
Blog: www.channelviewpublications.wordpress.com

The policy of Multilingual Matters/Channel View Publications is to use papers that are
natural, renewable and recyclable products, made from wood grown in sustainable for-
ests. In the manufacturing process of our books, and to further support our policy, prefer-
ence is given to printers that have FSC and PEFC Chain of Custody certification. The FSC
and/or PEFC logos will appear on those books where full certification has been granted
to the printer concerned.

Typeset by Techset Composition India (P) Ltd., Bangalore and Chennai, India.
Printed and bound in Great Britain by Short Run Press Ltd.

He felt himself at last beginning to be a teacher, which is simply a man to whom his book is true, to whom is given a dignity of art that has little to do with his foolishness or weakness or inadequacy as a man.

John Williams (1965) *Stoner*

Contents

Figures

Tables

Acknowledgements

My wife Alison has played an important supporting role in the writing of this book, transcribing recorded interviews, close-editing the text and commenting on it from the all-important perspective of the lay person. A colleague at Sheffield Hallam University, Paul Fallon, proofread a first draft, and otherwise encouraged me. I am hugely grateful to the 21 urban destination marketing professionals who unstintingly gave of their valuable time to take part in the interviews which form the empirical heart of this book. They spoke candidly and with much passion and pride about their work, enabling me to portray 'in their own words' (and 'warts and all') the praxis of urban destination marketing as it is being undertaken in Europe in the early part of the 21st century. Particular thanks are due to Aileen Crawford, Claes Bjerkne, Fritz Craft, Gillian Cruddas, David James, Camilla Nymen, Martin Peters and Scott Taylor for stimulating and otherwise irrigating my mind. I am also grateful to professors Anne Gregory, Bill Bramwell and Chris Cooper for pointing me in the direction of the sayings of Abraham Lincoln, 'globalisation' and 'service sector dominant logic', respectively. The broadly sociological 'in their own words' mode of narrative adopted in the book, and the related concern with paradigms and ultimate 'truth', reflect my formal education at school and university in which my thinking was greatly influenced by the writings of Albert Camus and Thomas S. Kuhn.

Foreword

Picture a scene that will be familiar to many. It might be a coffee break during a conference or small talk at a cocktail party. The dreaded question – 'so what do you do?' That alone is bad enough as you know the answer will require a lengthy explanation to impress upon the enquirer the vital importance of place marketing. How many destination marketing practitioners default to saying 'it's like a tourist board'?

However, many a time I have downed an over-hot coffee risking serious burns to the throat in order to be able to move on before the usually inevitable follow-on question is delivered: 'Do you ever wish you looked after a place that was easier to sell?'

You know the person in front of you means York, Bath, Edinburgh, but do you really want to enter into a long conversation about the common intricacies of developing the visitor economy in *any* destination, regardless of what natural advantages they may seem to have? Downing the coffee and moving on swiftly is usually the best option.

For as long as I can remember, case studies, textbooks and received wisdom in tourism and place marketing have drilled into us that unless we are able to replicate what was achieved in the past by the likes of Bradford and Glasgow then we will retire as failures. I'm sure I'm not alone in having been told too many times by colleagues and stakeholders 'can't we just do what they did in . . . ?'

I've known and worked alongside John Heeley for many years. Our views on tourism and the approaches we have adopted towards place marketing have differed at times, but there are few people I enjoy discussing the subject with more. It was in slightly hushed tones during such a discussion a while ago that he raised the unthinkable: 'What if we've all been pursuing something that's wrong?'

Like colleagues across the UK and beyond, I've been involved in my fair share of destination branding exercises and the eternal search for a 'USP'. Brands, logos and straplines have come and have gone. What remains in the more astute destinations are strong foundations of tactical tourism development and marketing that drive new business, growth and expansion. The

'Stay, Play and Explore' campaign initiated by my organisation and referred to in this book is one such initiative.

As John and I started to unpack thoughts on competitive advantage, I was reminded of a conversation with a larger-than-life tourism PR guru from way back who achieved amazing national coverage for a rather revolutionary short-break package at a hotel he worked with. He admitted that in spite of a level of coverage we would all dream of, not a single booking for the break in question had been received. 'It's a good thing really,' he said. 'As the package doesn't actually exist. But occupancy levels at the hotel have gone through the roof.'

Could it be that the successes of Glasgow and Bradford and others was more to do with the 'noise' that surrounded the destinations rather than a specific strategic approach they were taking? What if the success of the destination practitioners was that they got everyone talking about those places – a point the author takes up at the beginning and towards the very end of this book.

We can all be guilty of becoming so immersed in the day-to-day pressures of the job that we neglect to step back and really think about what we are doing and why, and this is why this text is as thought-provoking as it is insightful and timely. The first half of the book 'tells it like it is', illustrated with comments from destination marketing practitioners like myself. In the second part we lose and then regain perspectives within which our world of urban destination marketing may be conceptualised and understood. For these reasons alone, *Urban Destination Marketing in Contemporary Europe: Uniting Theory and Practice* deserves to be widely read and highly respected. Most importantly, however, in tackling the 'unthinkable', there is revolutionary food for thought here – for academics as well as practitioners.

May I end with a plea? If you ever come across me at a conference or cocktail party, feel free to talk about global warming, world politics or quantum physics. Just don't ask me what I do.

Martin Peters
Chief Executive, Leicester Shire Promotions

Preface: Bradford, 1980–2014

> *One theory was so far out in front of all the others ... It became*
> *what we knew.*
> James Robertson (2013) *The Professor of Truth*

> *Led by a new paradigm, scientists adopt new instruments and look in new*
> *places ... scientists see new and different things when looking with familiar*
> *instruments in places they have looked before. It is rather as if the*
> *professional community had been suddenly transported to another planet*
> *where familiar objects are seen in a different light and are joined by*
> *unfamiliar ones as well. ... What were ducks in the scientist's world before*
> *the revolution are rabbits afterwards.*
> Thomas S. Kuhn (1962) *The Structure of Scientific Revolutions*

In 1980 something quite remarkable appeared to be happening in the world of urban destination marketing. Tourists started visiting a rather bleak and nondescript northern industrial city in England known as Bradford. Their arrival was down to an enterprising local government officer, Eddie Fenn, who headed up a small marketing section from within the local authority's Economic Development Unit (EDU). Based on its industrial heritage and nearby literary associations, Fenn reasoned that Bradford had 'something to sell' and that he could make an 'impact on the market' (Fenn, 1988: 61). Utilising £100,000 of municipal 'seed-corn' monies, he established a destination marketing organisation (DMO) as a self-contained entity within the EDU. So it was that in 1980 this DMO began to promote weekend breaks in Bradford; initially these featured the city's industrial past and its proximity to nearby Haworth with its Bronte sisters' connections. Modest numbers bought into these packages: 2000 in that first year. However, the media coverage generated by the arrival of tourists in Bradford was significant, albeit on a UK-wide only basis, and with a rather predictably negative 'shock-horror' storyline along the following lines: 'Would you believe people are actually choosing to spend their hard-earned cash taking holidays in a northern industrial town?' Further themed packages were developed, notably 'Flavours of Asia', as well as ones associated with the TV series *Last of the Summer Wine* and *Emmerdale Farm*.

By the end of the decade and well into the next, the so-called 'Bradford story' had become a much talked-about urban destination marketing success. Academics used it as an exemplar of how tourism could be attracted to so-called 'difficult areas' (Buckley & Witt, 1985), consultants trumpeted it as best practice and advised other places to follow suit, tourist industry institutions heaped prestigious awards upon it (the author himself was among the judges making one such award!), and towns and cities queued up to replicate it. Eddie Fenn's simple and direct message was to package and sell:

> The basic rule is develop products (in this case holiday packages) that the consumer wants – then tell those consumers about your products and keep telling them. After all, holidays are competing for a share of the consumer's expendable income. (Fenn, 1988: 65)

In this way, the 'Bradford story' became a role model for urban tourism marketing with its two reassuring subplots. First, it appeared that even the most unlikely of urban locations could succeed in tourism, as long as they energetically marketed a convenient unique selling point (USP) or two. In 1985, no fewer than 28,000 Bradford short-break packages were reputedly sold by the ground-handling agencies to which EDU outsourced this work (Fenn, 1988: 63). Secondly, success could be achieved more or less 'on the cheap'. For sure, £100,000 (£250,000 in 2014 monies) must have seemed a relatively small price to pay for the delivery of urban tourism and the resultant boost to the local economy. For the year 1985, Fenn cited the value of overnight stay leisure tourism to the Bradford economy as being in the region of £4.5 million, thereby positing a rate of return on the ongoing municipal revenue investment of 1:45 (Fenn, 1988: 63).

I first met Eddie Fenn in 1986 when we shared a platform at a conference held in Belfast. By then, Eddie had 'moved on' and was Head of Public Relations and Marketing at Wakefield Metropolitan District Council, although it was noteworthy that his conference paper addressed nothing other than the 'Bradford story'. Our paths crossed again four years later when I pipped him to the newly created post of Director of Tourism for the City of Sheffield. At the final interview, I can vouch for the fact that Eddie was still telling that same story! Six months on from that, I started my career as an urban destination marketing practitioner, taking strength from the 'Bradford story' with its demonstration that every place could find a suitably priced niche for itself in tourism. The 'Bradford story' made sense to me from the perspective of the academic community I had just left, and the practitioner one I had just joined. As per the title quote to this Preface, Bradford's tourism success had become part and parcel of 'what we knew' and of how we saw and understood the world of urban destination marketing. Moreover, there was a real sense in which the 'Bradford story' was what we all – academics and practitioners alike – *wanted* to believe. In this book, I style this particular 'way of seeing' and understanding urban destination marketing as the 'theory of marketing competitive advantage', and henceforth I will use the term paradigm to denote such a perspective. As defined by Thomas Kuhn in his seminal essay entitled *The Structure of Scientific Revolutions*, a paradigm 'stands for the entire constellation of beliefs, values, techniques, and so on shared by members of a given community' (Kuhn, 1970: 175).

As I write this book, I now view the 'Bradford story' less as a formula for success and more as a clever, yet ultimately ephemeral, piece of PR opportunism – a flawed panacea if ever there was one, whose beneficial and otherwise regenerative effects were certainly short lived and probably much exaggerated. In practice, there are no easy shortcuts and 'quick-win' solutions leading to success in urban tourism marketing. Rather, the marketing of urban destinations – as this book demonstrates – is a marathon as opposed to a sprint, and it is one in which the participating DMOs must overcome powerful obstacles and constraints if they are ever to cross the finishing line. As one of the DMO chiefs interviewed for this book opines: 'There are many shortcuts to failure, but there are no shortcuts to true success' (Nymen, 2013).

Success in urban tourism is, then, quintessentially problematic. Reflecting this, the 'Bradford story' is nowadays more or less forgotten, and any serious evaluation would surely conclude that its legacy is at best a marginal one. Indeed, it is instructive briefly to chart how Bradford's pioneering foray into urban destination marketing evolved from the 1990s onwards. In 1990, Bradford City Council was obliged by central government to make a series of year-by-year reductions to its budget. The political inclination of the Council's ruling Labour Group was to prioritise and protect so-called 'pavement issues', especially environmental health, housing, education and social services. The other side of the coin was to 'rationalise' (i.e. cut) non-statutory and therefore discretionary activities such as destination marketing. There followed a period of introspection and debate in which the political leadership of Bradford City Council and its senior officers began to voice doubts as to whether the 'Bradford story' had really been as successful as had originally been made out. The city's image appeared as poor as ever, as did its fragile economy. Its hotels base remained stubbornly small. Moreover, as other towns and cities across the length and breadth of Europe jumped on to what became the urban tourism bandwagon of the 1990s (Heeley, 2011: Chapter 1), the novelty value of Bradford's pioneering short-break packages quickly wore thin. An academic piece reviewing the city's trail-blazing efforts in the field of urban destination marketing highlighted the emergent problem areas, including 'the difficulty in collecting data to prove whether or not tourism contributes to the local economy' (Hope & Klemm, 2001: 634). EDU claims that Bradford was now selling upward of 30,000 packages each year, as well as hosting in the region of six million overseas tourists, were being greeted with increasing scepticism (Hope & Klemm, 2001: 634).

In 1995, the City Council effectively disengaged itself from the tourism policy it had so enthusiastically embraced in the 1980s, serving redundancy notices on all but one of the six staff then employed in the DMO, and consigning the remaining officer to work on business as opposed to leisure tourism promotions. In effect, there was now 'nobody doing active marketing' (Tillotson, 2014). A year before the dismemberment of the DMO, the travel writer Bill Bryson had written trenchantly about the realities and reputation of Bradford as a tourism destination:

> I reached Bradford in plenty of time – nearly three hours early, in fact, which made me tremble, for what is one to do in Bradford with three hours to kill? Bradford's role in life is to make every place else in the world look better in comparison, and it does this very well. Nowhere on this trip would I see a city more palpably forlorn. Nowhere would I pass more vacant shops ... Bradford seemed steeped in a perilous and irreversible decline. Once this was one of the greatest congregations of Victorian architecture anywhere, but you would scarcely guess it now. (Bryson, 1997: 196–197)

Having destroyed so much of that fine architecture, Bryson castigated the municipal authority for the 'ironic' and 'pathetic' manner in which it was now 'desperately trying to promote their meagre stock of old buildings' (Bryson, 1997: 198). He also alluded to an emergent 'dark tourism' reputation as the place where 'the Yorkshire Ripper (a sadistic serial murderer) used to hang out' (Bryson, 1997: 200). Bradford's image took a further knock in 1998 when it formed the backdrop to a television drama series called *Band of Gold*, which majored on drugs and prostitution. The infamous 'Bradford riots' of 2001 cemented an already dismal identity, emphasising once again the hollowness of the city's much lampooned 'Bradford's Bouncing Back' campaign initiated back in 1986 (Fenn, 1988: 68).

Superficially, tourism to Bradford might nowadays appear to have 'bounced back'! There are currently press releases to the effect that tourism is a 'booming' growth industry, with 'official' figures indicating it is now worth over half a billion pounds annually to the local economy (see below). Moreover, a Bradford DMO has more or less resurrected itself. Known as *Visit Bradford*, it comprises a Tourism Manager and her assistant, and no less than four tourist information centres. All of the staff are employed by Bradford Metropolitan District Council, working to an annual budget of just over £500,000. The Tourism Manager defines the role of *Visit Bradford* as follows:

> Our job is to promote Bradford as a tourism destination. We aim to encourage overnight stays by packaging things up, working with the hotels and the theatre. (Tillotson, 2014)

In essence, however, *Visit Bradford* is dedicated to reactive visitor servicing, *viz.* the production and distribution of brochures and guides, the operation of an information-only website, and the provision of tourist information centre services. There is ample good intent underpinning these visitor servicing operations, but the proactive element of urban destination marketing is now more or less absent. Few media visits are organised, and there is no equivalent nowadays to those innovative weekend breaks hatched in the 1980s. As far as business tourism is concerned, gone is any semblance of bidding for 'footloose' meetings. Indeed, unsolicited conference enquiries on behalf of Bradford are fielded by a neighbouring DMO (viz. *Conference Leeds*, a division of *Leeds and Partners*). In 2010, Bradford even suffered the indignity of being ranked as the least visited UK city (behind Wakefield, Dundee and Sunderland), with the media unfairly but predictably headlining it as 'dangerous, ugly and boring' (*Daily Telegraph*, 2010). A year later, a local government reorganisation of senior management roles within Bradford Metropolitan District Council led to the incumbent Director of Culture, Tourism and Sport being made redundant, with her post being deemed surplus-to-requirements (*Bradford Telegraph*, 2011a).

In this way, urban destination marketing in Bradford has over time become much less of a priority, and in the process a DMO has been more or less emasculated, moving from proactive to reactive mode. In effect, the city has turned its back on what Eddie Fenn was once hailing as a 'new and viable industry' which gave 'an excellent return on investment' (Fenn, 1988: 68–69). Of course, things don't have to pan out in this way. Interestingly, while the urban destination marketing 'stories' of Bradford and Glasgow began at roughly the same time (we highlight the latter's achievements throughout this text), the tourism outcomes from the vantage point of 2014 appear diametrically polarised. Urban destination marketing has helped transform the city of Glasgow, while in Bradford it has done little or nothing to change either the place or its still nascent tourist sector. Claims that tourism is worth £538 million to the local economy of Bradford appear to contradict this assessment (*Bradford Telegraph*, 2011b), but they should be treated with caution. Such figures include the spending associated with various categories of visitor that few in the general public would deem to be 'tourists' in their everyday understanding of the word, notably the overnight stays attributable to non-discretionary business travel and VFR (visits to friends and relatives), as well as day trips for shopping and other purposes. Because the spending of the above-mentioned categories is defined as 'tourism' for purposes of collecting the 'official' statistics, all manner of incongruity arises when the data are reported, some of it bordering on the incredulous. For instance, the £538 million figure cited above by Bradford's Tourism Manager (Tillotson, 2014) is in excess of the comparable £443 million value figure for the Yorkshire tourist honeypot of York (Visit York, 2012: 1), all of which defies 'common sense' and is redolent of Disraeli's 'lies, dammed lies, and statistics'!

However, I did not begin my book with Bradford in order to highlight the esoteric and frustrating inadequacies of UK tourism statistics, and the ways in which these data may be misinterpreted or even abused (more about these matters later). The 'Bradford story' is worth telling because it is a fine example of how the 'theory of marketing competitive advantage' – as the paradigm through which academic and practitioner communities portray, evaluate and otherwise account for urban destination marketing – does not accord with practice and reality. As I seek to demonstrate in this book, in nearly all of Europe's towns and cities the 'theory of marketing competitive advantage' fails to 'tell it like it is'. Specifically and most strikingly, it is impossible to square this theory, predicated as it is on exploiting genuinely unique and compelling differences between towns and cities, with a 'real' world in which most urban destinations take a more or less undifferentiated product to the marketplace. On the one hand, the vast bulk of towns and cities lack compelling USPs and thus any competitive advantage with which these might be associated. On the other, uniformity of message and imagery invariably characterises the content of destination marketing operations – what I refer to in Chapter 4 of this book as a DMO 'marketing of everything' approach (the marketing materials produced by *Visit Bradford* are a classic case in point). Within the 'theory of marketing competitive advantage', taking undifferentiated product to market can have no place whatsoever. In the context of what we have earlier defined as a paradigm, such behaviour constitutes an 'anomaly' which cannot be explained away (Kuhn, 1970: 52–53).

Take, for instance, my career as an urban destination marketing practitioner. During those 22 long years (1990–2012), I subscribed wholeheartedly in thought and word to the 'theory of marketing competitive advantage'. A stock-in-trade sound-bite was that the role of the DMO I was then heading up was to 'market the difference' or 'market competitive advantage'. In practice, however, I did exactly the opposite! The guides, videos, DVDs and brochures my DMOs produced invariably included everything remotely pleasant about the destination – the very opposite of 'marketing the difference' or 'marketing competitive advantage'. In saying one thing and doing another ('talking the talk', but not 'walking the walk'), I was not consciously being deceitful. To be sure, paradigms for the most part work at a subliminal level; we don't call up Newton's three laws of motion each and every time we take a walk or ride a bike. Physicists pre-Einstein were neither charlatans nor obscurantists; Einstein's theory of relativity simply proved them wrong.

During the course of writing this book, my somewhat belated recognition of the above 'marketing of everything' anomaly prompted me to question all of the 'explicit and fundamental generalisations of the paradigm' (Kuhn, 1970: 82) I have chosen to call the 'theory of marketing competitive advantage'. In particular, I began to doubt the efficacy of USPs as primary motivators of tourist travel (which in this book I dub as passing the 'Johnson test'), and then the capacity of DMOs to create significant numbers of visitors. In respect of the latter, I confess during my practitioner career to having had niggling suspicions-cum-fears that DMO marketing operations were at best marginal in the tourist's decision to visit a particular place. Related to this was a deeper scepticism as to the figures from marketing evaluation studies which purported scientifically to demonstrate ample 'conversion' from the campaigns my DMO had been orchestrating. However, as a practitioner, I consigned such nagging and heretical doubts to the long grass. I chose to shine the torchlight elsewhere, for reasons which must be all too obvious to the reader.

In this book, I argue that the 'theory of marketing competitive advantage' fails comprehensively to account for urban destination marketing. With just a few exceptions, towns and cities do *not* differentiate themselves on the basis of USPs, nor do their DMOs take competitive advantage to market. Instead, DMOs promote a more or less undifferentiated product which is typically inclusive of everything remotely attractive about their respective towns and cities – the above-mentioned 'marketing of everything' approach. In turn, these marketing operations for the main part fail to 'bring in the business' in the way envisaged or implied in the 'theory of marketing competitive advantage'. For these reasons, the latter theory cries out for reappraisal and reshaping, which is why in this book (with a good deal of humility and trepidation) I am advancing a new and revised conceptual model. In other words, I am arguing the case for a change of paradigm in which broadly the same data are placed within a different framework, so that the former concepts and some new ones 'fall into new relationships one with the other' (Kuhn, 1970: 149). In Chapter 5, I label this new and adjusted paradigm as the 'dynamics of urban destination marketing'.

It remains to be seen whether or not academics and practitioners will be convinced by this new theory and, if so, on what basis they will amend the existing one. 'Buy-in' will not come about easily. Paradigm change is rarely achieved quickly or painlessly and – if steadfastly resisted – may never happen at all. From a personal standpoint, debunking one theory and developing another has been hard work, as well as a somewhat humbling experience. As I have made clear already, throughout my long career in urban destination marketing I adhered resolutely to the principles of what I am here calling the 'theory of marketing competitive advantage'. In this sense, 'what we knew' then (as per the title quote to this Preface) was what I, too, honestly thought to be the case. I am obliged in this book to acknowledge that a theory which I had once viewed as 'far out in front' is in fact demonstrably 'way out' in terms of its predictive capabilities and all-round veracity.

The alternative theory I am proposing in this book (which, to reiterate, I term the 'dynamics of urban destination marketing') is grounded in empirical evidence, the greater part of it based on in-depth interviews with leading destination marketing practitioners. This new theory aims to capture the complexity and interconnections of a constraining and complex 'real' world in which the scope and content of urban tourism marketing is shaped by a host of often conflicting and contradictory influences, and where DMO outputs and outcomes are typically problematic. In such a context, urban destination marketing begins philosophically to resonate with Bob Dylan musing that 'there's no success like failure, and failure's no success at all' (*The Times*, 2006: 220). This is an equivocation to which I return in the Epilogue to this book. By now, the reader may well be forgiven if he or she has become a tad perplexed, but read on and all will hopefully become much clearer. In Part 1 I will appraise urban destination marketing in contemporary Europe, as a prelude in Part 2 to deconstructing and adjusting the existing paradigm so as better to unite theory with practice. At that point, and with reference to the quote by Kuhn heading up this Preface, what were ducks in the reader's mind before reading this book may well be rabbits afterwards!

1 Introduction

A world view or dominant logic is never clearly stated but more or less
seeps into the individual and collective mind-set of scientists in a discipline.
Stephen Vargo and Robert Lusch (2004) *Evolving to a*
New Dominant Logic for Marketing

This book is a sequel to my first one, *Inside City Tourism: A European Perspective*, which sought to provide an overview of urban destination marketing (Heeley, 2011). On its back cover, the book was described as a 'cross-over text'. What the reviewer (Brian Wheeller) meant by this was that while I had a considerable grounding in the academic study of tourism, the book had essentially been written from 'the practitioner's perspective'. He was referring to a career which had begun as a tourism researcher and lecturer (1972–1990), but which was followed by more than 20 years as a chief executive officer (CEO) of urban destination marketing organisations. Another reviewer pointed out that I had utilised a language which was 'less formal than is often the case' with academic texts, making the book accessible and 'easy to read' (Pirnar, 2012: 211). The book which follows is written in a similar vein, adopting as it does a more or less practitioner perspective – the 'less' a reference to recent academic experience as mentioned later on in this chapter – and aiming to be just as readable as its predecessor.

The reasons for once more putting pen to paper are threefold. They are discussed below in descending order of significance, and are interlinked and overlapping. Indeed, respectively they form a grand aim, a consequence, and a means to an end.

1.1 The Grand Aim: Uniting Theory and Practice

In writing a second book, I wanted to elaborate upon and take forward a point I had mentioned only in passing three years ago in *Inside City Tourism*, viz. the gap between the academic literature on urban destination marketing and the manner in which it is actually undertaken (Heeley, 2011: xix). At that time, it seemed to the author that the 'theory' conjured up an essentially different world from that of day-to-day 'practice', without my then being able to put my finger upon the 'why' and 'how' of it all. After leaving my last practitioner job in April 2012 as CEO of *European Cities Marketing* (ECM), this gap between the theory and practice of urban destination marketing came into ever-sharper focus as a result of my taking up undergraduate and postgraduate teaching responsibilities, beginning in October 2012 at MCI Innsbruck. Specifically, I found myself teaching on destination marketing modules in which I was obliged to familiarise myself with the now voluminous academic literature on the subject, a literature comprehensively and adeptly summarised by Pike and Page (2014) in their recent review. Progressively immersing myself in this literature, I was puzzled by its preoccupation with 'destination branding' and 'market positioning' and with techniques such as market segmentation and the various types of resource audits. Over my 22 long years as an urban destination marketing practitioner, such matters had hardly loomed large, whereas the politics, finance and partnering which had been such dominating factors scarcely received mention in the literature.

An all-important 'light-bulb' moment occurred in April 2013 as I was researching this book, conducting interviews with senior staff in the offices of the *Vienna Tourist Board* (VTB). Contrary to what the books and journal articles were positing, it dawned on me in those offices that the content of urban destination marketing in contemporary Europe was 'much of a muchness'. It was strikingly similar both in form and content. While convergence in respect of form came as no surprise (among towns and cities there is, as we shall see in Chapter 3, a more or less standard DMO 'marketing template'), a pervasive uniformity of content in respect of imagery and messages was most surprising, bordering on astonishing, given that academics and practitioners alike adhere overwhelmingly to the view that urban destination marketing is a process of marketing competitive advantage based on uniqueness and differentiation. Pike and Page themselves could not be more definitive when stating that 'the quintessential goal of all DMOs ... is sustained destination competitiveness', and that fundamental to this is a 'comparative advantage' based on attractions characterised by their 'relative uniqueness' and 'unimitability' (Pike & Page, 2014: 206–207). As already discussed in the Preface, this 'way of seeing' represents a Kuhnian paradigm, a shared belief-system through whose values, concepts and propositions the world of destination marketing is made sense of by academics and practitioners alike (Kuhn, 1970). As per my comments in the Preface, I refer to the paradigm-cum-mantra operative in the field of urban destination marketing as the 'theory of marketing competitive advantage'. Pike and Page (2014: 218) entitle it the '4Ps marketing paradigm'. Whatever the label, my Viennese 'light-bulb' moment was at long last to recognise that a central tenet of the '4Ps marketing paradigm' was manifestly at odds with the mainstream DMO approach to urban destination marketing. Instead of bringing a differentiated offer to market based on more or less unique selling propositions, DMOs overwhelmingly did exactly the opposite in an approach I characterise in Chapter 4 as the 'marketing of everything'. The fact that this moment of realisation occurred in Vienna was down to the DMO there being almost unique in using its destination branding to systematically market competitive advantage in the way ordained by the paradigm (refer to Section 4.4 of Chapter 4).

The ambitious intent of this book is to provide a critique of the 'theory of marketing competitive advantage' across all its central tenets, and to establish the foundation for a new and revised paradigm within which academics and practitioners can more readily and convincingly account for urban destination marketing – hence the theory and practice parts of the book's title. Having been a DMO CEO for over 20 years, I therefore find myself critiquing the very theory of which I had been such an enthusiastic and earnest supporter. Ironically enough, one of my last major projects as the outgoing CEO of ECM had been to organise a seminar held in Sofia for which I recruited as keynote speaker Eddie Friel, a much respected tourism consultant and former Glasgow tourism chief. His address in the Bulgarian capital represented in pure, unadulterated form the 'theory of marketing competitive advantage'. In it, he referred to DMOs as the 'champions' of cities, and to their marketing 'competitive difference' as enshrined in 'powerful narratives' (Friel, 2011). The audience of senior DMO executives nodded contentedly and knowingly, and otherwise lapped up all that Eddie had to say. Immersed as they were in the paradigm, most if not all of them would have been hard put to name its parts and recognise it as a 'collective mind-set' (Vargo & Lusch, 2004: 2). That's how paradigms work – they seep unrecognised, but nonetheless powerfully into the psyches of academic and practitioner communities. Piling on the irony for the author, it had been Eddie – some time back in the early 1980s when I was a tourism lecturer in Glasgow at Strathclyde University – who had introduced me to the basic idea underpinning what I am now calling the 'theory of marketing competitive advantage'. Eddie's simple but nonetheless compelling message to me then was that the essence of promoting and selling cities was 'marketing the difference'.

To be fair, the gap between theory and practice in destination marketing is recognised by some of the academics specialising in this field (see, for instance, Pike & Schultz, 2009). This, however, still begs the question of why there should ever be, at any one point in time, such a gap. Taking academe first, I think it fair to say that much the greater part of how teachers and researchers account for urban destination marketing is conceived from an 'ivory tower' position; such detachment is, after all, a fundamental part of the academic ethos. Referencing my long years as a practitioner, I hardly ever encountered academics observing urban destination marketing, let alone participating in policy making or day-to-day operations. As a general rule, academics 'find it difficult to gain access to the inner sanctum of DMO decision making' (Pike & Page, 2014: 209). When academics do 'soil their hands' in this way, the experience may well turn out to be strange and even uncomfortable. One academic alludes to his anxieties in an account of his tenure as a board member of a regional-level DMO, *Welcome to Yorkshire* (Thomas, 2011). Although 'constrained from reflecting openly' (Thomas, 2011: 497), he questions the unevidenced and seemingly irrational manner in which large amounts of public money were being used to attract events to Yorkshire whose local economic impact was highly questionable – notably a 'one-off' Royal Ascot staged at York, and the International Indian Film Academy Awards held in Sheffield (Thomas, 2011: 498).

Scholarly writing on urban destination marketing is typically grounded neither in experience nor empirical observation. As a consequence, principles and procedures advanced in conventional academic descriptions may come to have no counterpart in practice; they may be unworkable and/or irrelevant and/or outmoded and/or done tokenistically. In ways which ultimately can only be conveyed by 'real life' experience and evidence (as in my previous book and in this one), urban destination marketing in practice is less a science and more the art of the possible; as such, pragmatism, opportunism, expediency and compromise loom large, and are major factors determining the scope and content of what is undertaken. Politics, in particular, 'is notoriously destructive to the marketing process' (Cooper & Hall, 2013: 234).

Turning to the practitioners, there is a sense in which urban destination marketing professionals (like all practitioners) are preoccupied with 'doing', to the extent that they rarely consciously 'test out' their own fundamental practitioner beliefs. Reflecting once again on my own experience as CEO of ECM (2009–2012), it is remarkable how this association's annual programme of seminars and workshops was throughout devoted to 'nitty-gritty' financial, administrative and operational matters, such as the latest budgetary projections or bookings software, the routine swopping of 'hot' convention leads, the modernisation or 'look and feel' of a particular tourist information centre, trends in visitor arrivals relating to, say, the burgeoning Chinese market, visitor card sales performance for the past year, etc. Rarely, if ever, was there discussion or debate about 'the bigger picture' – those fundamental, paradigmatic tenets which comprise the 'theory of marketing competitive advantage' (or Pike and Page's '4Ps marketing paradigm'). Whether or not we were conscious of the fact, all of us at ECM subscribed to this theory as a paradigm. It was there as 'background', so that whenever one of its axioms surfaced explicitly – as recounted above with Eddie Friel's call to market 'competitive difference' – we would wisely nod our heads, purr contentedly, and otherwise feel soothed and reassured. This is the way paradigms work for practitioner communities; they are 'givens' that are accepted, working essentially out of view. They are only from time to time articulated, by industry 'gurus' like Eddie Friel and by the university lecturers who write 'authoritative' texts and journal articles for their students and peers. As a practitioner, the day-to-day job is one of 'doing the business' as opposed to reflecting on the theory of it all. It is, of course, an entirely separate matter as to whether or not the axioms or fundamental generalisations of a theory hold true in practice at any given point in time. Even if the 'facts' or experience appear to contradict elements of the theory, the latter may still be accepted because it is 'neater, more suitable, and simpler' (Kuhn, 1970: 155). It is in this sense that 'theory' can and often does become more or less divorced from reality. Neat, suitable and simple, by the way, are the very adjectives I would use to describe the 'theory of marketing competitive advantage'.

1.2 The Consequence: Closing the Quest for the Holy Grail of What Makes Urban Destination Marketing Succeed or Fail

A related motivation for writing a second book was suggested in another review of my first:

> Informally the book (*Inside City Tourism*) can be read as the quest of a city tourism practitioner seeking the holy grail of what makes city tourism succeed or fail – and Heeley is to be credited for also recognising that not all attempts to develop city tourism are successful. (Clarke, 2012: 366)

Although the 'holy grail' referred to by Clarke was most certainly a thread running through *Inside City Tourism: A European Perspective*, the book was essentially an overview of urban tourism marketing. As a result, it skirted around what made for success and therefore best practice, as opposed to delineating and explaining these matters 'full on'. It presented examples of best as well as worst practice, and advocated public–private partnership (PPP) as an organisational way forward. However, it fell short of developing a theory with which to understand and appraise the practice of urban destination marketing in terms of the effectiveness or otherwise of the bespoke delivery mechanisms established to take forward these tasks, viz. the destination marketing organisations (DMOs). Notwithstanding the truism that 'achieving success in tourism is challenging and ill understood' (Bornhorst *et al.*, 2010), the academic literature is remarkably non-committal as to whether or not destination marketing operations are effective in delivering the turnover, employment and other benefits on which they are premised, although there is recognition of the widespread lack of rigorous performance monitoring, and the related difficulties faced by DMOs in arriving at meaningful key performance indicators (Pike & Page, 2014: 210, 212–213). The literature, as it were, sidesteps the question of the efficacy or otherwise of destination marketing, and is more or less silent as to precisely where best practice is to be found. Nowhere does it identify the DMO 'leaders of the pack'.

Building on the author's previous book (Heeley, 2011: especially Chapters 4, 6 and 8), this text breaks new ground in setting out a conceptual model within which success or failure can be evaluated and best practice identified and adumbrated. Its conclusion for many academics and practitioners will be as surprising as it is controversial; viz. remarkably few DMOs in a town or city context are really 'making a difference' to the urban economy and profile, mainly because the practice of urban destination marketing presents formidable challenges and obstacles with which these organisations in the main are ill-equipped to deal. European best practice in urban destination marketing is limited to only a handful of DMOs; they are referred to in Chapter 5, with the *Glasgow City Marketing Bureau* (GCMB) and VTB emerging as the outstanding 'leaders of the pack'.

The holy grail of what makes for success and failure in urban destination marketing runs through Part 1 of the book, which profiles and then appraises how DMOs are organised and financed, with DMO professionals 'in their own words' portraying how they conduct their operations (another sense in which this book breaks new ground). Success or failure is also a cross-cutting theme running through Part 2, inasmuch as the 'theory of marketing competitive advantage', and my proposed revision and reshaping of it, both contain strong normative dimensions. As such, the existing and revised theories set out the principles and practices which a DMO has perforce to follow if it wishes to be effective, reach operational targets, deliver desired outcomes in terms of urban economy and profile, attain best practice standards and otherwise possess leading-edge capabilities and infrastructure. As we shall see in Chapter 5, the starting point for the new theory adumbrated in this book is that success in urban destination marketing is an end-state in which the net local economic impact of tourism is being maximised. This, in turn, is conditional upon the interplay of four variables whose outcomes in practice mean that remarkably few urban DMOs end up optimising that net local economic impact. Set against the latter criterion, DMO destination 'losers' predominate over DMO destination 'winners.'

The Epilogue found at the end of this book seeks closure in an historical and ultimately philosophical manner of the author's quest for the holy grail of what makes for success and failure in urban destination marketing.

1.3 The Means to an End: Towards a Theory of the Mid-range

The third reason for writing this book relates to methodology. In attempting a synthesis of theory and practice in respect of urban destination marketing, I have in mind what the American sociologist Robert Merton referred to long ago as 'middle-range' theory (Merton, 1949). Merton classically defined theory as 'logically interconnected sets of propositions from which empirical uniformities can be derived' (Merton, 1949: 39). For Merton, 'middle-range' theories were intermediate between what another American sociologist (Wright Mills, 1959) termed 'abstracted empiricism' and 'grand theory'. The former comprised empirically based studies which assembled 'facts and figures' on behaviour, organisation and change, but without reference to wider, explanatory frameworks of concepts and propositions. The latter – 'grand theory' – comprised all-embracing, interconnected conceptual systems whose generalisations were so distant from observed data that they could not in any meaningful senses be tested or verified (Wright Mills, 1959: Chapters 2 and 3).

It is my view that tourism as a domain of study will only progress significantly on the basis of 'middle-range' theories of the sort propounded by Merton and Wright Mills. Progress in that direction has undoubtedly been made during the past half-century of tourism studies, and in this respect the 'theory of marketing competitive advantage' may be seen to lie somewhere equidistant between 'abstracted empiricism' and 'grand theory'. Having said that, the 'theory of marketing competitive advantage' is critically deficient in that its component 'middle-range' propositions have in the main neither been tested empirically nor otherwise grounded in practice. In contrast, the new theory proposed in Chapter 5 is most certainly of the 'middle-range', in that it seeks to make sense of a delimited yet important aspect of behaviour (viz. urban destination marketing) by reference to a set of generalisations which are based both on the author's practitioner experience and (more importantly) upon empirically based researches conducted specifically for the purposes of writing this book. The latter consist of a series of 21 in-depth interviews with DMO executives, and a review of 62 DMO websites (as outlined further in the penultimate section of this chapter). In this way, the 'middle-range' theory forming the final chapter of this book is one grounded in empirical evidence. The sum total of all of this evidential material (Part 1) provides a valid and sound basis on which to unite theory and practice in the field of urban destination marketing (Part 2) in a more systematic and verifiable manner than has hitherto been the case.

It may well be that over time a build-up of related and overlapping 'middle-range' conceptual schemas will yield a general theory of urban tourism. A good example of one such related and overlapping schema would be the theoretical foundation Hankinson is attempting in respect of destination branding (Hankinson, 2009). Interestingly, an academic review written over a decade ago pointed out that 'theoretical analysis of the complexity and interlinkages of the urban tourism phenomena have been few and far between and received scant attention until of late' (Godfrey, 2001: 77). A little later, Selby (2004) commented to the same effect, just as Maitland and Ritchie (2009: 2) have done more recently in citing Selby. From these observations, we must surely conclude that little progress has been made over the past decade in synthesising a general theory of urban tourism. Perhaps this is too herculean a task and it will never happen, and theories of the mid-range such as the one proposed here will have to suffice.

1.4 The Author's Perspective

At this juncture, it is worth reiterating the personal position from which I have written all that follows. After an early career as an academic specialising in tourism (1972–1990), I spent the next 19 years as a UK urban tourism practitioner, all of them at a senior level, as the founder CEO of four DMOs for the cities of Sheffield, Coventry, Birmingham and Nottingham. For a further period (2009–2012), I held senior executive positions in *European Cities Marketing*, a voluntary association whose *raison d'être* is to network urban DMOs so as to facilitate the exchange of best practice and of market and other intelligence. In April 2012 I left ECM, after which I made a gradual and somewhat unexpected part-time return to academe. This started with a keynote 'practitioner' address at the inaugural *Advances in Destination Management* conference held at the University of St Gallen in June 2012, and was followed by ad hoc teaching engagements at various universities, principally in my home town at Sheffield Hallam University (SHU) where, in 2013, I eventually took up an associate lectureship. This year (2014) I have commenced a three-year visiting fellowship at SHU, developing teaching and research in the field of destination marketing. My partial re-socialisation into the mores and practices of academe has alerted me to how this book would have been more or less impossible to write during my years of practice. Partly this would have been through lack of time, but mainly it would have been an inability then to see the paradigmatic 'big picture'. The truth is that one has to exit the practice of urban destination marketing before attempting seriously to critique its existing theories and, in so doing, develop alternative paradigms!

A final point on perspective is worth making. Inasmuch as I am suggesting that the existing paradigm currently shared by academics and practitioners alike is out of kilter with reality and needs to change, there is inevitably a sense in which this book embodies a one-person perspective. Challenging that paradigm's fundamental axioms is always going to make the author (for the time being at least) in a minority of one! Setting aside that inevitability, what follows nonetheless represents a comprehensive and hopefully objective overview of the field across both academic and practitioner dimensions. As for the former, I have in Chapter 4 systematically appraised the academic literature in the field of destination marketing in order to chronicle the evolution of the 'theory of marketing competitive advantage', isolating seminal and representative texts, essays and articles. In respect of the latter, the interviews with practitioners forming the evidential or empirical basis of the book (as set out in Chapters 2 and 3) was designed specifically to avoid the subjective and one-person perspective which, with hindsight, was a weakness of my first book, especially in its Chapters 5 and 7 (Heeley, 2011). Through the practitioner interviews, I try in this book to let the practitioners speak for themselves, using their words to demonstrate just how much the content of the current academic literature (conditioned as it is by the 'theory of marketing competitive advantage' paradigm) does not accord well with reality.

1.5 Defining and Disentangling Urban Destination Marketing, Destination Management, the DMO, Place Marketing, City Marketing, City Branding and Integrated City Marketing Agencies

While a universally accepted definition of the term 'destination' may be lacking, it has been suggested that 'a destination is best defined as a geographical space in which a cluster of tourism resources exists, rather than somewhere that is delineated by political boundaries' (Fyall & Garrod, 2012: 1). Although few would disagree with this statement, it is worth recognising from the onset that the geographical remit of DMOs is nearly always configured precisely on the basis of political boundaries, and that the problems to which this gives rise could well form the subject of a separate book! To cite just one example, here is one DMO chief executive venting his frustrations:

> Place branding? Well, it's all down to politics isn't it? The city of Derby chooses to market itself differently to the county, Derbyshire. Woe betide the two of them ever coming together, through ourselves, to place market the county of Derbyshire to include a dynamic and thriving city called Derby. Logically, this is an obvious thing to do, but politics gets in the way. Politicians being politicians means that you have a tourism officer team for Derby, as well as my organisation, the Peak District and Derbyshire DMO. So you get two bodies instead of one, and that doesn't help. (James, 2013)

Setting aside such administrative niceties, delineation of the destination starts from recognition that tourism is 'essentially a local phenomena, tending to be concentrated in a very small percentage of the land area of a given country' (Young, 1973: 111). It follows from this that destinations are 'the fundamental unit of analysis in the tourism system' (Fyall & Garrod, 2012: 1). As with the term destination itself, a definitive definition of destination marketing to the best of my knowledge does not exist, and surrounding it is a degree of terminological confusion arguably equivalent to that which existed for the term 'tourism' itself in the 1980s (Heeley, 1980). Probably the principal reason for this is 'the recent tendency by some authors to refer to destination marketing organisations (DMOs) as destination management organisations' (Pike, 2013: 247). The latter convention has also been adopted by some practitioners. For example, in this country, *Visit England*, the official national tourist organisation, encourages DMOs at the regional and local scales to refer to themselves as destination management organisations or partnerships. In this way, *Visit County Durham*, the DMO for the city of Durham and the wider administrative area, refers to itself on the corporate pages of its website 'as the tourism management agency for County Durham'. Pike correctly observes that usage of the term destination management is 'contentious' (Pike, 2013: 247), and it merits further discussion as a prelude to my formally defining urban destination marketing for the purposes of this book.

Referring to urban destination marketing organisations as destination management organisations is in the view of this author as confusing as it is erroneous. To be sure, the responses of towns and cities to the opportunities and problems presented by urban tourism have, since time immemorial, centred on two distinct but related roles. On the one hand, there has been *urban tourism marketing* (the subject of this book), aiming to enhance destination profile and create more customers. On the other hand, there has been *urban tourism planning and management*, a much more diffuse and essentially non-commercial set of activities designed inter alia to facilitate and/or regulate the development of tourist infrastructure and superstructure, and to maintain standards and otherwise enhance the quality of the visitor experience (Heeley, 1981). Those academics and practitioners who choose to refer to destination marketing organisations as destination management organisations in effect combine both of the above roles into one organisational concept, so that their 'destination management organisation' ends up encompassing an altogether heady mix of tourism marketing, planning and management functions.

To be fair, the DMO as we have entitled it – namely the DMO as the destination marketing organisation – can in an urban context occasionally be both marketer and manager. In some central and eastern European countries, for instance, DMOs have apparently been renamed as Tourism Destination Management Organisations to 'emphasise the role in tourism management, policy, product development, training and marketing' (Clarke, 2012: 367). As a general rule, however, this is not the case, so that in practice the vast majority of DMOs in Europe major on the marketing dimension, having at best only a tangential role in respect of planning and management issues. The same is true, broadly speaking, of North America (Getz *et al.*, 1998: 338). As Pike neatly and crucially remarks, the phrase 'destination management organisation' is problematic because it 'infers control over destination resources, a level of influence that is in reality held by few DMOs' (Pike, 2013: 247). To the extent that urban tourism management matters are consciously and corporately dealt with in towns and cities, they are overwhelmingly the domain of a multiplicity of agencies other than the DMO, especially the various departments and committees of local government. For practitioners like myself, it is misleading to refer to the two roles – urban tourism marketing and urban tourism planning and management – as 'destination management', and it is remiss to describe the agencies responsible for implementing the various disparate functions as the 'destination management organisation'. I experienced at first hand the deep and ultimately unnecessary misunderstanding to which this gives rise in listening to otherwise interesting presentations delivered in 2012 at the inaugural *Advances in Destination Management* conference, to which I have made previous reference.

Moreover, it is my experience that practitioners in the main prefer the 'M' in the DMO acronym to stand for 'marketing' as opposed to 'management'. The Chief Executive of *Leicester Shire Promotions* says:

> We don't claim to be a destination management organisation. Here in Leicester we have an elected city mayor who has more influence over what happens in the city than we as the DMO could ever dream of having. There is a massive investment programme under way across the city at the moment, and it is driven by him as city mayor. It's not the DMO that's driving that; we're playing a part in it, we're supporting the marketing, we're providing some of the data and intelligence on which investment decisions are being made. But the local authority is always the custodian of the destination, and is best placed to influence the visitor experience more than anybody else. Because with destination management, you come down to very basic things like parking, street signs, cleanliness, and toilets – the 'basics' in other words, and that's what the local authority provides. (Peters, 2014)

Or, as Gillian Cruddas, former CEO of *Visit York*, crisply states:

> Abroad, DMO tends to mean destination marketing organisation. As a marketer, I prefer the term destination marketing organisation. (Cruddas, 2014)

Reflecting the above arguments, whenever I henceforth use the DMO acronym in this book I am referring only to the destination marketing organisation and to the urban tourism marketing it undertakes. In this way, I have chosen formally to define urban destination marketing as **the deployment of proactive promotional, sales and fulfilment techniques aimed at attracting and servicing tourists in order to raise profile and otherwise generate net local economic benefit for a town or city**. The urban DMO may then be viewed as the bespoke delivery mechanism established by a town or city for the purposes of urban destination marketing. In other words, urban destination marketing is what DMOs 'do' – it is their day-to-day business. DMOs are 'the main vehicle to compete and attract visitors to their distinctive place or visitor space' (Pike & Page, 2014: 202).

Defined in this way, urban destination marketing may be subsumed under the term *'place marketing'* or, specifically in an urban context, *'city marketing'*. Here it joins several other strands of urban marketing in which specific audiences other than tourism ones are addressed (notably film producers, inward investors, local residents, prospective students and potential occupiers of property). A final, 'generic' strand is sometimes applied in the form of an 'umbrella' awareness-raising promotional platform upon which the DMO and 'sister' urban marketing agencies may more effectively pursue their targeted approaches. In an urban context, this final and some would argue crucial coordinating strand is usually referred to as *'city branding'* or the 'city brand' (Heeley, 2011: Chapters 7–8). Arguably the best known examples of such brands currently are 'I Amsterdam', 'Only Lyon', 'People Make Glasgow', 'Copenhagen: Open for You' and 'Be Berlin'. By way of illustration the marketing campaign associated with the latter city brand is implemented on a truly herculean scale by a bespoke PPP called the *Berlin Partners*. Bringing together city government and over 200 private sector companies, the partners undertake what Americans refer to as 'civic boosterism'; every Berliner is communicated with personally, there are promotional toolkits called 'Berlin boxes', and an army of 'Berlin ambassadors' busily fashion their own online 'Berlin stories'. At the national and international scales, *Berlin Partners* employ a flexible 'the place to be' slogan which enables specific themes to be highlighted: viz. Berlin as the place to be for conventions, for creative industries, for fashion, and so forth. High profile 'Berlin Days' are organised in the world's most important capital cities, targeting VIPs and potential inward-investor audiences (Grupp, 2010). It is worth noting here that *Berlin Partners* have an annual budget of circa €20 million, over half of which is derived from private sector donations, and the organisation employs 125 staff (Steden & Holtgrewe, 2013). As an organisational entity, it is larger than (and is entirely separate from) the city's DMO, *Visit Berlin*. While city branding of late has certainly moved up the urban policy making agenda, its effectiveness remains problematic and its practical implementation is fraught with difficulty (Heeley, 2011).

An important and related trend affecting DMOs in recent years has been the rationalisation of the various strands of urban marketing referred to above to create *integrated city marketing agencies*. A good example is *Amsterdam Marketing* formed last year by merging the hitherto separate city branding authority (*Amsterdam Partners*), the DMO (*Amsterdam Tourism and Conventions*), the inward investment bureau (*Amsterdam Business*), and the *UIT* agency responsible for promoting and staging municipal events (Diender, 2011). In England, the author helped engineer two prototypes of the integrated city marketing agency (*CVI* in Coventry and *Marketing Birmingham*). *Marketing Manchester*, set up as the Manchester Visitor and Convention Bureau in 1991 (Heeley, 2001: 278), has over the years evolved into an integrated city marketing agency. More recent amalgamations have spawned *Cardiff & Co*, *London & Partners*, *Leeds and Partners* and *Marketing Edinburgh*. As I write, York is following suit with the establishment of an integrated city marketing agency. The 'jury is still out' as to whether 'joining things up' in this way really leads to greater efficiency and effectiveness, mindful of the fact that achieving cost reductions has been an underlying objective, that two of the integrated city marketing agencies (*CVI* and *Cardiff & Co*) have already been wound up, and that the organisations set up for Leeds and Edinburgh have experienced considerable 'teething troubles'.

1.6 Research Method

To gather the information and data on which to review urban destination marketing in contemporary Europe from the vantage point of practice, on the one hand, and the adequacy or otherwise of current academic and practitioner theorising on the other, I have employed a four-pronged method. First, I undertook a review of the academic and practitioner literature on urban destination marketing, as presented in Sections 4.1–4.2 of Chapter 4. Secondly, I conducted an online investigation of urban destination marketing in 62 European towns and cities; in each case, I was already familiar with the place and the work of its DMO delivery mechanism, and the principal online sources consulted were the corporate and consumer pages of the DMO website. The resultant information informed Chapter 4, enabling Figure 4.2 to be compiled.

A third strand of research comprised in-depth interviews with the DMO departmental heads of GCMB and VTB, for use throughout Chapters 2–5. Each interview was recorded digitally for subsequent transcription, and was conducted on the basis of a semi-structured interview schedule. The DMO departmental heads interviewed at GCMB were: Joe Aitken, Head of Major Events; Aileen Crawford, Head of Conventions; and Tom Rice, Head of Marketing and Communications. In the case of VTB, the interviewees were: Gudrun Engl, Director, Market and Media Management; Bernard Klein, Head, Brand Communications and International Advertising; Christian Mutschlechner, Director, Vienna Convention Bureau; and Markus Penz, Head, Strategic Destination Development.

Fourthly, interviews were arranged with 13 current or former DMO executive heads in order to:

• develop the empirical basis of Chapters 2–3 which reviews the practice of urban destination marketing in contemporary Europe;
• help critique the 'theory of marketing competitive advantage' in Chapter 4;
• strengthen and otherwise empirically validate the 'dynamics of urban destination marketing' theory set out in Chapter 5.

As before, the interviews deployed a semi-structured interview schedule, and were recorded digitally before being transcribed. All 13 interviewees were experienced and respected professionals, 11 of them working (or having worked) in DMOs whose status was that of a PPP. The two exceptions were local government tourism officers. The interviewees may be seen as representing various urban destination types as per Law's pioneering classification (Law, 1992: 600), viz.: large (Gdansk, Glasgow and Gothenburg); smaller (Bradford, Derby, Hull and Leicester); historic (Chester and York); seaside (Blackpool and Scarborough); and ski (Innsbruck). The DMO executive heads interviewed were Stella Birks, Visitor Services Development Manager, *Derby Tourism Team*; Claes Bjerkne, former CEO, *Gothenburg & Co*; Friedrich Kraft, Director, *Innsbruck Tourism*; Gillian Cruddas, former Chief Executive, *Visit York*; Anna Górska, CEO, *Gdansk Tourism Organisation*; David James, Chief Executive, *Visit Peak District and Derbyshire* (covering the city of Derby); Kate McMullen, Head, *Visit York*; Katrina Michel, CEO, *Marketing Cheshire* (covering the city of Chester); Camilla Nymen, Acting CEO, *Gothenburg & Co*; Martin Peters, Chief Executive, *Leicester Shire Promotions* (covering the city of Leicester); Scott Taylor, Chief Executive, *Glasgow City Marketing Bureau*; Patricia Tillotson, Tourism Manager, *Visit Bradford*; and Mike Wilkinson, former CEO of DMOs covering Hull and the seaside resorts of Scarborough and Blackpool.

All 21 interviews took place over a 15-month period, beginning January 2013 and ending March 2014.

1.7 Format of the Remainder of the Book

The rest of the book is organised into two parts. Part 1 examines the practice of urban destination marketing in contemporary Europe, building on my first book, but focusing on the practitioners and their work. Chapter 2 profiles the bespoke DMO delivery mechanisms established by towns and cities for the purposes of urban destination marketing, making reference to the following parameters: nomenclature and core purpose; status and structure; and finance and partnering. The next chapter is necessarily a long one, in that I wanted to encapsulate in a single episode of continuous text what the imperfect and constrained world of urban destination marketing is really like – 'warts and all', as the phrase goes. As such, the reportage and analysis serves as an antidote to the idealised, normative and unproblematic picture of the DMO world conveyed in much the greater part of the academic and practitioner literature. To this end, it introduces the DMO 'marketing template' in order to classify and then exemplify operations across media and travel trade relations, advertising and promotions, conventions and business tourism, sporting and cultural events, and supporting web/digital, print and visitor servicing activities. Having reviewed the template, Chapter 3 goes on to consider the brand and planning frameworks within which marketing operations are conducted. Finally in this chapter, we assess how outputs and outcomes are typically appraised, making reference to the DMO 'measurement tool kit'.

Having established an empirically based urban destination marketing context in Part 1, we switch to a comparison of theory and practice in Part 2, with Chapter 4 appraising the current, dominant explanatory paradigm, labelling it as the 'theory of marketing competitive advantage'. This chapter demonstrates that a remarkable gap exists between the 'theory of competitive advantage' and actual practice. In particular, the theory is unable to account for the uniformity of content which characterises mainstream urban destination marketing throughout contemporary Europe. The latter typically comprises a 'marketing of everything' approach which, in turn, reduces to a theming of 'urban sameness'. In the chapter which follows, a revised perspective is advanced in the form of a four-variable model entitled the 'dynamics of urban destination marketing'. The model, in effect, is a drawing together of key findings and observations established in Chapters 2–4 and, as such, is a 'middle-range theory' grounded in empiricism and praxis. It is based on the author's own practitioner experience and – more importantly – the findings from the interviews conducted with DMO practitioners. Crucially, the new theory accommodates the anomalies and counter-instances associated with the existing paradigm. The concluding sections of Chapter 5 highlight principal implications of the theory, as these relate both to academe and to practice. In this way, we come full circle, returning to the starting point of this chapter and, in particular, to the quest for the holy grail of what makes for success and failure in urban destination marketing and – even more importantly – to uniting theory and practice, linked to which is the weighty question of what mission in future might best underpin urban DMO marketing operations.

Self-evidently, the intention to unite theory and practice in urban destination marketing as it relates to the quest for the holy grail of what makes for success or failure is an ambitious one. It will be up to the student, academic or practitioner reading this text to judge for himself or herself whether or not *Urban Destination Marketing in Contemporary Europe: Uniting Theory and Practice* delivers on that ambition. Will it enable the reader to 'know' and evaluate what the world of urban destination marketing is really like? As ever, the proof of the pudding will be in the eating!

Part 1
Practice

2 The Practitioners: Profiling the Ubiquitous DMO

Character is like a tree and reputation like a shadow.
The shadow is what we think of it; the tree is the real thing.
Abraham Lincoln, an undated quote popularly attributed to him

With public sentiment, nothing can fail; without it nothing can succeed.
Abraham Lincoln (1858) First debate with
Stephen A. Douglas at Ottawa, Illinois
Goodwin, D.K. (2013: 206)

2.1 Introducing Urban DMOs

The scale and extent of urban destination marketing and the prevalence of its DMO delivery mechanisms are well attested to in the literature (e.g. Ashworth & Page, 2011). The DMOs themselves 'act as umbrella marketing organisations and consolidate the role of destination partners' (Cooper & Hall, 2013: 212). Geographically, this chapter presents a pan-European overview of urban DMOs; the DMOs that are to be found in just about every European town and city – from *Visit Reykjavik* in Europe's northern extremities to the *Istanbul Convention and Visitors Bureau* in its far south-westerly reaches. It sets an organisational context for the chapter which follows on DMO marketing operations. Together, the two chapters provides an empirical basis on which we can in the remaining Chapters 4 and 5 compare and contrast theory and practice in urban destination marketing. In setting out the DMO organisational context, the principal parameters under consideration in this chapter are nomenclature, purpose, status, structure, finance and partnering arrangements. Finance (or the lack of it) is especially important as it, to a large extent, drives the mode of organisational status adopted, and the scope and content of partnering arrangements, and it goes on to determine the scale of the subsequent inputs, outputs and outcomes with which urban destination marketing is associated.

Dry and technical as these six organisational parameters are, they provide that indispensable foundation or platform upon which DMOs are able to undertake their urban destination marketing. Take it away and DMOs are reduced literally to nothing, and urban destination marketing does not take place. In this sense, it is nomenclature, purpose, status, structure, finance and partnering arrangements which are the essence of the DMO – Lincoln's 'real thing'. Unfortunately, their influence is understated in the academic and practitioner literature, precisely because the six parameters are prosaic matters and they are overshadowed by the marketing operations they make possible. Scant research has been undertaken of 'the relationship between governance, organisation, strategy and achievement of DMO objectives to guide destination marketers on what constitutes an effective organisation' (Pike & Page, 2014: 210). Moreover, it may be argued that academic, industry and wider public understanding and appreciation of DMOs is aggravated by a widespread failure on their part clearly to define who they are and what they do! This is a critical failure inasmuch as no activity which is in the public domain succeeds in the long term if it does not have on its side what Lincoln alludes to as 'public sentiment' – a point to which we return at the end of this chapter. Before reviewing each of the six organisational parameters, a little history is set out below in order to widen understanding and provide context.

2.2 A Potted History of Urban DMOs

Two dates may be viewed retrospectively as being of signal importance in the historical evolution of urban DMOs in contemporary Europe, and both are quintessentially British institutions. The first was Richard 'Beau' Nash's civic appointment in 1705 as Master of Ceremonies in the spa town of Bath (Pimlott, 1947: 37). A professional gambler possessed of a flamboyant and eccentric character, Nash oversaw a department of local government which was 'responsible for organising entertainments and diversions', and he took it upon himself personally to promote and otherwise safeguard the reputation of the town as a health resort and to welcome distinguished visitors to the city (Tames & Tames, 2009: 97–100). Nash's message to traders and the municipal authority alike was that to win and retain the patronage of Bath's fashionable and upmarket visitors, standards had to apply across accommodation, amenities, attractions, entertainments and public spaces (Pimlott, 1947: 36). To that end, Nash drew up codes of conduct, for instance, outlawing duelling in the streets. In places of public entertainment, he instituted rules and regulations which, for instance, banned the wearing of swords at card tables. At dances and balls, young and elderly ladies were enjoined to occupy the 'Second Bench' due to their being 'past, or not come to Perfection' (Pimlott, 1947: 48). His appointment as master of ceremonies for what was arguably the world's first purpose-built tourist township represented in embryonic form the beginning of that nexus between the local public and private sectors in tourism which we nowadays refer to as the

DMO. Eventually, on the boot heels of Bath, other spas and seaside towns introduced the post of master of ceremonies in order to promote their reputations and otherwise ensure that the highest possible standards obtained (Pimlott, 1947: 42, 59).

DMOs in a recognisably more modern form first began to appear in Europe during the second half of the 19th century, especially in Britain, Switzerland and Austria (Heeley, 2011: 7). For example, in 1888 a *Municipal Council for the Improvement of Tourism in Innsbruck* was established:

> (It) took on the status of a public organisation for the promotion of tourism. People started to organise offers for guests and to actively advertise them near and far. From 1888, the Commission saw ensuring the establishment of a 'Bed Information Service' *Bettenauskunftsdienst* at the railway station as one of its most important functions. In later years this information service was expanded into a Tourist Information Office and exists as such even today. (Innsbruck Tourism, 2013: 8)

However, the second and even more momentous date in the evolution of urban destination marketing takes us back to Britain, to the year 1879, to the fast-developing Lancastrian seaside resort of Blackpool, and to a bizarre mistake on the part of national government! Despite the then relevant national government department (the Local Government Board) being steadfastly opposed to local authorities promoting themselves as tourist destinations, an oversight on its part in 1879 enabled one municipal authority – Blackpool Corporation – to levy a two penny rate specifically for the purpose of mounting advertising campaigns 'stating the attractions and amusements of the town' (Walton, 1983: 150). Armed with these unique powers, the Corporation established the *Blackpool Advertising Committee* under whose auspices an annual budget of £4000 (£390,000 in today's currency) was being expended by the outbreak of the Great War. Working 'hand in glove' with railway companies, the principal medium employed by the Advertising Committee was the picture poster, supported by visiting exhibitions and other publicity stunts. By promoting itself in Yorkshire and the Midlands, and eventually in London and Glasgow, the *Blackpool Advertising Committee* cleverly used its urban destination marketing monopoly to extend awareness of itself as a seaside resort and in so doing it enlarged its visitor catchment area, thereby lessening its dependence on the custom of adjacent Lancashire cotton towns. By the turn of the 20th century, Blackpool had established for itself a national reputation as the UK's premier seaside resort (Walton, 1983: 150–151).

Courtesy of an oversight on the part of national government, Blackpool therefore pioneered the concept and techniques of proactive urban destination marketing. Similar fiduciary arrangements with which to fund urban destination marketing only became available to other British spas and seaside towns following legislation in 1921 and 1936. These long-awaited powers were eagerly lapped up outside Blackpool, so that one social historian writing in the aftermath of World War II could assert that:

> ...every important resort has its own publicity department, either organised directly under the local authority or, where it is provided by voluntary arrangements, sponsored by them. (Pimlott, 1947: 44)

The essential 'tools of the trade' in respect of resort publicity, as urban destination marketing was termed in the inter- and post-war periods, became less the erstwhile poster and more the annual guide; the former continued to carry slogans, some of which became household names such as 'Skegness is so bracing', while the latter became of pivotal importance, as it sought to strike a judicious balance between picture, text and advertising content, on the one hand, and the amount of text given over to accommodation, as opposed to attractions and amenities, on the other (Yates, 1988). In the next two decades a highly effective sales formula was introduced, based on New Year media advertising supported by the production of an annual holiday guide. The practice survives to this day, as recalled by the former tourist chief of a prominent English seaside resort:

> When I started work here in Scarborough in 1998, the holiday guide was the prime means of attracting visitors to the area. About 70,000 guides were produced each year. We'd get them ready for Christmas and the New Year, so that we could advertise in certain publications, notably the TV magazines and newspapers. We invited readers to fill in a coupon so that they could send away for their free holiday guide. This worked wonders, and it is still going on. When I first arrived, the main guide had around 100 pages, of which 40 or so were given over to saying what a great place Scarborough was, and the rest was taken up with accommodation. We carried out some research on people requesting a guide, and found out that about half said they were 'definitely coming' and another quarter said they were 'likely to come'. Now most of the 70% or so of those who were 'coming' or 'likely to come' sort of intimated that they'd already decided they were going to visit Scarborough before they even requested the guide. They wanted the guide as an information source; in particular, they wanted maps so they could see where their holiday apartment or hotel was in relation to the rest of the town. In addition, they wanted festival and other event listings. So in other words, we were wasting 30 or 40 pages trying to sell a destination that most of our customers had more or less already decided they would be going to! That wastage was expensive in print terms. So the following year we reduced the size of the main guide; I remember it went down from 96 to 64 pages. Print costs came down dramatically, and we only devoted 8 pages to selling the resort – two on coast, two on culture, two on countryside, and

two just general stuff. The rest was accommodation and events information. (Wilkinson, 2014)

The dominant part played by local government in the first two and a half centuries of urban destination marketing (1705–1955) reflected what we might now term as a situation of 'market failure' in which such marketing offered (then as now) little or no prospect of generating a rate of return on investment sufficient to attract private capital. However, the hegemony of city and town governments in this field began to be challenged by the advent of public–private partnership (PPP) arrangements during the post-war period – sporadically at first (e.g. the *Vienna Tourist Board* (VTB) in 1955), and then in a more sustained manner from the late 1970s onwards as the DMO form of organisation spread its wings to embrace not only Europe's 'great capitals' and inland and coastal resorts, but also other urban types, notably former industrial centres and so-called heritage towns (Heeley, 2001: 276–282). At the time of writing, the urban DMO is now more or less ubiquitous in towns and cities across the length and breadth of Europe, split roughly evenly (and perhaps irrationally) between the local government and PPP models which we discuss below. Whether public sector or PPP, DMOs vary markedly across the six key parameters referred to in Section 2.1 above. Arguably, it is this extreme variability which is their most remarkable and seemingly inexplicable feature. Taking finance and citing just one example: VTB at the time of writing has an operating budget of £16,260,000 which is 271 times greater than the £60,000 available to *Marketing Sheffield* – the DMO promoting my home city. In the remainder of this chapter, we spotlight this variability in respect of all six of the key organisational parameters, beginning with nomenclature and core purpose.

2.3 Nomenclature and Core Purpose

While the work of, say, a local newspaper, education authority or pharmaceutical company is more or less readily intelligible to the layperson from its title (it is what it 'says on the tin', so to speak), the same cannot be said of the urban DMO. Moreover, public understanding as to who the urban DMO is and what its role involves is aggravated by the diffuse manner in which urban DMOs choose to name themselves and to define their core purpose. Taking nomenclature first, it can be seen that as a genre urban DMOs variously refer to themselves as tourist boards, tourist organisations, destination marketing organisations, destination management organisations, tourism destination management organisations, destination marketing or destination management partnerships, place marketing organisations, and city or destination branding authorities – the list seems almost endless.

As for the corporate titles themselves, there is a quite remarkable diversity evident across Europe. Although now somewhat *passé*, urban DMOs sometimes ape North American practice by styling themselves as visitor and convention bureaux (e.g. *Derry Visitor and Convention Bureau*). Some use the prefix 'destination' (e.g. *Destination Uppsala* and *Destination Bristol*), whereas others opt for 'marketing' (e.g. *Marketing Dresden* and *Marketing Manchester*), or 'visit' (e.g. *Visit Brussels* and *Visit York*), or even 'discover' or 'experience' (e.g. *Discover Stratford* and *Experience Nottinghamshire*). A recent practice is to allude to the essentially rural hinterland of a town or city (e.g. *Bath Tourism Plus* and *Leicester Shire Promotions*) or to a rooting in PPP (e.g. *Gothenburg & Co* and *London & Partners*). More prosaically, we have the use of 'tourism' or 'tourist office' or 'visitors board' or 'tourist board' after the name of the city (e.g. *Antwerp Tourism, Luxembourg Tourist Office, Stockholm Visitors Board*); usually, but not always, the latter descriptors are applied by DMOs organised as departments of city and town government, as opposed to DMOs constituted as PPPs. A handful of DMO names give little or no indication whatsoever as to their destination marketing role (e.g. *Newcastle Gateshead Initiative* and *Wonderful Copenhagen*). Such heterogeneity in nomenclature reflects the essentially 'bottom up' way in which local tourism administration has evolved throughout Europe (Heeley, 2011: 6–18), although needless to say this does little to aid public perception and appreciation of who and what the DMOs are!

In a similar vein, among DMOs there is a self-inflicted and widespread obscurantism as to their core purpose. In my experience, DMOs typically fail to set out explicitly what their core purpose is, or else do so in rather an unclear manner. As an example, in 2010 the *Belfast Convention and Visitor Bureau* (now *Visit Belfast*) formally defined its core purpose as being:

> ...to promote Belfast as a world class visitor destination by increasing the contribution that tourism makes to the economy in such a way that is customer focussed, delivering a quality solution in a cost effective way, respecting the environment, is acceptable to the local economy and offers sustainable growth. (Heeley, 2012a: 22)

The same is true of the following core purpose devised by *Bournemouth Tourism* as per the 'about us' pages of its destination website: 'to provide Bournemouth with the best possible leisure, cultural and tourism services, generating economic, environmental and social benefits for residents, visitors and local business'. Worthy as they are, both the above statements are self-evidently too complicated, unwieldy and unmeasurable to serve as a meaningful core purpose. It goes without saying that the latter should succinctly encapsulate the organisation's fundamental reason for being in existence.

As might be expected, academic conceptualisations of DMO core purpose (and to a lesser extent practitioner ones) diverge along the destination management versus destination marketing distinction appraised in Section 1.5 of the previous chapter. Hence, some academics argue that the urban DMO is essentially a 'marketing organisation whose *raison d'être* is creating customers for the destination' (e.g. Pike, 2008), whereas others view the DMO as a 'management' organisation (responsible for planning and management as well as marketing functions) whose mission centres upon leadership and coordination, ensuring suitable provision of tourist superstructure and infrastructure, and leadership, advocacy and liaison (e.g. Ritchie & Crouch, 2003). Similarly, another academic considers the management role as inclusive of 'leadership and coordination, planning and research, product development, marketing and promotion, partnership and team-building, and community relations' (Morrison, 2013: 7).

Clearly, in the light of how we have defined urban destination marketing in Chapter 1, the conceptualisation of core purpose more appropriate to this text is that which derives from Pike and, if you like, the destination marketing (as opposed to management) school of thought. Pike (a practitioner turned academic) sums up DMO core purpose by quoting the President and CEO of the *San Francisco Convention and Visitors Bureau*:

> The primary reason cities created destination marketing organisations hasn't changed in more than 100 years: 'Bring in the business'. (Pike, 2008: 35)

In a like vein, Eddie Friel (this time a practitioner turned consultant) combatively asserts that DMOs have 'no right to exist if they do not create customers for the destination' (Friel, 2011). For a relevant, albeit regrettably rare example of a DMO clearly and comprehensively defining its core purpose as per the 'destination marketing school', I refer the reader to the *Glasgow City Marketing Bureau* (GCMB):

> GCMB is the Destination Marketing Organisation (DMO) for Glasgow. Our role is to position Glasgow to its key markets, to create customers, generate inward investment and sustainable net economic benefit. Our mission statement is simple: GCMB Creates Customers. (GCMB, 2012)

The essence of DMO core purpose as defined above is therefore the creation of visitors through marketing activity, with the raising of urban profile as an important, yet subsidiary objective. Commenting on this statement of core purpose, GCMB's Chief Executive suggests that it gives the organisation's stakeholders and employees a shared sense of what the Bureau is there to do:

> It's just three words, but basically that's what we do for a living. If someone says 'what do you do for a living'? We say, 'we create customers'. So at the very heart of our cultural wheel is 'we create customers'. (Taylor, 2013)

In some cases, defining core purpose may expose tensions. Reflecting on her long tenure (1995–2013) as Chief Executive of *Visit York*, Gillian Cruddas notes:

> The core purpose when *Visit York* was established was to deliver busi-ness to the commercial members. The emphasis was that way because it was businesses, not the local council, who had set up *Visit York* back in 1987. This steered all the decisions really; we were constantly driven by hanging on to the commercial members and keeping them happy. It was only when the local authority came on board in 1995 that we had more of a dilemma; looking back it would have been better if we had amended our core purpose at that time, so that it was one stage removed from the commercial members, to be, for instance, about growing the visitor economy. We never really tackled this dilemma. (Cruddas, 2014)

A penultimate example shows how a 'heads in bed' core purpose was arrived at by *Leicester Shire Promotions*:

> What we've agreed with our core partners (the city and county council) is that the fundamental purpose of the organisation is to generate over-night stays. And the reason we're focussing on that is basically because it's the one thing we can say we can do as a DMO that is unique to us and isn't being duplicated. The usual question we then get asked is: 'why are you not promoting for day visits?' Day visits are important, to be sure, but that is a market that all of our individual visitor attractions are addressing and spending their resources on. They're all going after the day visit market, and collectively are spending far more than we could ever spend and doing it very well. So they look after the day visit market, and we focus on the overnight stuff which, in turn, brings them (the visitor attractions) some new business. (Peters, 2014)

The importance of accurately and meaningfully defining DMO core pur-pose is attested to in the comments above by Taylor, Cruddas and Peters. It is a matter to which we return in the concluding parts of Chapters 3 and 5. For the moment, we reiterate that the core purpose of urban destination marketing, as defined by academics of the 'destination marketing school' and by the vast bulk of practitioners, is that of generating overnight stays and bednights in commercial accommodation outlets, with the raising of profile being a related, secondary aim. The primacy of creating visitors, and the subsidiary role played by profile generation, is captured in this remark by Simon Anholt, writing in the Introduction to the World Tourism Organisation's *Handbook on Tourism Destination Branding*. Having rather naively opined that 'destination marketing is a relatively straightforward business' in which a DMO 'can be fairly sure of increasing tourism arrivals' as long as it has 'enough marketing expertise, resources and patience', he goes on to say:

> So it follows that destination marketing, in addition to its primary purpose of encouraging visits, can play an important secondary role in helping visitors to form a compelling personal narrative about the country, which enhances their power as 'viral agents' or informal advocates for the country's brand once they return home. The way in which the destination is marketed, the 'brand story' that it tells, is passed on by satisfied visitors to other prospects, and eventually becomes a powerful agent for widespread social marketing effects. (WTO/ETC, 2009: 7)

Looking back over his long career as an urban destination marketer, Mike Wilkinson is clear that core purpose reduces to creating visitors and 'bringing in the business':

> The role of the destination marketing organisation is always to attract new visitors – those who would not otherwise have come – and so create new business. (Wilkinson, 2014)

The phrases 'bringing in the business' and putting 'heads in beds' neatly convey this core purpose. To this end, urban DMOs discharge two related roles; the first aims to foster a 'generic' awareness of the destination, while the second may or may not use this as a basis on which to mount 'tactical' sales activities designed to create new overnight customers for a town or city across business, leisure and event tourism audiences.

2.4 Organisational Status and Structure

With respect to organisational status, a fundamental division is evident among Europe's urban-based DMOs between those administered from within local government and those which are constituted as PPPs. A membership survey undertaken by the author on behalf of *European Cities Marketing* (ECM) indicated that over a third of ECM's members (39%) were town and city government based DMOs, with the remainder (61%) adopting the PPP model (ECM, 2011). In the latter set of circumstances, the municipality effectively 'lets go', ceasing directly to undertake destination marketing tasks itself in order to join forces with the local private sector (especially tourist trader interests) in more or less independent, so-called 'arms-length' arrangements. As such, the PPPs typically form themselves into not-for-profit companies, foundations and trusts, and endeavour to run themselves more or less commercially along the lines of a private company, albeit with varying degrees of independence from their stakeholders, viz. the city or town government, the private sector, and other key urban institutions such as the universities. In contrast, local government based DMOs are either departments of the local authority or sections of such departments.

Over the past three decades, a marked trend in favour of the PPP model of DMO organisation is discernible, driven by the potential advantages and benefits it affords; PPP enables earned and private sector income streams to be exploited on a significant scale, and it otherwise facilitates the introduction of an organisational culture in which the DMO may be run in a business-like and results-orientated fashion (Heeley, 2001). The Head of Marketing at *Visit York* alludes to this when she says:

> For me the independence of being a public–private partnership is key, alongside the accountability it gives back to the private sector. Their (the private sector's) input to our marketing campaigns goes well beyond financial contributions, important as that is. Of course, we want their money. But over and above that is their marketing 'know-how' and experience; many of our private sector partners are doing the same job as us, albeit they are marketing hotels, attractions etc. We test-run campaign ideas with them. I am not convinced you would get that working in a local authority. Also, when opportunities present themselves, we can take decisions and move quickly; there is much less bureaucracy. Public–private partnership is a much more sustainable model going forward, allowing us to be inventive and creative. It works for both sides. Both parties – the local authority and the private sector – see a value in us acting as middleman: we are a broker communicating backwards and forwards. (McMullen, 2014)

It is the author's view that the continued existence of the town/city government model in urban destination marketing is difficult to justify in the light of the demonstrable financial and operational advantages afforded by PPPs. Remarking on the Swedish capital's city government based DMO, the Acting CEO of *Gothenburg & Co* opines:

> By being a capital you always have so many advantages. You can get away with being successful, though not as successful as you could have been if you were a PPP. Stockholm is one of the world's most beautiful cities and it is trendy, with fine food etc. However, if we had established a public sector DMO in Gothenburg, we would have been dead. (Nymen, 2013)

The Director of Strategic Destination Development at VTB highlights two operational advantages of PPP:

> A big advantage is that the CEO can hire professionals and he can fire people, too, if he is not satisfied with them. I would say that the freedom

to 'hire and fire' and appoint appropriate people to the various jobs is a great advantage, and is one which by and large does not apply in public sector bodies. A second big advantage is that issues are dealt with in a speedy and professional manner, as opposed to a time-consuming and political one. (Penz, 2013)

The Director of *Innsbruck Tourism* put matters even more concisely:

> The advantage of PPP is that normally there is no political influence; the experts and professionals are allowed to get on with the job. Of course, we are subject to pressures of a sort from our 12,000 commercial members, especially the hotels, but we can handle that. (Kraft, 2013)

A final DMO respondent opined on this matter as follows:

> I know this sounds a little twee, but the key to a DMO is partnership. The public sector simply can't do it on their own, and the reality is that it has to be a relationship between the public and private sectors, with the public sector looking to the longer-term, and with the industry wanting to get quick returns. If the DMO is just a council arrangement full of local politicians and tourist officers, then it just doesn't work. (James, 2013)

The opportunities and benefits flowing from PPP are therefore vital in shaping the success or otherwise of the destination marketing undertaken by a DMO, and is a matter to which we shall return in Part 2.

Whether a part of town or city government or run as a PPP, DMO structure divides along governance and executive lines, as shown in the organisation charts for *Visit Oslo*, *Visit York*, VTB and GCMB, forming Figures 2.1–2.4. In the PPP model, a board of part-time and 'volunteer' non-executive directors generally serves as the governance, while the permanent executive comprises professional staff employed on a full (and occasionally part-time) basis, and organised into departments. Staff are recruited from diverse backgrounds, with marketing, business, media, the arts, information and technology, administration and finance well represented. In local government based DMOs, the permanent professional staff are local government officers reporting either to their departmental or section heads, and/or to committees of elected politicians. For instance, the *Derby Tourism Team* employed by the city council comprises a staffing complement of just four and a half full-time equivalent (FTE) posts. It is headed by a Visitor Services Development Manager who oversees a small tourism marketing unit and a tourist information centre, with a reporting line which leads eventually to the Council's Director of Regeneration (Birks, 2013). On a far different scale, *Stockholm Visitor Board* (SVB) has 40 FTE positions, being one of two operating subsidiaries of the Stockholm Business Region (SBR). SBR as an organisational entity is a department of city government, and its governance in 2012 was formed by a board of six city councillors nominated by the Moderate Party who at that time were the majority party controlling Stockholm City Council. A small Executive Board of senior officers, including the CEO of the SVB subsidiary, reported directly to this governing board (Stockholm Business Region, 2013). Across the local government–PPP divide, the permanent employees of urban DMOs nearly always exhibit a pronounced gender imbalance; females predominate, and it is usual for them to account for upwards of 70% of all staff appointments. For example, VTB employs a total of 114 staff, 76% of whom are women (VTB, 2013a: 2).

The organisation chart in Figure 2.1 illustrates the division between governance and executive in the case of *Visit Oslo*. Its governance – the Board of Directors – in the 2012/2013 year was chaired by Tarje Hellebust, General Manager of the city's Radisson Blu Plaza Hotel (Omberg, 2012). The 'main', full-time jobs of the remaining board members were as follows:

- Marketing Manager, Oslo Concert Hall;
- General Manager, SAS France, Spain and Portugal;
- Director of Business Development and Real Estate at Oslo Airport;
- Marketing and Communications Director, Norwegian National Opera and Ballet;

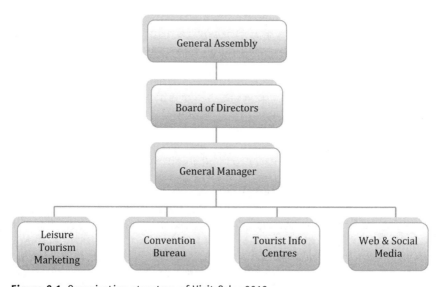

Figure 2.1 Organisation structure of Visit Oslo, 2013

- Managing Director, Fursetgruppen restaurant group;
- Two senior city hoteliers.

In the above example, the eight directors are elected to serve on the board as representatives of particular sectors of the tourist trade, viz. hotels, transport, catering and visitor attractions. The alternative model is for appointments to be made on an 'individual' as opposed to 'representative' basis. The advantages and limitations of both models are neatly articulated by the former CEO of *Visit York*, whose organisation structure is shown in Figure 2.2:

> We took a conscious decision to go down the non-representational route in order to get 'good' and able people who were prepared to put in time and effort. The flaw in that was that different industry sectors – the large hotels and retailers for instance – felt they didn't have a voice at Board level, so we had to develop alternative ways of working with them. (Cruddas, 2014)

Interestingly, despite Oslo City Council providing *Visit Oslo* with nearly half (48%) of its €4.6 million income during the 2012/2013 year (Rodven, 2012), it is noteworthy that no nominees of city government serve on the DMO's Board of Directors. This reflects *Visit Oslo* being constituted as a limited company owned by 150 private sector shareholders drawn from the local tourist industries. The votes of the various shareholders at the elections

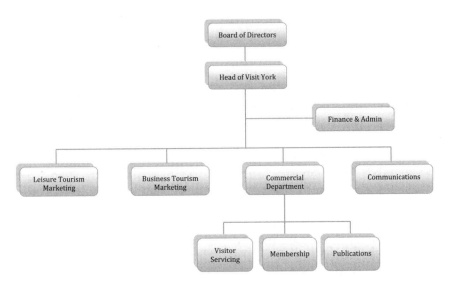

Figure 2.2 Organisation structure of Visit York, 2013

which form part of the agenda of the company's annual general meeting determine the composition of *Visit Oslo*'s Board of Directors. Reporting directly to the Board of Directors is a six-strong Senior Management Team led by a CEO, with departmental heads for marketing and communications, web and digital media, conventions, visitor servicing, and finance and administrative support services, respectively (see Figure 2.1). *Visit Oslo*'s full-time staffing complement, inclusive of the CEO and spread across these five departments, numbers 27 employees.

In formal terms, a summing up of the respective roles and responsibilities of governance and executive would be that the former determines policy and ensures accountability in respect of how public and private monies are being expended, while the latter administers policy in an efficient and otherwise expedient manner. In reality, the emphasis of policy formulation usually lies less with governance and more with the executive. For instance, the Chief Executive of *Visit York* said of the Board of Directors to whom she reported (see Figure 2.2):

> I think it is fair to say they act as a sounding board in several areas and are mainly a reporting-back thing. Most of the creative energy and thinking comes from the executive. A lot of the Board members simply do not understand the main issues and priorities, or even their responsibilities as directors of a limited company delivering business for its members and satisfying the council with the service-level agreement. They have full-time jobs elsewhere, so realistically they can only dip in and out. (Cruddas, 2014)

The Director of *Innsbruck Tourism* says this of the three-person Executive Board to whom he reports:

> They don't lay down the marketing approach. Of course, they have the right to ask questions and get answers, and the President of the Board is by law responsible for what happens, down to the discharge of daily duties. The reality is that it is me who is responsible. (Kraft, 2013)

In a similar vein, VTB's Director of Strategic Destination Development stressed that the Commission forming VTB's governance (see Figure 2.3) is essentially a consensual, reporting-back mechanism:

> The Commission meets four times a year. In its entire history since the formation of the Board in 1955, the Commission has never gone to a vote, let alone overruled the CEO. The Commissioners proceed on the basis of consensus and partnership, and they have always 'okayed' proposals from the executive. (Penz, 2013)

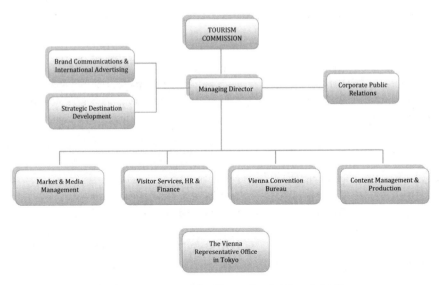

Figure 2.3 Organisation structure of the Vienna Tourist Board, 2013

The Commission in this case is headed by its President; at the time of writing this was a senior local government councillor, Renate Brauner, Vice-Mayor of Vienna City Council and portfolio holder for finance and economic affairs. The President and most of the remaining 17 commissioners are appointed by the municipality (VTB, 2013a: 1).

The Chief Executive of GCMB emphasised the close, day-to-day relationships he enjoyed with the six non-executive directors of the Board to whom he reports (see Figure 2.4 and Table 2.1), saying 'they're doing a good job for us, they're helping us, they're giving us strategic direction, they're working for us as a city and as a board' (Taylor, 2013). In contrast to *Visit Oslo*, GCMB's Board of Directors is an equal mix of public and non-governmental sectors; there are three public sector representatives, all of them local politicians nominated by Glasgow District Council, one of whom is the political head of the

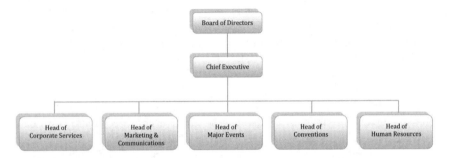

Figure 2.4 Organisation structure of the Glasgow City Marketing Bureau, 2013

Table 2.1 Board of Directors of *Glasgow City Marketing Bureau* as at January 2013

Status	Individual	Main job
Chairman	Councillor Gordon Matheson	Labour Party representing *Glasgow City Council*: he is Leader of the City Council ruling group
Vice-chairman	Bailie Liz Cameron	Labour Party representing *Glasgow City Council*
Board member	Councillor Graeme Hendry	Scottish Nationalist representing *Glasgow City Council*; he is Leader of the opposition
Board member	Dr Lesley Sawers	Chief Executive of the *Scottish Council for Development and Industry*
Board member	Geoff Ellis	CEO of *DF Concerts and Events*, a prominent Scottish event management company
Co-opted	Professor Anton Muscatelli	Principal and Vice-chancellor of *Glasgow University*
Executive Director	Scott Taylor	Chief Executive of *Glasgow City Marketing Bureau*

Source: Glasgow City Marketing Bureau.

current administration while another is leader of the main opposition party. The other three board members are co-opted by the above politicians on an individual as opposed to a representative basis, although it can be seen from Table 2.1 that all three are drawn from non-governmental institutions and companies. As with VTB's governing commission, this arrangement enables the local authority to exercise a degree of influence over what is ostensibly an arms-length arrangement. Indeed, GCMB's Chief Executive concedes that 'we would never say "no" to what our main parent wants us to do', humorously describing the Bureau as a 'short arms-length company of the council'! He goes on to remark that it is a 'special purpose vehicle that allows the local authority to do things it wouldn't normally do':

> The board is designed not to be unwieldy. It's a city owned company. So the company needs to have a structure that ensures that the council retains control of the board. So it's not a public–private partnership with private members like, say, Oslo. Indeed, it's nothing like the *Visit Oslo* situation where commercial members get on the board. I wouldn't want that sort of arrangement. (Taylor, 2013)

In turn, Vienna and Glasgow may instructively be compared with the governance arrangements for Gothenburg. In the 2012/2013 year there were no less than 21 board members of *Gothenburg & Co*: five nominees were from city government, two of whom – respectively the Chairman and Vice-Chairman of the board – were the Mayor and Deputy Mayor of the Gothenburg city administration. The remaining 16 board members were representatives of the private sector and key city institutions, notably the universities (Gothenburg & Co, 2013: 46). Here, the five political representatives are viewed as affording the executive of *Gothenburg & Co* and its private sector board members an all-important 'direct access to the top political level' (Nymen, 2013), while the predominance of private/institutional sector representatives means that all the main industry and commercial sectors are seen to be committed to the work of the DMO. As the Acting CEO of *Gothenburg & Co* says:

> The City Council has only five seats on the Board. The rest are private companies, many of whom have formed networks so as to have a share-holding in *Gothenburg & Co*. Every one of these networks – the hotels, restaurants, shops and so on – can then send someone to serve on the Board. That means that everyone is there within the industry, taking on a huge responsibility. (Nymen, 2013)

As can be seen from Figures 2.1–2.4, executive structure is more or less similar from one DMO to the next, in that there are typically departments or sections for communications, leisure marketing, conventions, visitor servicing, finance and administration, and occasionally ones covering sporting and cultural events. In the latter cases, this can range from the production of festivals and/ or coordinating the process of bidding for championships or cultural events, through to their subsequent hosting on behalf of the town or city concerned. Contrasting with the broad uniformity evident in respect of executive struc-ture, we have seen above that governance arrangements vary significantly in terms of their size and composition, especially the nature of the balance between the public and the private/institutional sectors, and the choice between 'representative' or 'individual' models. Ultimately, the composition of DMO governance in any one town or city will reflect local circumstances, reducing to an often complex interplay of historical, geographical and political factors. For instance, in the case of the *Belfast Visitor and Convention Bureau* (now *Visit Belfast*), its 12-strong board of directors in 2011 mirrored the 'troubles' and compromise peace arrangements which have characterised the country since the 1970s (Belfast Visitor and Convention Bureau, 2011). Chaired by the Managing Director of Botanic Inns Ltd, the rest of the Bureau's board com-prised nine representatives of the tourist trade and eight local politicians. The latter were councillors nominated on a co-equal basis by Sinn Féin (four) and the various unionist parties (four). All in all, it is arguably fair to say that there is no 'one size fits all' best solution to the structure of DMO governance.

2.5 Finance and Partnering

The member survey mentioned in the section directly above and under-taken in 2010 sought to take stock of key financial parameters as these currently obtained for the network of urban-based DMOs known as *European Cities Marketing* (ECM); the 41% response rate furnishes results that are more or less representative and reasonably up to date (ECM, 2011). Moreover, a broadly similar survey had been undertaken during 2003, providing an important source with which to compare beginning and end points of the first decade of the new millennium. The paragraphs below summarise the main findings of the survey.

In respect of finance, a quite remarkable variation is evident from one urban DMO to the next with, broadly speaking, four income bands being discernible. The DMOs for Gothenburg and Vienna recorded annual budgets in excess of €20 million, reflected in relatively large staffing complements of 97 and 112, respectively. A second, four-strong band comprised the DMOs for Copenhagen, Lisbon, Brussels and Paris, registering annual incomes of between €10 million and €19 million. A third band followed, made up of DMOs with annual incomes greater than €5 million, but less than €10 million (viz. Amsterdam, Barcelona, Geneva, Lucerne, Luxembourg, Lyon, Oslo, Stockholm and Stuttgart). The remaining 59% of DMOs, nearly two-thirds of the sample, financed their activities from within budgets of €5 million or less. The operating as opposed to overhead expenses of the urban DMOs taking part in the study comprised on average some 43% of the annual budget, meaning that roughly two-thirds worked to operating budgets each year of less than €2 million. Inasmuch as ECM is made up mainly of larger cities and towns, operating cash elsewhere is typically much less than €2 million, as we shall see in due course when we examine the 'size matters' dimension as part of Chapter 5. In England, the author estimates that the vast bulk of urban DMOs have operating budgets of less than £1 million a year. Suffice to say, scale in respect of operating budget strongly influences the degree to which a DMO can maximise the net local economic benefits of tourism.

In the ECM survey, the share of income attributable to public and earned/private sector sources in the 2010 year revealed an average reliance on public sector grants of 48%. The comparable figure taken from the 2003 survey was 65%, indicating that over the intervening seven-year period a pronounced shift in the locus of DMO funding had taken place – away from the public sector towards earned/private sector income streams. The survey findings confirm what we would have expected to be the case as per the discussion above in respect of the PPP and local government modes of DMO organisation, in that those DMOs which were departments of local government turned out to be heavily dependent on public sector grant support. In the case of the *Bratislava Tourist Board*, for instance, there was complete reliance on the public purse. On average in 2010, DMOs that were branches of city government received nearly three-quarters (69%) of their funding from the public sector, whereas for PPPs the comparable figure was less than half (43%). The ECM survey revealed that the amounts of earned/private sector funding leveraged by some PPPs on their 'core' funding was quite striking, e.g. for every €1 of core funding grant from the municipality and chamber of commerce, *Barcelona Tourism* levered €32 of trading income, the greater part of it earned from sales in the network of tourist information centres, souvenir shops and tourist bus services it operates. DMOs in Bergen, Oslo and York also demonstrated that they were adept at maximising revenues from earned and private sector sources, to the point where such monies formed 95%, 74% and 72%, respectively, of gross annual income. It should be noted that revenues from hypothecated tourist taxation were available to just over a quarter of the 2010 survey respondents, notably city tourist offices and convention bureaux in the countries of Croatia, Austria, Slovenia and Switzerland. VTB, for instance, derived nearly half of its annual income from this source, forming one leg of a relatively stable three-legged stool; the remaining two legs were city government grant and earned/private sector revenues. *Ljubljana Tourism* obtained a comparable amount of its annual income from tourist taxation, although in this case casinos as well as hotels were the basis of the tax revenues collected.

As far as the conventional breakdown into overheads and operating costs is concerned, the ECM survey reported labour and other overhead accounting on average for just over half of DMO gross expenditure (52%). The remaining 48% comprised operating expenses, i.e. the actual marketing cash available to the DMO. The 2010 overhead to operating ratio of 52:48 compared with 46:54 reported in 2003.

Unsurprisingly, within these averages, there was considerable variation by individual DMOs. Indeed, the 2010 survey showed that the proportion spent on operating varied from a low of 14% (Dijon) to a high of 80% (Lisbon). In respect of how operating monies were spent, the ECM survey indicated the dominant expenditure categories were, unsurprisingly, marketing and communications (57%) and visitor servicing (22%), the former targeting short breaks/city breaks and conventions/meetings, and the latter attributable to the management of tourist information centres and related expenses (typically visitor cards, apps, and training courses for the local tourist sector in customer handling and product knowledge). Attracting, hosting and in some cases producing major events – typically sporting championships and festivals – was also an important expenditure head for some cities and towns (10%). It should be noted that the 10% figure is an average, as only just over a quarter of the DMOs surveyed possessed an events capability of a sporting/cultural kind (see Section 3.5 of the next chapter). The remaining 5% of operating budget was devoted to research and intelligence.

Three further points in respect of DMO finances are worth emphasising. First, the relative prowess of PPP-based DMOs in generating earned and private sector income streams tends to have a disproportionately large effect on the sum of operating monies which they then have at their disposal. This is exemplified in Table 2.2, showing the income and expenditure of £6 million for

Table 2.2 *Glasgow City Marketing Bureau* budget, 2012/2013

Income	£ million	Expenditure	£ million
City government grant	3.9	Labour	2.1
Membership fees	0.2	Other overheads	0.6
Commissions	0.2	Operating	3.3
Private sector contributions	1.7		
Gross income	**6.0**	**Gross expenditure**	**6.0**

Source: Glasgow City Marketing Bureau.

which GCMB budgeted in the 2012/2013 financial year. As far as expenditure is concerned, just under a half (45%) goes on overheads, especially wages and salaries, leaving operating monies (i.e. marketing cash) of £3.3 million. On income, it can be seen from Table 2.2 that city government core funding of £3.9 million more than covers the overhead in the sense that there is a residual £1.2 million which can be used for marketing purposes. In a hypothetical situation in which GCMB levered no earned and private sector income (as would largely be the case if it were a local government based DMO), this residual amount would in effect be GCMB's marketing budget. The impact of the £2.1 million grossed from earned and private sector income streams was therefore to swell operating budgets by some 175%, i.e. from £1.2 million to £3.3 million, resulting at the same time in a much healthier ratio of overhead to operating expense (viz. from £1.0:£0.40 or 69:31, to £1.0:£1.22 or 45:55). In the case of the *Belfast Convention and Visitor Bureau* (now *Visit Belfast*), the proportionate impact of earned and private sector income streams is lessened as a result of the Bureau operating a comprehensive and labour-intensive network of tourist information centres associated with which are operating costs of just over £1 million (see Table 2.3). GCMB, it should be noted, undertakes no visitor-servicing activities and therefore carries no such overhead. So in the case of the *Belfast Convention and Visitor Bureau*, budgeted earned income for 2011/2012 brought about an 86% increase in operating budget, as the earned income of £0.9 million levered on the public sector core funding of £2.6 million boosted operating cash from just over £600,000 to £1.1 million (see Table 2.3). Clearly, however, whatever the proportionate impact, the lesson to be drawn is that income earned from trading and that garnered from the private sector is of critical significance in providing the DMO with its working capital or operating cash. In turn, and as mentioned above, these revenue-earning capabilities depend strongly on the DMO having PPP status.

Secondly, for those PPPs that do not have recourse to hypothecated tax revenues and/or relatively generous levels of public sector grant, the requirement to maximise earned income from trading and private sector

Table 2.3 *Belfast Visitor and Convention Bureau* budget, 2011/2012

	£
Income	
Belfast City Council grant	1,942,000
Other local authority grant	100,000
Northern Ireland Tourist Board grants	601,000
Public sector sub-total	**2,643,000**
Private sector income streams	690,000
Visitor servicing – gross margin on trading and other income	328,000
Private sector and earned sub-total	**1,018,000**
Total income	**3,661,000**
Expenditure	
Labour – marketing and administration	630,000
Overhead – marketing and administration	318,000
Visitor servicing overhead	1,093,000
Overhead sub-total	**2,041,000**
Leisure tourism marketing	800,000
Leisure tourism marketing support	389,000
Business tourism marketing	155,000
Communications	171,000
Web and digital	105,000
Operations sub-total	**1,620,000**
Total expenditure	**3,661,000**

Source: Belfast Visitor and Convention Bureau.

contributions will be the basis of the DMO's very survival in the sense of it remaining in accounting terms 'a going concern'. Inasmuch as (1) earned income levels are by their very nature always somewhat problematic from one year to the next; and (2) core funding from the public sector has been progressively reduced in many European countries in recent years, a climate of financial uncertainty currently pervades DMO operations (Coles *et al.*, 2012). One of our interviewees spoke graphically about how his DMO was now obliged to eke out a precarious financial existence:

> We desperately need to shoot this 30 second ad as we speak. Everything is agreed; the production company are lined up, the script and storyboard have been agreed, but I haven't got the cash. We've got no reserves upon which I can draw. We have buttons for money nowadays. My marketing

budget this year is just £450,000; it sounds a lot to Mrs Jones down the road, but it costs me £100,000 just to produce the visitor guide. You are constantly battling for cash. I am dealing with lots of local authorities who are giving me little bits and pieces of cash. There are so many eggs in the basket, and you are reliant on them all staying in, but budgets are so tight for the local authorities nowadays. For instance, Sheffield used to put £25,000 a year into us, but recently they reduced that to £10,000. So what do I do? I spend most of my time going round with a begging bowl. (James, 2013)

Another example is provided by *Visit York*. Table 2.4 reveals the organisation's heavy dependency on earned income streams, with 81% of its £1.7 million income being assembled in this way during the 2011/2012 year. In a situation where core funding had been significantly reduced from that obtaining in the previous year, the organisation's existence became 'precarious and hand-to-mouth' (Cruddas, 2014). Table 2.4 shows that the actual level of earned income by the end of the financial year had fallen short of that originally budgeted for by some £98,000 (6%), resulting in a trading deficit of £67,000.

Table 2.4 *Visit York* income and expenditure 2011/2012, budget versus actual

	Budget (£)	Actual (£)
Income		
Core funding	313,000	313,000
Membership fees	372,000	369,000
Publications advertising revenues	284,000	259,000
Web revenues	53,000	52,000
Visitor card sales	348,000	297,000
Partner contributions: leisure tourism campaigns	40,000	59,000
Partner contributions: conventions	138,000	105,000
Tourist information centre gross profit margin and other sales	177,000	164,000
Other	32,000	41,000
Total income	**1,757,000**	**1,659,000**
Expenditure		
Head office – marketing and administration	1,382,000	1,364,000
Tourist information centre	379,000	362,000
Total expenditure	**1,761,000**	**1,726,000**
	(–4,000)	(–67,000)

Source: Visit York.

For a not-for-profit company aiming to balance its books year-in year-out, this represented a financially unsustainable situation 'going forward', necessitating an unwanted reduction in 'head-count'.

A further illustration of the financial knife-edge on which many DMOs find themselves is provided by *Marketing Cheshire*, the DMO for Chester and its rural hinterland. This DMO has registered a 90% cut in its public sector grant income between 2011 and 2014, to the point where core funding now forms only 20% of annual income, with labour costs having to be pared by 30% in the 2013/2014 year (Michel, 2014a). The CEO there referred to the 'piddly' amounts of operating monies now at her disposal, and to how raising money had come to lie at the heart of the DMO's day-to-day relationships with its various partners and commercial members:

> DMOs are under massive funding pressures. We have hardly any money. Our concept of partnership now has to be that we both get something out of it. If you come into my office asking me to help you, it has got be clear that there is money in it for both of us. Otherwise, I'm not going to be very co-operative. (Michel, 2014b)

Marketing Cheshire increasingly has recourse to selling consultancy services to external clients, exploiting the fact that 'our rate is pitched about 40% below local competitors' (Michel, 2014b).

A final example is *Bath Tourism Plus*, whose overall reliance on public sector income has fallen from 50% to 29% in the space of just four years (Brook-Sykes, 2014). The situation in England to a large extent mirrors that in other 'Euro-debt' countries such as France, Portugal, Spain, Italy and Greece, but contrasts sharply with the relative stability of funding regimes elsewhere in Europe, notably Scandinavia, Belgium and Germany, but especially in Austria and Switzerland where hypothecated tourism taxation levied on businesses and/or on visitors provides both a surety and scale of income denied to the majority of European DMOs. For instance, nearly three-quarters (69%) of VTB's budget for 2013 of €24.6 million derived from a local accommodation tax (VTB, 2013a: 1–2), whereas *Innsbruck Tourism* received virtually all of its 2013 income of circa €50 million from taxes levied on enterprises and visitors (Kraft, 2013).

Thirdly, there is among DMOs a strong and proper concern with financial probity, albeit practices designed to ensure this vary according to whether or not the organisation is PPP or local government based. In the PPP model, accounts are each year the subject of independent, external audit, and on a day-to-day basis appropriate processes and systems are put in place to regulate expenditure and the receipt of income. The Chief Executive of GCMB refers to the need to be 'whiter than white' when spending what is in effect 'somebody else's money', even to the point of reimbursing funding partners in cases of underspend on specific projects (Taylor, 2013). The former Chief

Executive of *Gothenburg & Co* summed up the financial probity requirement by saying of his tenure (1991–2008):

> We never lost any money. We always kept the financial situation under good control. No scandals. One big mistake, one dishonest thing, and you're done for. (Bjerkne, 2013)

Intimately connected to finance is the question of partnering, associated with which are two types of scheme, viz. commercial and corporate. For reasons already discussed, such schemes are found only in DMOs organised as PPPs, where they are premised on the notion of effectively engaging the local private sector as financial and operational partners. While commercial membership schemes have routinely been applied in PPP-based DMOs throughout England and parts of Europe, corporate schemes are far from commonplace, but where they do exist they can be highly successful in terms of income generation. Table 2.5 summarises the partnering schemes run by 10 leading UK DMOs, indicating a mean income level from commercial membership fees of £127,000, whereas the comparable figure for corporate schemes is £314,000. Having said that, it must be borne in mind that the fee element of commercial membership is essentially an 'entry-level' charge, and in that sense it represents only the visible tip of an iceberg of funding with which it is associated. In other words, commercial membership usually delivers a set of private sector budgetary inputs from a combination of membership fees and additional opportunities to invest in DMO projects and campaigns. The entry-level fee delivers the member a basic level of exposure

Table 2.5 Commercial partnering in 10 UK DMOs, 2011/2012

Name of DMO	Number of commercial members	Fee total (£)	Number of corporate members	Donor income (£)
Bath Tourism Plus	482	96,000	X	X
Visit Belfast	512	153,000	X	X
Cardiff and Co	200	80,000	19	260,000
Experience Nottinghamshire	250	140,000	X	X
Glasgow City Marketing Bureau	250	165,000	X	X
Marketing Birmingham	300	160,000	93	408,000
Marketing Leeds	X	X	53	150,000
Liverpool City Region LEP	470	173,000	100	500,000
Newcastle Gateshead Initiative	99	40,000	14	251,000
Visit York	700	270,000	X	X

Source: Heeley (2012b).

for his or her business in terms of listings on the DMO's consumer-facing website and in core visitor and other publications. Potentially, there are then five additional levels of contribution, comprising: (1) commissions paid by members on direct business referrals by the DMO (typically those levied on hotel, venue and ticketing sales); (2) charges to secure participation in trade shows and other events via, for example, print collateral and/or 'stand-share'; (3) advertising fees, so that a member gains enhanced exposure on the consumer-facing website and in the main visitor publications, and the chance to be featured in specific marketing campaigns; (4) in-kind or discounted contributions in respect of DMO-organised site inspections and media visits; and (5) charges levied on members for specific items such as training, literature supplies and sales missions. The extent to which these five additional levels of contribution are presented as member benefits varies from one DMO to the next, as does the degree of member exclusivity. For example, some DMOs will offer level 4 marketing opportunities and others will not, while some DMOs will make level 5 'member only' and others will not. Such variation reflects the essentially historic and pragmatic way in which membership schemes have evolved in the UK. The twin challenges for DMOs are to delineate and communicate in the clearest and most compelling way what is or isn't a member benefit, and to present a benefits package which is as comprehensive as possible. In this way, the value of the entry-level membership fees may be trebled. For instance, in the case of *Visit Belfast*, 2011/2012 fee income from its 385 commercial members grossed £153,000 and was then accompanied by further financial contributions totalling £420,000. These came in the form of commissions and contributions towards various DMO marketing campaigns, publications and other projects. Viewed in this way, every £1 of fee income was associated with an additional financial commitment of £2.74 (Heeley, 2012b: 24). A similar 1:3 ratio is reported by *Bath Tourism Plus* (Brook-Sykes, 2014). As one DMO succinctly put it: 'what the member buys into is key, the entry fee is just that' (Simpson, 2014).

Commercial as opposed to corporate membership draws on the local tourist trades of towns and cities and, as such, the membership is predominantly small to medium-sized enterprises (SMEs). The commercial membership scheme run by *Bath Tourism Plus*, for instance, enlists just over 500 businesses, of which 85% are SMEs (Brook-Sykes, 2014). Unsurprisingly, accommodation providers are numerically the most important category; in the membership schemes operating in York and Bath, for instance, they make up 50% and 43%, respectively, of the total. Catering, retail and visitor attractions swallow up the bulk of the remainder: 36% in York and 34% in Bath (Heeley, 2012b: 23). Membership fees vary by category and size of enterprise, but in the 2011/2012 year the average fee obtaining in the nine membership schemes referred to in Table 2.5 came within a £199–£660 range. Conceptually, commercial membership schemes may be seen as having a dual function; first, they furnish the DMO with a regular and potentially crucial set of private sector income streams; secondly, they enable the DMO to maximise the involvement of the local tourist industry in its marketing and visitor servicing operations. No individual trader, large or small, has the ability or wherewithal to undertake marketing and visitor-servicing operations on behalf of the destination as a whole (self-evidently, that is the unique role of the DMO). Through membership of the DMO, however, an individual trader is able both to contribute financially and participate operationally, deriving (at least potentially) commercial 'bottom-line' benefit. As his or her enterprise collaborates with other members in activities orchestrated by the DMO, the member enjoys networking and other B2B gains. The relationship between member and DMO is therefore one of mutual benefit, although arguably more emphasis nowadays is placed by the DMO on the networking gains as opposed to the more direct commercial benefits. As the former Chief Executive of the DMO for the city of York suggests:

> Our message to the commercial tourist sector in the city is that they **have** to be a part of *Visit York* through membership. It's all about networking them so that they feel they are part of a club; it's particularly important to have connections with kindred businesses, especially when you're just starting up. The reality is, however, that when member businesses are doing well, they don't really need the DMO. Third party booking agencies mean we are able to provide our hotels and other accommodation providers with fewer and fewer bookings. If members measured the direct benefit they got from us, then most of them wouldn't get a return, but most of them don't bother (to measure the benefit), and in any case you hope they see the bigger picture. (Cruddas, 2014)

Membership prospectuses and other collateral produced by DMOs naturally highlight the importance of partnership and the networking and business benefit fundamentals. For instance, *Visit York*'s membership prospectus is entitled *'Good for Business'* and its members' handbook *Showcasing York to the World* suggests membership means 'you are automatically benefiting from our collective efforts to market York, Yorkshire and England' (Heeley, 2012b: 12). The *Newcastle Gateshead Initiative* (NGI) publishes a partnership charter setting out the aims and philosophy which lie at the back of its commercial membership scheme. In return for 'networking, marketing and business' benefits, it asks its members to commit to being 'a vocal and positive advocate' for the city region (Heeley, 2012b: 12). Similarly, *Marketing Birmingham* suggests that its commercial members are 'more than members'; they are 'partners on the road to an even more successful Birmingham and West Midlands' (Heeley, 2012b: 13).

It should be noted that commercial membership schemes are difficult for DMOs to 'get right' for four main reasons. First, the aims and philosophy underpinning commercial membership are often poorly articulated by the DMO at the time of the scheme's inception, and/or get 'lost in time' once the scheme 'beds in' and becomes established. Secondly, members are in general reluctant to part with the monies represented by their fees and the additional 'marketing opportunities' into which they are encouraged to invest. As time goes on, it is all too easy for DMOs to take members (and their financial contributions) for granted and to stereotype them as continually 'carping' or 'moaning' about their contributions. The vicious circle is completed when member attitudes harden in the form of perceptions that the DMO is parasitic, peripheral and underperforming. Thirdly, commercial membership schemes tend to have a large number of passive members; a 'knock on' problem associated with this is that it can contribute to membership scheme inertia as DMOs 'let sleeping dogs lie' rather than proactively seek to tackle the reasons for passivity. Fourthly, DMO reporting arrangements to record member details and involvement are often inadequate, which in turn makes it difficult and time consuming to communicate value for money and 'payback' to members (Heeley, 2012b). For the above-mentioned reasons, commercial membership is entered into reluctantly by most DMOs, driven as it is by financial exigencies. As much is captured in these remarks by the Chief Executive of *Leicester Shire Promotions*:

> Well, we dropped the commercial membership scheme we had developed on the conference side because it fundamentally affected the relationship we had with the hotels and other venues. As a DMO, what we need is to have the industry's support, and to know that they are 100% on our side. As soon as we introduced a commercial membership scheme, everything changed and suddenly the relationship was very much based on commercial criteria. Every year when we went to talk to the hotels and venues about their membership fee, it was a case of 'well let's have a look at what we've had from you'. And it all became very mercenary and materialistic, and the only thing that seemed to count in their eyes was 'how much business have we had from you?' The minute we started to charge them a fee, we also found ourselves spending a lot of time chasing commission, arguing whether or not this was due on a booking we had generated for them. They would say 'we were talking to that conference buyer before you anyway'. Another disadvantage is that we started to get inaccurate data from the hotels and venues because – if they declared a conference booking – then they feared we'd try and charge a commission. We were between a rock and a hard place. So eventually, sometime in the late 1990s, we met with the hotels and venues and decided to scrap the membership fee. So we moved over to a shopping list approach in which any commercial operator could voluntarily buy into a raft of marketing projects and campaigns. And we've never looked back to be honest. There is a wider angle, too. A word most

destination organisations use to describe themselves is 'official' – the official tourism website, the official tourism guide, the official tourism body, and so on. By using that word, you imply a degree of impartiality. The second you introduce a membership fee you become partial. You lose your impartiality as a DMO, and that gives me a concern from a consumer point of view, because the one thing that a consumer ought to get from a DMO is an unbiased overview of what that destination offers. They're not getting that if you've got a membership fee because the members get priority. (Peters, 2014)

Corporate as opposed to commercial membership schemes are a relatively recent phenomenon, having been pioneered in the 1990s by *Gothenburg & Co* and the *Merseyside Partnership* (an organisation now subsumed within the Liverpool City Region Local Enterprise Partnership), with a handful of similar city-based initiatives emerging in the following decade. Interestingly, *Gothenburg & Co* from the onset rejected partnering based on commercial membership and associated fee collection in favour of a corporate network. As the founder Chief Executive of the company reflected:

We went on a study tour in the US and discovered that the visitor and convention bureaux there had to work really hard at attracting commercial members. They had to hire a lot of people to do this who, at the end of the day, were costing nearly as much as they brought in! We also found most of the members were not happy; the bureaux were never able to do enough to satisfy them, and it changed the focus of the actual marketing away from what was attractive about the destination to promoting individual properties owned by the member – their brand of restaurant, hotel or whatever was uppermost and not the destination as a whole. So we at *Gothenburg & Co* never had commercial members. We turned the matter on its head, and went instead for the top 20 or so companies who could really make a difference. Some of these were from the tourist industry – the ferry lines and the Liseberg amusement park, for example – but most were from real estate, financial services, manufacturing and so on, including the universities. We got Volvo involved. When the big players had all agreed to come on board, we were really on our way. (Bjerkne, 2013)

At the time of writing, the involvement of these companies within *Gothenburg & Co* is discharged primarily through a standing committee of the company known as the Trade and Industry Group. There are 26 companies in total, and each makes a €25,000 annual donation, with the resultant €1.4 million being expended on a variety of projects designed to enhance the image of the destination. There is no expectation on their part of commercial 'payback'; instead there is a commitment to 'sharing the spirit of being engaged in the city of which they are part' (Nymen, 2013).

As far as the UK is concerned, Table 2.5 indicates the number of 'corporates' recruited to five leading DMO schemes and the income with which they were associated. The pioneering Liverpool scheme is nowadays based on a flat-rate donation of £5000 a year, yielding a £500,000 income stream. In 2002, *Marketing Birmingham* (through the author who was then its founder CEO) launched a corporate scheme which it dubbed 'Championing Birmingham'; this attracted into membership the likes of the three universities, Aston Villa Football Club, property companies, law firms and accountants, as well as world-class brands such as Jaguar and Cadbury Schweppes. 'Champs' donated annually a sum of money of their choice of between £5000 and £15,000, contracted over a three-year period (Heeley, 2011: 95–96). Corporate membership schemes prove attractive to medium- to large-scale businesses which view themselves as having a commitment to corporate social responsibility (CSR) and/or as having strong local roots and presence in the city or town in question. In contrast to commercial membership, recruitment to corporate schemes majors not on mutual financial benefit, but on CSR and 'love of place' (Heeley, 2011: 90), as reflected in the following extract from recruitment materials associated with the NGI corporate membership scheme:

> A gold partner is one of North East England's most influential businesses or organisations; one which shares Newcastle Gateshead Initiative's high ambitions for the region and is absolutely integral to the successful development of Newcastle and Gateshead. (Heeley, 2012b: 26)

Numbered among the recruits are: the Arts Council (North East England); the local airport, universities and colleges; Newcastle United Football Club; Virgin Money; Ryder Architecture; Nexus (transport) and Ward Hadaway (legal).

In return for their donations, corporate members expect high-level connectivity through networking events with civic leaders and fellow 'corporates', as well as the enhanced company profile that comes from being seen to support the city or town. As a generalisation, it would be fair to say that establishing a corporate membership scheme within a DMO context is problematic, precisely because the organisation is typically perceived by business leaders as being 'tourism' and about overnight stay generation, with a linked accountability to the local tourist trade. To assuage such sentiments, recruitment of corporate members places great emphasis on the important role that the DMO plays in raising the urban profile generally and projecting positive perceptions of a town or city as a fine place in which to live, work and invest. This is exemplified in recruitment material for 'Cardiff City Champions':

> The initiative offers companies the opportunity to contribute to and be associated with the efforts to promote the city-region. Becoming a Cardiff City Champion will result in widespread recognition of your company's

investment in the promotion of Wales' capital city, which will, in turn, help raise your profile in a positive way. (Heeley, 2012b: 26)

Taken together, commercial and corporate membership provide PPP-based DMOs with vital financial contributions as well as 'root and branch' foundations in partnership working. As we have seen, optimising the benefits flowing from such schemes presents a formidable set of challenges. If the DMO is denied scale and surety of funding from public sector grant and/or hypothecated tourist taxation sources – as is nowadays increasingly the case – then the DMO must perforce overcome these challenges if it is to obtain a level of resourcing within which it can have a realistic prospect of succeeding in its urban destination marketing. However reluctantly they may be entered into, robust and productive commercial and corporate membership schemes may be viewed as a necessary precondition of effective urban destination marketing.

2.6 Commentary

At the time of writing, virtually every town or city has a DMO, sometimes as a part of local government, but increasingly as a more or less independent PPP. There is nowadays, as one DMO chief says, almost 'blanket coverage' (Brook-Sykes, 2014). In the author's view, the role and make-up of such organisations is weakly understood by its customers and stakeholders and by society at large, a situation aggravated by the DMOs themselves in respect of the rather confusing manner in which they so often choose to name themselves and to articulate their core purpose. So, in respect of the ubiquitous European DMO, what is its essential character? What, as in one of the title-quotes to this chapter, is its 'real thing'?

As demonstrated in this chapter, DMO organisation everywhere bifurcates into governance and executive; whereas the size, function and composition of the former varies widely according to local circumstance, executive structure is demonstrably more uniform. The PPP model of DMO organisation is growing in popularity at the expense of its local government counterpart, its ascendency attributable to the financial and operational advantages with which it is associated. In general, however, lack of resourcing characterises most urban DMOs; as we have seen, almost two-thirds of the DMO respondents taking part in the 2010 ECM survey had annual operating budgets of €2 million or less. Inasmuch as ECM members tend to be more prominent and larger DMOs, many of them representing the larger capital and 'second' cities, then the resourcing available to the remainder of Europe's DMOs is considerably less than this average figure (as we have exemplified above and will elaborate upon in the final chapter). The relatively small operating budgets which typically obtain inevitably restrict what can be achieved operationally, while an increasing dependence on trading and 'earned' private sector income streams means that many DMOs are financially vulnerable, eking out a more or less precarious existence. Successful partnering via commercial and corporate membership schemes is becoming ever more critical to the build-up of operating budget and, in some cases, is crucial to ongoing viability, but this comes at a cost. Partnering is time consuming and carries with it administrative burdens. In the case of commercial membership, we have seen how it can have deleterious effects on a DMO's relationships with the tourist trade, and also lead to a loss of customer focus.

Throughout the DMO world, money (or more accurately the lack of it) is nearly always a dominant concern, and few practitioners would disagree with the proposition that most of Europe's DMOs face financially uncertain futures. Indeed, in this chapter I have endeavoured to show that DMO structures are shaped as much by financial exigencies as they are by the quest for operational effectiveness and impact. Many of the comments made above by DMO senior executives bear ample witness to the often pressing requirement to access the necessary financial wherewithal on which to survive and then operate. Equally (if not more) important, however, is the need for DMOs to access what Lincoln, as per one of the title quotes to this chapter, refers to as 'public sentiment'. This is the requirement to mould public opinion, so that stakeholders, customers and society at large gain a better and more positive understanding of the purpose and role of official DMOs. In contrast to the preoccupation with matters financial, this aspect is rarely to the fore of DMO thought and action. As a result, DMOs for the most part pay only lip service to corporate public relations and this, in turn, helps explain why they are obscure and opaque as to their core purpose and role (although more fundamental reasons are at work here as we shall discover in the chapter which follows). With the possible exception of VTB, the author cannot instance a case of a DMO developing and disseminating a truly coherent *corporate* vision and narrative for the organisation, defining and communicating its essential character and values (Lincoln's 'real thing') so as meaningfully to engage stakeholders, customers and society at large, and thereby gain their more or less fulsome appreciation and backing (Lincoln's 'public sentiment'). Without such 'public sentiment', ultimately, as per Lincoln's stricture, 'nothing can succeed'. No wonder, then, in the Foreword to this book, our DMO Chief Executive struggles when faced with the simple but 'dreaded' 'so what do you do?' question. Just as in August 2004 I struggled when the newly appointed Chairman of *Experience Nottinghamshire* (EN), to whom I as EN's Chief Executive was just about to start reporting, questioned me on the organisation's core purpose, challenging me to demonstrate that DMOs were something other than the 'woolly marketing organisations' he suspected they were (Heeley, 2011: 97). It is to these allegedly 'woolly' marketing operations that we now turn.

3 Urban Destination Marketing Operations

I felt a pleasure in ... walking about any town to which I am not accustomed. There is an immediate sensation of novelty; and one speculates on the way in which life is spent in it, which although there is a sameness everywhere upon the whole, is yet minutely diversified. The minute diversities in everything are wonderful.

Samuel Johnson, Friday 19 September 1777, as recorded in Boswell (2008) *The Life of Samuel Johnson*

The dream should be promoted ... the most wonderful cathedrals, the most delightful architecture, fine music and friendly people. Two weeks will cost you X dollars and you can hire a car for Y pounds.

Advertising agency chief, David Ogilvy (1973)

3.1 Introducing the DMO Urban Destination Marketing Template

In Chapter 1, I suggested destination marketing operations as these are presented in the academic literature (e.g. Ritchie & Crouch, 2003; Morrison, 2013; Pike, 2008) are somewhat different from the 'real-life' ones undertaken by DMOs – the organisations that actually 'do' urban destination marketing. In particular, the literature distorts reality because of its emphasis on destination brand and market positioning and on techniques such as market segmentation and the various types of resource audit. Destination brand, for instance, is viewed as the 'glue that holds the marketing of the destination together' and, as such, is 'central to the contemporary destination marketing process' (Cooper & Hall, 2013: 212, 222). For Pike and Page, everything a DMO does should reinforce the brand identity; DMOs attempt in all their marketing and communications activities to 'communicate the brand position ... as per the brand identity focus' (Pike & Page, 2014: 212). One text effectively reduces destination marketing to destination branding (Morgan *et al.*, 2008). In practice, destination branding is the relatively unimportant, routine and unproblematic manner in which DMOs create a 'look and feel' around their marketing materials (see Section 3.7 below and Heeley, 2011). In this and several other ways, the academic literature fails to 'tell it like it is', conditioned as it is by a paradigm which is in need of radical appraisal.

I will be elaborating upon this gulf between theory and practice and the need for paradigm change in Chapter 4, but before attempting to do this we must first provide an accurate and up-to-date evidential base covering the practice of urban destination marketing in contemporary Europe, acquainting the reader with the principal operational aspects – just as we did in the previous chapter in respect of DMO organisational parameters. To help the reader to 'cut into' and then penetrate the somewhat arcane, but 'real-life' world of urban destination marketing operations, he or she is referred to the DMO marketing template shown in Figure 3.1. There are five principal activity areas which DMO departmental organisation more or less mirrors, as can be confirmed from a perusal of the organisation charts forming Figures 2.1–2.4. Four of these activity areas comprise 'core' marketing operations, and the fifth is supporting web/digital, print and visitor-servicing tasks. While the template summarises how destination marketing is undertaken in contemporary Europe, on its own it tells us little about what is actually involved within each of the five activity areas. To, as it were, put flesh on the skeleton provided by Figure 3.1, Sections 3.2–3.6 of this chapter consider and exemplify each of the five activity areas in turn, hopefully simplifying and demystifying urban destination operations for the reader, while at the same time 'telling it like it is' in the words of the practitioners themselves. In a like manner, we go on in Sections 3.7 and 3.8 to appraise the branding, planning and performance management frameworks within which urban DMO operations are discharged.

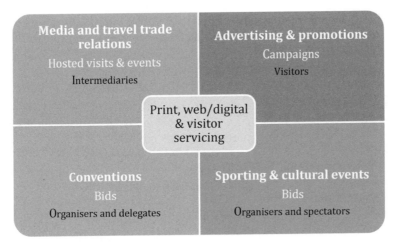

Figure 3.1 The DMO marketing template

3.2 Media and Travel Trade Relations

Media and travel trade relations comprise the first of our five activity areas and are essentially B2B (business to business); on the one hand, media relations seek to persuade journalists and other media to write positive 'pieces' about the destination and to otherwise give it constructive and helpful exposure; on the other hand, travel trade relations encourage tour operators, travel agencies and other intermediaries to handle specific destination products available in a town or city, such as weekend breaks, events, overnight stopovers and week-long holidays. The principal mechanism for targeting both of these audiences is the 'hosted' visit in which journalists and travel trade operators and intermediaries visit the town or city in order to sample its 'tourist offer'. Nearly always, the visit revolves around an itinerary put together by the DMO; the standard formula is one of sightseeing interspersed with refreshments and meals, with the itineraries spotlighting key aspects of the 'offer', 'spoon-feeding' relevant strands of information to journalists and travel trade in an imaginative as well as a comprehensive fashion. As we shall exemplify in the next chapter, the financial outlay from hosting such visits is modest in comparison to the tangible and measurable returns. The efficacy of hosted visits is widely appreciated by DMO chiefs:

> Don't underestimate press and PR. That doesn't cost you an awful lot of money. If you can get stories and coverage in newspapers like the Guardian or Daily Telegraph or better still, the quality Sundays, who all have travel supplements, then it's worth thousands of pounds. We measure this by something called advertising equivalence value, so that a full page of coverage in the Guardian, say, is worth about £10,000. And it costs you peanuts. You put the journalist up in a nice hotel, wine and dine them, and then you more or less tell them what you want them to write. People believe what they read in newspapers. (Wilkinson, 2014)

In a similar vein:

> It's my view that people don't like to be sold anything; they're suspicious of advertising. PR is different. When a journalist has written some glowing piece about the destination, then people believe it – even though it will have been our PR guys who will have written most of it! The journalists often just cut and paste into the Sunday Times Colour Supplement, or whatever. PR is very powerful in tourism. (James, 2013)

For instance, a press visit by *Air France Magazine* hosted by the *Glasgow City Marketing Bureau* (GCMB) over a five-day period (18–22 October 2012) resulted in a 14-page piece. Entitled '10 raisons d'aller Glasgow', this article appeared in the February 2013 edition of the in-flight *Air France Magazine*, whose readership at that time was put at 451,000 (Dyer, 2013). Were an equivalent amount of advertising to have been bought in this magazine, then the cost to the Bureau would have been €378,000 – a metric already mentioned above and referred to as advertising equivalence value (AEV). It is worth noting that this press trip was just one of eight organised by GCMB for French media in 2012 (Dyer, 2013). Although media and travel trade relations are a cost-effective and central aspect of DMO marketing operations, it is noteworthy that this topic receives scant attention in the academic literature. For instance, Pike's text *Destination Marketing* devotes just two of its 400 or so pages to press trips (Pike, 2008).

We go on to highlight exemplary media and travel trade relations activities in Section 5.6 of Chapter 5, as part of the best-practice case study of *Vienna Tourist Board*'s leisure tourism marketing.

3.3 Advertising and Promotions

The second main activity area identified in Figure 3.1 is advertising and promotions, which is arguably the one most readily associated with DMO marketing operations. In contrast to media and travel trade relations, it is essentially a set of B2C (business to consumer) operations. The central unit of this activity area is the campaign; in urban destination marketing these are invariably 'themed' upon some or other aspect of the urban tourism 'offer', targeting audiences on a more or less 'broad-brush' geographical basis. For instance, in Section 5.5 of Chapter 5 as part of the best-practice case study of VTB's leisure tourism marketing, we show how the main thrust of the Board's advertising and promotions is centred on a 'Vienna: Now or Never' offer taken to the capitals of 16 European countries. As another example, *Visit Belfast* promotes its short-break 'packages' to the rest of Ireland and the conurbations of northern England. In this connection, it should be noted that praxis in urban destination marketing rarely involves a recourse to the fine-tuned market positioning and segmentation exercises so dear to academic texts on this subject, and to the paradigm we are calling the 'theory of marketing competitive advantage'.

Urban DMOs in their campaigns have traditionally deployed a range of media formats in order to reach their projected audience: ranging from billboards and the backs of buses to advertisements in newspapers and journals, through to the production of brochures, TV and cinema commercials and promotional videos. Until late on in the last century, DMO advertising and promotions centred on posters and the production and distribution of guides and brochures, together with linked newspaper and magazine advertising (see Section 2.2 of Chapter 2). In the last decade of the 20th century and into the first two decades of the present one, the web/internet and, latterly, social media have become increasingly important mediums (Heeley, 2011).

Nowadays, much of the form and content of DMO advertising and promotional activities revolves around Facebook, YouTube, Twitter and Flickr. Relationships with booking engines such as Late Rooms and user-generated websites (notably TripAdvisor) are also important, as are mobile and digital formats generally. Interestingly, one factor contributing to the dominance of 'new media' is pragmatic considerations of cost; that is to say the relatively small operating budgets typifying urban destination marketing (see Chapter 2) mean that social media represents a low-cost alternative to 'traditional' and expensive forms of media advertising. It will doubtless surprise many readers that DMOs are often unable to afford television and other above-the-line expedients. Referring to his tenure as the Chief Executive of the *Lancashire and Blackpool Tourist Board* (2004–2012), Mike Wilkinson says:

> I had an annual budget of over £3 million, and 24 staff, but there was no above-the-line advertising in our campaigns. We didn't have that sort of money – so we had to be more inventive. (Wilkinson, 2014)

A mix of conventional and 'new media' formats is well illustrated in campaigns orchestrated throughout the 2012/2013 year by *Visit Belfast*'s 11-strong Department of Marketing and Communications. In that year, the Department was set to undertake five campaigns aimed at the UK/Ireland city break market, for which operational monies totalling £380,000 were budgeted (Heeley, 2012a). In autumn 2012 the first of these campaigns, based on a TV commercial, was undertaken in conjunction with a principal carrier (Stena Line Ferries) at a cost of £110,000. As this campaign was underway, flag protests and rioting adversely affected city centre trading (trading and other losses were estimated at £15 million), generating a rising tide of negative publicity for the destination. As a consequence, *Visit Belfast* radically revised its marketing plans, initiating a £700,000 'Backin' Belfast' campaign, made possible by additional funding from DETI (the Northern Ireland Department of Trade and Industry) and Belfast City Council, which staked £300,000 and £250,000, respectively (McMullan, 2013). The campaign plan was coordinated by *Visit Belfast*'s Director of Marketing and Communications, developed in conjunction with key stakeholders, and executed by her marketing and communications department, with the help of an advertising agency (Ardmore Advertising). Posters, a TV commercial, and several 'vox pops' on radio and television stations were produced. Press advertising was conducted locally and in the *Daily Mail*, and street theatre and other events were used to animate the city centre. As well as a dedicated 'Backin' Belfast' website, bespoke YouTube and Twitter pages were introduced. *Visit Belfast* commercial members and key institutions in the city were encouraged to offer in-kind contributions or to otherwise support the campaign. In this way, a radio station (Cool FM) made its presenters available, the drinks company DIAGEO came up with £140,000 of alcoholic products, hotels stumped up complimentary rooms, and the *Belfast Telegraph* replaced their rather draconian call to 'Save our City' with the altogether more inspiring 'We're Backing Belfast'.

'Backin' Belfast' is a classic example of the rear-guard marketing campaigns initiated by DMOs in response to crises and disasters, as discussed in the academic literature (e.g. Pike, 2008: Chapter 18). The 'normal' situation is one in which the DMO each year orchestrates one or a handful of campaigns working in conjunction with its members and partners, and relying on them for cash and in-kind support. For instance, prior to a radical change of approach which is highlighted in the next chapter, VTB for several years undertook two major 'shoulder month' campaigns. Entitled 'Wine & Design' and 'Shop & Win', the campaigns were telescoped within October/November and January/February periods, respectively (Weiss, 2009). Both campaigns were print and advertising led, targeting in a 'broad-brush' manner the capitals of Italy, Germany, Switzerland and England, as well as major towns and cities in Austria itself. Media advertising each year was supported by the production of 110,000 brochures and 2.7 million newspaper/magazine supplements. The emphasis on 'shoulder month' timing is important, as clearly it is counterproductive for a DMO to seek to increase tourism traffic at periods when hotels and other accommodation providers are already full, and when attractions and catering outlets are busy. Reflecting this, GCMB runs three leisure tourism campaigns corresponding to spring and autumn 'low seasons' and to the Christmas period (Rice, 2013). The thrust of *Marketing Manchester*'s advertising and promotions work is currently centred on two campaigns addressing high summer and Christmas (Simpson, 2014); the former is typically a so-called 'graveyard' period for urban accommodation outlets when convention and corporate custom dries up, and rural and seaside tourism is at its height. Christmas-based campaigns are extremely common among DMOs. The 2012 'Gothenburg Christmas City' campaign, for instance, carried through a love theme, and was spearheaded by *Gothenburg & Co* with the Liseberg theme park and ferry and hotel operators as strategic partners. The principal campaign medium was 1.5 million copies of a printed brochure, supported by outdoor advertising, as well as web and digital marketing (Gothenburg & Co, 2013: 21).

The main aim of the DMO leisure tourism marketing campaigns we have considered so far is to raise awareness, and in this sense a broad division is evident between campaigns which are 'generic' as opposed to more 'tactical', sales-driven ones, albeit there may be some overlap between the two. An interesting example of a tactical, sales-orientated initiative is 'Stay, Play and Explore', a demonstrably successful short-break campaign introduced by *Leicester Shire Promotions* in 2006. The Chief Executive of the DMO takes up the story:

'Stay, Play and Explore' came out of a chance conversation with one of our more switched on general managers. In 2006 he had taken up his post at a large, four star 150 bedroom hotel situated at Hinkley Island, just off the M1 motorway. At that time it had an almost exclusively business profile: it was classic 'four-sevenths of the week' trade, Monday to Thursday usage. As a result, during high summer the hotel was basically mothballed for 6–8 weeks; staff were either laid off or deployed to other hotels in the group. Things just ran on a skeletal basis. It was a case of bed and breakfast for a limited amount of passing trade. The general manager was keen to turn the space, capacity and *in situ* leisure facilities to better use, and was also willing to offer extremely competitive rates. Every hotel room is a perishable asset. So together we developed a concept, and then ran a campaign called 'Must See Three', which was a simple package of overnight accommodation and admission to three neighbouring visitor attractions, including the National Space Centre. This proved to be a great success, expanding in subsequent years to embrace more attractions and hotels, evolving into 'Stay, Play and Explore' and becoming more flexible. There are now three hotels and five attractions, from which customers can choose their hotel and the three attractions they are going to visit. So it has become a 'pick and mix' affair. There is nowadays a suite of six separate breaks, but they are all of them still focussing on the M1 corridor. And the hotel from where it all started is now as busy during the summer as it is for the rest of the year, and the general manager no longer has to lay off staff. What's the real secret of this campaign's success? Well, it does what it says on the tin. For a family of four it will cost you just £109, and for that you can go to three top visitor attractions and stay overnight in a four star hotel. That – more than anything else – is why it works so well. (Peters, 2014)

In the first year (2007/2008), bookings of 'Stay, Play and Explore' numbered 2708. These have risen steadily to reach 5646 in 2012/2013, which translates itself into approximately 22,000 bednights and £600,000 worth of revenue for the participating hotels and attractions. The target demographic is environmentally and socially conscious ABC1 families who are receptive to short-break offers featuring learning experiences for children. Marketing activity is supported by leaflet production and distribution, as well as 'niche' advertising, but is centred on various online promotions including e-direct mail and, increasingly, social media (Peters, 2014).

In contrast, the more 'generic' awareness-raising marketing campaigns undertaken by DMOs nearly always centre upon a principal media element, supported by poster advertisements at high-profile sites and associated advertising and press and PR. Early in 2014, for instance, *Visit York* commenced its main campaign for that year entitled 'When Was the Last Time You Had a First Time?':

We call it the first time campaign for ease. It's a big headline campaign specifically targeting first-time visitors to the city aged between 25–65 years. Though we know we have an ageing demographic, the campaign is using iconic, traditional York imagery. It is running in London and the South East, and in Scotland, with posters at high profile sites such as Kings Cross underground. For the first-time ever, we will be rolling out a planned schedule of TV advertising. We will be doing TV and cinema in Glasgow, and just cinema in London because the budget doesn't run to TV in London. We are partnered with East Coast Rail as well as a boutique hotel chain – Mr and Mrs Smith Hotels – and High 50 (a life-style website for the over-50s). Our main media partnership is with the Telegraph and Independent, so there will be destination pieces, videos and travel blogging, including stuff from Simon Calder (a well known travel journalist). The first phase of the campaign takes us to April when we will evaluate and take stock. (McMullen, 2014)

An earlier winter campaign undertaken by *Visit York* over a six-month 'off-peak' period (October 2012–March 2013) had been executed under the heading 'York Wrapped Up'. It sought to encourage UK residents to book a short-break holiday using the East Coast railway:

It was a play on words. Wrap yourself up warm and enjoy seasonal York, but also consider giving a visit to York as a Christmas present. We had posters at various railway stations – Newcastle, Victoria, Paddington and Euston – as well as on London underground stops. We also used 3D screens at Covent Garden, and did some effective national press advertising and linked press and PR. We advertised in the Guardian, Observer, Telegraph, Independent, Metro and the London Evening Standard. For two months during the campaign, the Independent's website ran a 20 minute video featuring the well known travel journalist Simon Calder, and we ran an online competition which attracted 13,000 entries. Some 7000 bednights were generated in the form of direct bookings from our website. That was a particularly successful campaign. (Cruddas, 2014)

In the light of the considerable expense involved in buying media time, DMOs frequently have recourse to creating short promotional films for onward distribution to free or low-cost terrestrial, satellite and social media channels. In addition, they seek to persuade members and partners to use their own channels to showcase these so-called 'promos'. In this manner, *Visit Cheshire* produced a ready-to-use 30-second commercial 'Chester: The Classical, Contemporary City', in August 2013, with a view to 'selling a weekend away in the city to female decision-makers' (Michel, 2014b). The commercial featured a mix of 'old' and 'new', emphasising the city's Roman origins and its 2000 years of heritage as a backdrop to a 21st-century lifestyle, with attendant opportunities for designer shopping, soothing spas and fine dining. The intent was to capture 'a beautiful setting, interesting but not too arduous things to do, independent shopping, and a great choice of restaurants and bars' (Marketing Cheshire, 2013). Explaining the rationale behind the choice of medium (Channel 4's 4oD), the Chief Executive of *Marketing Cheshire* remarks:

> We used it (the commercial) on our own website and on YouTube, and we ran it on 4oD – the equivalent of BBC iPlayer for Channel 4. Although you are not reaching huge amounts of people with 4oD, what you do know is that you have got an audience; they can't skip the ad like they can on TV. My audience is ABC1 women 30+ years old, so that the programming we would have gone into is what they like – cookery and beauty programmes and American series. It's better to have done 4oD than nothing at all, but in an ideal world, say if I had had £25,000, then I would have gone for a very 'light' campaign on digital Sky. That puts you into a bigger group; you get a greater reach. I wouldn't choose ITV even if the proverbial fairy godmother came up with the money. A very low rating, month-long campaign on ITV would start at around £100,000, but potentially this would generate so much demand that the hotels would not be able to cope. What we need is a steady drip of people responding. Low-level, 'drippy' campaigns in the shoulder months are what we need. (Michel, 2014b)

Advertising and promotional activities telescoped into campaigns and supplemented by media and travel trade relations activities lie at the heart of DMO leisure tourism marketing. The other side of the coin is business tourism marketing, and it is to this that we now turn our attention.

3.4 Conventions or Business Tourism

Conventions or business tourism marketing functions are occasionally discharged by a stand-alone organisational entity (e.g. the *Prague Convention Bureau*), but for the most part convention bureaux are part of wider DMO entities. For instance, the *Gdansk Convention Bureau* is one of four departments comprising the *Gdansk Tourism Organisation*: a PPP constituted as an association, with the city council as its principal member and strategic partner, together with a further 130 fee-paying commercial members (Górska, 2013). The Convention Bureau department is made up of just four staff, led by the organisation's Chief Executive Officer. Staffing complements and associated annual budgets devoted to convention bureau activities range from literally one person and an annual budget of a few thousand pounds (e.g. the *Sheffield Convention Bureau* which is part of *Marketing Sheffield*) to the likes of the convention department of GCMB with its 18 staff members; this department forms the best-practice case study in Section 5.7 of Chapter 5.

Another well-resourced and effective operation is the *Wonderful Copenhagen Convention Bureau*; for the 2012 year, it could boast 15 staff and a €2.4 million budget (Jakobsen, 2012). The latter budget, high though it is in European terms, is small when compared to leading convention bureaux in Australia and North America. For example, the *Melbourne Convention and Visitors Bureau* has no less than 48 staff and a 2011/2012 budget of €9.1 million (Melbourne Convention Bureau, 2013).

The activities of DMO convention bureaux or business tourism departments centre on bids for 'footloose' association and corporate meetings, and on assisting with the subsequent delivery or hosting of such events. There is often intense competition between bureaux to secure meetings, reflecting the relatively high average per capita daily expenditure of business tourists which, in turn, translates into much sought after employment and other economic gains. At a national level, for instance, a recently published study estimates the gross economic contribution of the UK meetings and events industry to be equivalent to 2.9% of GDP and 423,000 full-time equivalent (FTE) jobs, making it the country's 17th most important industry (MPI, 2013: 3). At the level of town and city, where the impact of conferences and linked events are concentrated, these economic effects are pronounced and visible, although perhaps somewhat obscured by the generally prosaic and esoteric titles of the meetings taking place. For example, VTB's successful bids for the annual congresses of the European Society for Radiotherapy and Oncology and the European Music Therapy Confederation (to be staged, respectively, in 2014 and 2016) are estimated to have a combined value of €12 million to the local economy (VTB, 2012). A further example is the five-day annual meeting of the European Society of Gastroenterology which – when held in Vienna in October 2014 – was expected to attract 14,000 delegates generating expenditure in excess of €27 million (VTB, 2013b). One of the largest conventions hosted by Vienna in recent years has been the European Congress in Radiology which was attended by no less than 20,000 delegates (VTB, 2013c).

In any one year, VTB's convention department (the *Vienna Convention Bureau*) will prepare upwards of 35–40 bid proposals (or 'bid books') for specific association or corporate events, often in response to an RFP, i.e. a request for proposals (Mutschlechner, 2013). In 2011 the *Wonderful Copenhagen Convention Bureau* made 103 such bids for specific international association and other meetings, of which just under a half (50) were confirmed (Jakobsen, 2012). From these events, the anticipated delegate numbers and expenditure were estimated at 80,136 and €150 million, respectively. The latter figure represented just under a third (32%) of total business tourism spending in the Copenhagen district in that year (Jakobsen, 2012). A simple division of the €150 million by the annual cost of the *Wonderful Copenhagen Convention Bureau* (€2.4 million) indicates an impressive rate of return on marketing investment (ROI) of 62:1. A final example is *Gothenburg & Co*, where the convention department originated or influenced the staging of 66 meetings in 2012, generating 48,000 delegates whose spending totalled €36 million (Gothenburg & Co, 2013: 25). One such event, the Astra Tech World Congress – won in the face of competition from Milan and London – attracted 3000 dental care specialists from 48 countries to the city (Gothenburg & Co, 2013).

The work of convention bureau departments in bidding for events and assisting in their hosting is supported by the following: participation in trade shows; compilation of statistical data; production of promotional materials, especially meeting planner guides which provide an overview of venues and other arrangements; site inspections at which association 'clients' or professional conference organisers review venues, access and other arrangements; participation in international organisations, especially the International Congress and Convention Association (ICCA) which maintains an important database of international association meetings from which potential 'leads' can be sourced; and the management of local ambassador networks in which bureaux enlist the support of academics, doctors and others who work locally in order to 'bring home' specific association and other meetings. GCMB's pioneering and much-copied conference ambassador scheme has at the time of writing over 1700 active members and, as we shall see in Chapter 5, is viewed as critical to the success of the Bureau's business tourism marketing and sales activities. Not all convention bureaux, however, adopt this expedient. According to the Director of VTB's convention department:

> You can argue a lot about ambassador programmes. The way we work is as follows; if we need a local representative, then we talk to that person. If he or she says 'yes I'm interested' then we move forward, and he or she becomes a kind of ambassador. I'm always anxious about systems which demand extra staff time, and what I have observed over the years is that there is a huge danger of ambassador programmes becoming a self-fulfilling prophecy, taking up quite a lot of cash plus a staff member, and I'm a little bit doubtful about the outcome. (Mutschlechner, 2013)

Another important difference between convention bureaux occurs in respect of membership schemes. As we have seen in Chapter 2, for GCMB this is an important source of income, but for VTB commercial membership represents an unnecessary distraction:

> A major reason for our success story is the way the convention bureau is structured. It's still more or less the same as it was back in 1969 when it was founded. We have no members, and that is key. Many bureaux in the world need to have membership, but it creates a lot of trouble and problems for the staff who get diverted from their real work in order to keep the members happy. That has never been the case for Vienna. The main point I kept stressing when we were set up in 1969 was that our Bureau

had to be a non-supported institution. Our clients – the event organisers and PCOs (professional conference organisers) – are the kings for us. We are driven by them, not the industry in Vienna. (Mutschlechner, 2013)

Characteristic features of the bid process for conventions are protracted lead times, as well as accommodating to rotational patterns and the wishes of event organisers, all of which emphasises the long-term nature of acquiring and hosting meetings. The Director of VTB's convention department remarks:

> Well a bid that comes immediately to my mind is the one we made for the World Lung Cancer Congress. We started working on it as far back as 1999, and made our first bid in 2000, but lost. We made a second bid for the event taking place in the 2011 year, and again we lost. A third bid for the 2017 event was successful. However, the association then came back to us and said they would like 2016 rather than 2017. Fortunately, we were able to offer them a date in that year. So this shows you the time dimension which underpins this business, in this case 1999 to 2016, nearly twenty years. Helping us with all three bids was a local professor. In this business, you sometimes need to lose pro-actively, so that you can win on the second or third try. You can't win all the bids. You are rather successful if you achieve a win ratio of about 50%. (Mutschlechner, 2013)

VTB's convention department is regarded as being one of the most effective in Europe. Its Director, Christian Mutschlechner, puts this down to the city's leading-edge infrastructure and venues, supported by the operations of his own department. In respect of the former, a critical factor had been the decision to develop the Austria Centre conference complex, which opened in 1987 with a capacity to accommodate up to 15,000 delegates at any one time:

> In the late '70s the plan was announced to build the Austria Centre which sparked off a national debate and eventually a referendum at which 1.8 million Austrians voted against the proposed venue being constructed. The Chancellor at that time had the vision and strength of mind to say that while he fully respected the views of the 1.8 million, he was also minded to consider the 5 million or so Austrians who hadn't bothered to vote. So the development went ahead. As a destination, we wouldn't be in the position we are today without the Austria Centre. (Mutschlechner, 2013)

Impressively, Mutschlechner's department commits to service RFPs within a 24-hour timescale, even if they are lodged over a weekend (Mutschlechner, 2014). He stresses the value of being able to appoint staff drawn from the private sector, creating a business culture within the *Vienna Convention Bureau* which embodies 'target and service orientated behaviour':

> There are simple rules. One of them is that no telephone should ring three times or more before it is picked up. Whoever picks it up, everybody hears it. I do the same. There are no barriers. Everybody can call me direct. We have a very flat operating structure which is completely and one hundred percent service-oriented to the customer. (Mutschlechner, 2013)

A final and critical point pertaining to convention bureau staff is the requirement to obtain a judicious split between the researchers who source potential leads using databases such as the ICCA one referred to above, and sales staff who convert and otherwise fulfil those leads once they have become 'live'. The Chief Executive of GCMB says:

> To win conferences, it takes a serious commitment to research. I recall ICCA conducted an analysis of the frequency that UK cities used their research database, and found that most cities never used what is at the end of the day a critical, if 'dry and dusty', resource. Paying to be a member of ICCA and attending the events, but not doing the basic research amounts to a pretence, and it has unintended and unfortunate consequences. The expectations of stakeholders and industry are falsely raised. Convention bureaux need to look at the resources they allocate to research and establish clear performance measures to ensure focus. The profile and skill-set of a researcher is completely different to that needed by a sales manager. Bureaux who fail to employ motivated people with the right skill-sets and business experience will always be behind the ones that do. The competition between bureaux for conferences is as much about staff competency, skill and focus as it is about anything else. (Taylor, 2013)

Along with the PPP-based convention departments for Berlin, Barcelona, Copenhagen and Gothenburg, Vienna and Glasgow are acknowledged as 'top' operators in what is a highly competitive field.

3.5 Sporting and Cultural Events

A fourth and final core DMO activity area is sporting and cultural events as depicted in Figure 3.1. An initial point worth stressing here is that relatively few DMOs major on this aspect. In general, the functions involved are discharged by local government and, in particular, departments dealing with sport, leisure and recreation. Having said that, a few towns and cities have opted for an arms-length DMO mechanism to coordinate bidding and/or hosting arrangements for 'flagship' cultural and sporting events (e.g. GCMB). In certain cases, this bidding and hosting role has been extended to producing an annual programme of 'hallmarking' cultural and other events (e.g. *Gothenburg & Co*). The event role of the *Munich Tourist Office*, for instance, comprises the organisation of the world-renowned 'Oktoberfest', while the *Split Tourist Board* undertakes summer season animation of key historic sites. *Visit Brussels* have an eight-strong Events Team which in 2011 produced and otherwise supported major events such as 'Brusselicious' (a gourmet food festival), 'Brussels Design Week', 'Brussels Mania Party' (for young people staying in the city for a short period of study or employment) and 'Winter Wonders' (Bontink, 2011).

The wide-ranging sporting and cultural events remit of *Gothenburg & Co* takes shape within a formal event-led strategy (Heeley, 2011: 51–54). Reflecting this, the company has been tasked with cultural programming to celebrate Gothenburg's 400th anniversary as a city in 2021. Its Events Department leads on bids for major sporting championships, such as those which led in 2013 to the city hosting European Indoor Athletics and Women's Euro Football (Gothenburg & Co, 2013: 5, 35). In that year, the Department bid successfully for 14 'footloose' sporting and cultural events, proving successful on no less than 12 occasions, and on the event production side it stage-managed annual cultural and science festivals, as well as a student fresher's programme (Gothenburg & Co, 2013: 33). Financial assistance was provided to a series of indigenous, 'home-grown' events such as the half-marathon run, the Gothia Cup and annual harbour festivities (Gothenburg & Co, 2013: 30).

GCMB has within its structure a seven-strong events department (see Figure 2.4). Staff are divided along sporting and cultural lines, as the Bureau's Head of Major Events explains:

> One thing in terms of departmental structure is worth pointing out. Although my two senior managers don't have culture or sport written into their job titles, that's the way that it shapes down. That's because how you develop or attract a cultural or sporting product demands different skills, contacts and experience. That's the way that it tends to go; the people you need are very different – almost polar opposites. (Aitken, 2013)

GCMB's event-bidding prowess across cultural and sporting events is widely acclaimed (Heeley, 2011: 38–44), and is reflected in it having published a major events charter. As the Head of Major Events put it:

> Few, if any cities can match our capacity to bid for and host events successfully. We believe we are the only city in the world which has a published Events Charter in which we set out a dozen promises to event

owners around financial and infrastructure support, as well as various other promises, all of which make it easier for events to choose Glasgow. (Aitken, 2013)

The work of GCMB's Events Department is shaped by the deliberations of an ad hoc standing committee known as the Glasgow Strategic Major Events Forum (SMEF). The Forum is chaired by the Chief Executive of Glasgow City Council, bringing together at CEO level the relevant national and local partners, including the regeneration, environmental health, and leisure and cultural departments of the local authority, as well as the Glasgow Chamber of Commerce, and the official national level agencies for economic development and event procurement, viz. Scottish Enterprise and Event Scotland, respectively (Glasgow City Council, 2009). SMEF ensures the event-bidding activities of the Bureau have the highest level credibility and support, and it encourages a 'Team Glasgow' approach to the sourcing and securing of specific events and their subsequent delivery. Under the auspices of the Forum, a framework of economic impact and other criteria have been established against which decisions are made as to whether or not a specific event is to be supported. As the Head of Events says:

> So essentially there is a Forum where broad agreements are reached about the city's events portfolio. This, in turn, anchors us. As a department, we have a rationale; we know what we are doing and why we are doing it, and this drives us. In the main, we look for events that are going to maximise economic impact and media profile. So numbers, spend and image are what we focus on in terms of the selection process as to what major events we should in the end go for. Within that, we will maybe ask questions around some of the 'softer' benefits of a social, cultural and environmental nature. But the core for us, what predominates, is the economic impact and profile dimensions. (Aitken, 2013)

In this way, the Events Department on a day-to-day basis seeks to procure, assist and otherwise facilitate events which have been agreed within the SMEF framework:

> In any one year there's a schedule of events we will be funding, as well as an agreed target list of events we are seeking to procure or help develop, with things coming on and off that list as we see fit. We also have new possibilities and requests coming in all the time. All enquiries are logged, and if there is an event there that doesn't hit our agenda, or fulfil the impact criteria, then we hand it on to somebody else – to another service or department who might decide that's it's an event they want to explore. We hand the file across and say 'well it's not for us, but see what you can make of it'. It might be for, say, environmental services or parks to pick

up, or a local community group. So there's different layers of events, but our concern is with the major events. (Aitken, 2013)

By way of illustration, GCMB's Major Events Department provided financial assistance totalling £463,000 to 10 major events during the 2010/2011 financial year, whose combined economic impact was assessed at £26.5 million, thereby indicating an ROI of 58 (Aitken, 2013). The events receiving subvention included the World Pipe Band Championship, the Snooker Grand Prix and the Glasgow International Comedy Festival. At the commencement of the 2013 year, the Department was proactively bidding for no less than 21 major events spanning the period to 2017, including the 2014 MTV Music Awards, the 2015 Turner Prize, the 2016 World Figure Skating Championships and the 2017 UEFA Champions League Final (Aitken, 2013). On 9 January 2013, GCMB was notified that its bid lodged in the previous September for the 2015 Turner Prize had been accepted, beating off competition from three other cities, and prompting the Bureau's CEO to remark:

So when we got the Turner Prize this morning at 10 o'clock we danced a jig. It was great. That will go to the press on Friday. That's a good win. A good start to the week. (Taylor, 2013)

In the light of the apparent advantages of arms-length PPP-based DMOs being made accountable for major event bidding, hosting and production arrangements, it is noteworthy how relatively few towns and cities have so far adopted this practice. The author's practitioner experience indicates a strong resistance within local government to 'letting go' in terms of sporting and cultural events portfolios, less on the producing side, but much more so in respect of coordinating the bidding and hosting arrangements.

3.6 Print, Web/Digital and Visitor-Servicing

The fifth and final activity area is print, web/digital and visitor-servicing as shown in Figure 3.1. As such, these functions may be viewed as providing collateral or support to the other four core activity areas, especially leisure tourism based promotions and advertising. While *print* may nowadays be relatively less important than web and digital formats, there is widespread consensus among DMOs that 'people still like print' (James, 2013). The scale upon which it is produced by them is substantial, feeding directly as it does into visitor-servicing operations as well as the core marketing functions referred to above. VTB, for instance, estimate that on an annual basis it is currently producing no less than 200 separate print items (VTB, 2013a). For less well resourced DMOs, the production and distribution of the annual, 'main' visitor guide may be *the* dominant budget item, with in one case the production and mail-out of 100,000 such items costing £150,000 (James, 2013).

However, there is no gainsaying the fact that *web* and *digital* activities are becoming ever more prominent, with urban DMOs constructing attractive and functional website platforms, and assiduously assembling Facebook 'friends', Twitter 'followers' and YouTube 'views'. VTB's consumer-facing website, www.vienna.info, comes in 13 languages, providing a comprehensive 'things to see and do' overview of the city, including an event calendar updated on a daily basis, as well as online accommodation booking and other services (VTB, 2013a). A downloadable version of the site is available for mobile appliances. For the 2012 year, the site registered 5.4 million unique users (VTB, 2013d: 21). Unsurprisingly, social media is used extensively by VTB, especially Facebook, but also YouTube, Foursquare, Flickr, Twitter, Xing and LinkedIn. An innovative exercise in 2012 saw the launch of www.socialmedia.wien.info as a social media newsroom, aggregating content from the above channels and making it available to all web users.

The *visitor-servicing* role discharged by urban DMOs everywhere centres on the provision of information, reservations and merchandise, although the emphasis placed on each aspect varies from one organisation to the next. The traditional heart of the visitor-servicing role is provided by tourist information centres (TICs). For example, visitor-servicing arrangements currently provided by *Visit Belfast* revolve around the operation of a new 'flagship' city centre TIC, supported by two 'satellite' TICs at the Belfast International and George Best airports. The three TICs service upwards of half a million enquiries a year, of which approximately three-quarters are counter based (Heeley, 2012c). Satellite airport TICs are a more or less standard feature of leading European city destinations, e.g. Amsterdam, Barcelona, Berlin, Birmingham, Brussels, Copenhagen, Dublin, Edinburgh, Lisbon, Liverpool, Rome, Sofia, Stockholm, St Petersburg and Vienna, to name but a few. Interestingly, Munich has recently introduced at its airport a virtual tourist information service *InfoGate*, using a real-time video-conference link. While DMO-managed TICs are able to recoup a significant proportion of their running costs from trading revenues (Tables 2.3 and 2.4 indicate 45% and 30% in the cases of Belfast and York, respectively), their inherently labour intensive nature, and the rental and other property expenses with which they are associated, render them relatively high cost items. This, alongside changing technology and consumer tastes, has led of late to a serious questioning of the future of TIC provision and operation. Notwithstanding this, a new breed of '21st-century' TICs has emerged during the past decade in selected European cities, e.g. Belfast, Manchester, York, London and Nottingham in the UK, and elsewhere in Europe at Aix-en-Provence, Bilbao, Brussels, Berlin, Ghent, Gratz, Innsbruck and Stockholm. Such centres are prominently sited, combining modernity with style and spaciousness. They embody the destination or city brand (see the next section), giving visitors a taste of the city's 'story' and using modern touch-screen and other technology to direct them to attractions, shows and events. Staff proactively 'meet and greet' so as to 'own' the customer and better manage the flow of visitors. Merchandise reflective of the city is displayed in an attractive and well-presented manner, and a full range of ticketing and other reservation services are on offer (Heeley, 2012c).

In addition to TIC management, the visitor-servicing role typically embraces 'outreach' projects and initiatives which might range from 'pop-up' information stands at major conferences and other events, through to the development and promotion of apps and programmes of industry engagement in which front-line staff (such as concierges, receptionists, waitresses, taxi drivers and sales assistants) are trained in customer handling, and advised as to new products and key destination 'messages'.

Several European cities have developed so-called integrated 'hub and spoke' approaches to visitor-servicing, notably in Gothenburg, Barcelona and Stockholm (Heeley, 2012c). In Gothenburg, for instance, there are two city centre TICs; the main one is situated halfway along the city's principal pedestrian thoroughfare, while a satellite unit is set amid a busy shopping mall. Radiating from the main city centre 'hub' with its ground floor TIC and first floor contact centre is a network of interactive visitor literature panels which are erected, racked and maintained by *Gothenburg & Co*. In effect, the panels act as the 'spokes', and are stationed in hotels and transport termini, as well as at leading visitor attractions. *Barcelona Tourism*, focusing as much on merchandising as on information and reservations, operates a network of no less than 15 TICs for which there is a complement of 74 FTE posts. The main centre (700 m^2) is situated in Place de Catalunya, serving as the 'hub' for a further 14 staffed units located at airports, the railway station and major attractions. In addition, there are three Barcelona Original shops retailing branded clothing items. The TICs and shops retail the Barcelona Card, bus and walking tours, an audio guide and souvenirs. Gross annual turnover from these various income streams is currently in the region of €25 million (Heeley, 2012c).

Finally, *Stockholm Visitors Board* operates one of the most modern and best performing 'hub' TICs in Europe, complete with multi-touch and digital systems through which customers can view information, and tourism businesses can promote themselves. As a result, a high proportion of callers 'self-service' and rental incomes are maximised. There is a large liquid crystal display (LCD) wall and a Bose sound system. The Stockholm Tourist Centre (STC) receives over 500,000 personal callers a year, and generates revenue sufficient to cover 60% of its cost base. Tourists are able to purchase and reserve a wide range of products, including tickets for events, hotel bookings and the hiring of bicycles. STC operations are supplemented by satellite TICs at the Stockholm Exhibition and Congress Centre, at the cruise terminal and at Arlanda Airport. While the latter facility is managed by the airport authority, it nonetheless has the same 'look and feel' as the STC-run centres. In a similar vein, private sector partners operate a TIC service at the Gallerian shopping mall. Other noteworthy outreach services provided by STC include innovative bicycle-based mobile information provision, as well as Stockholm knowledge courses for 'frontline' staff (Heeley, 2012c).

3.7 Brand and Planning Frameworks

All DMO marketing operations take place within brand and planning frameworks. In urban destination marketing, the former is referred to as the *destination brand*. In its most integrated form, the destination brand has six principal components, viz. core values, logo, slogan, font, colours, and language or tone of voice. It is more or less standard DMO procedure to bring together the 'do's and don'ts' of using these components in a brand manual or style guide, and to express them in brand imagery or so-called 'signature shots' (Heeley, 2011: 127–130). Guided in this way by manual and imagery, all DMO marketing and visitor-servicing activity as summarised in Figure 3.1 comes to embody and otherwise reflect the destination brand. As such, usage of the destination brand is normally routine and unproblematic, shaping the content as well as the 'look and feel' of DMO marketing materials and visitor-servicing arrangements. From one DMO to the next, the destination brand will be more or less rigidly applied, and from time to time it will be modified or 'refreshed'. Eventually, it will be discarded and replaced by a new one in a 'rebranding' exercise.

As a general rule, destination branding only becomes problematic when it is utilised as a wider place or city brand. In this respect, the issues may simply be ones of finance and commitment, as application of the destination brand goes beyond the DMO to embrace other partners and organisations, as captured in this remark by the Chief Executive Officer of *Marketing Cheshire*:

> We have a manual for the Chester brand which we developed with the design arm of the City Council. There is a particular typeface we use, as well as colour palettes; we have heritage colours and we have different ones for family fun-days out. We use the brand in our publications; we used it on the TV ad and we will be using it on the new website. I'd like to see it out more on the streets; the obvious things are street signage, welcome to Chester boards, and bus stops. We could also put it up on the hoardings around building works. The issues here are funding; the Council don't want to provide any funding for the brand, and they seem incapable of persuading anyone to use it. (Michel, 2014b)

Questions of ownership nearly always arise whenever a destination brand is used as a place brand for the town or city as a whole, to the point where implementation of urban branding invites controversy and debate as to its efficacy and purpose (Heeley, 2011: Chapters 7 and 8). For example, the destination brand utilised by GCMB between 2004 and 2012 was entitled 'Glasgow: Scotland with Style', and from the onset it was intended as a wider city brand for which the Bureau was to act as custodian. The latter role centred on gaining urban-wide visibility for the brand, ensuring that it was directly applied in the form of street furniture applications, while at the same time persuading Bureau stakeholders and other city organisations to make use of the logo, slogan and signature shots. In this way and especially in 2004 following its launch, the 'Glasgow: Scotland with Style' brand appeared in banners, pennants, bus shelters, billboards and signage, and was adopted (albeit selectively and fitfully) by local government, universities, hotels, shops and visitor attractions. Leading hotels in the city might, for instance, integrate the logo and brand signature shots into their reception desk areas. While 'Glasgow: Scotland with Style' worked well as a destination brand, its limitations as a place or city brand are well brought out by the Head of Marketing and Communications of GCMB:

> The word 'style' meant that the brand was perceived by many as being biased in favour of retail, anchored as it was in Mackintosh and the associated 'Glasgow style' (a reference to the Glasgow-born artist and designer Charles Rennie Mackintosh). The 'Glasgow: Scotland with style' brand was also construed as being too heavily focussed on the work of our Bureau – tourism, major events and conventions – sense of place in that context. So while the brand served the Glasgow City Marketing Bureau well, it didn't in the end really reach sectors like financial services who are now looking for a city brand to be developed which is something a bit more specific to their sector. Even the universities and colleges, who in the past utilised 'Glasgow: Scotland with Style' to communicate the advantages of Glasgow as a place in which to study, are nowadays calling for something which is more clearly a differentiator for their particular sector. So as far as 'Glasgow: Scotland with Style' is concerned at this particular point in time (January 2013), it is a case of 'the brand is dead, long live the brand'. My Chief Executive is very clear on this. (Rice, 2013)

In June 2013, GCMB therefore launched 'People Make Glasgow' as a new destination-cum-city brand; here the supportive stance of local media contrasted with the more predictably hostile one taken by selected national news channels (e.g. McKenna, 2013).

As we will see in Chapter 4, the academic literature affords destination and place branding a pivotal strategic role, inasmuch as it is used to ensure that the content of DMO marketing enshrines competitive advantage. Although rarely used by DMOs in this way (the next chapter highlights VTB as the prime exception), among practitioners there has nonetheless been a sense in which the destination or place brand has been vested with an almost mystical yet ultimately nebulous strategic significance, prompting one DMO chief to remark:

> Largely because of what was seen to be achieved by the 'Glasgow's Miles Better' city brand in the 1980s, I think other destinations have looked to find something similar which will somehow or other work wonders and transform the place into a successful tourism destination. We all got caught up in this, being led to believe that the 'be all and end all' of anything we did had got to be about destination branding. I've started to question that recently because Leicester is making good progress, but without any such brand. In hindsight, I'd say we've put a ridiculous amount of money and effort over the years into trying to find the one, ideal brand. Though we had some short-lived successes that made a bit of difference at the time, initiatives like 'Leicester: City full of surprises' never fundamentally shifted external image. And then, when something like Richard III comes along – which more or less overnight immeasurably changed external perceptions of the city – you can't help but conclude that a transformation of that magnitude could never have been achieved by a destination or city brand, no matter how much money we spent. So it started raising in my mind the whole issue of destination branding, and whether or not it has been a bit of a smoke and mirrors job. For a while now, I have begun to think that the importance we have all attached to destination branding has been misplaced. The idea it can pull out advantage and then transform a place is basically flawed. (Peters, 2014)

The *planning* as opposed to brand framework established by DMOs is typically a three- to five-year strategy which each year is broken down and otherwise refined to form the annual marketing plan and/or annual business or budget plan. For example, GCMB is currently working to a five-year, citywide tourism strategy. It is anticipated that successful implementation of the plan by 2016 will have grown tourist revenues by some 60%, with an associated expansion of employment and hotel capacity. There are other aspirations in the strategy, all of them linked to specific measures, and designed to instil a 'service excellence culture', to enhance cityscape and environment, to provide for a 'seamless travel experience', and to further develop venues and attractions (GCMB, 2011). A steering group monitors progress on implementation of the five-year strategy, made up of representatives of the Bureau, Glasgow City Council, Visit Scotland and Scottish Enterprise Glasgow.

Similarly, VTB's current strategy is entitled the 'Vienna Tourism Concept', establishing growth targets for the volume and value of tourism which centre upon the achievement of a 10% increase in overnight stays from 10 to 11 million between 2011 and 2015, as well as adumbrating a series of planning and development priorities, e.g. airport expansion, improved visitor welcome arrangements at key entry points and the introduction in shops of more 'visitor-friendly' opening hours (VTB, 2009). The concept document is updated each year, and every five years a completely new plan is produced, so that the next one to emerge at the end of 2014 will cover the period to 2020 (Penz, 2013). Realisation of the planning and development priorities identified in the strategy nearly always emphasises collaboration with industry partners and other organisations. For the DMO this can form an important action-based agenda of change, as instanced here by VTB's Head of Strategic Destination Development:

> The issues in respect of planning and development are basically qualitative and relate to 'the customer journey'. If the destination is to stay competitive, then it has to address nitty-gritty issues such as, for instance, having announcements in English on the underground. We have so many English-speaking tourists here in Vienna. A big problem identified in the current strategy is the standard of taxi services. So we have worked hard on this by lobbying. For two years we tried to persuade the industry to get its act together, but they just ignored us, so in the end we said 'enough is enough' and went public, voicing our concerns on TV and in the press. The result is that we got the law changed, so that taxi drivers can no longer smoke in their cabs, or use their mobiles, or refuse to take disabled people and their guide dogs. Cabs in Vienna nowadays have to have air conditioning. So all these matters were addressed, and we forced the taxi industry to accredit drivers and improve their cars. (Penz, 2013)

Within the context of the overall strategy, the Board publishes in late autumn its marketing plan for the following year (Penz, 2013).

In England, DMOs are enjoined by the national tourist organisation (Visit England) to formulate tourism strategies in the form of 'destination management plans'. The city of Chester, for instance, is covered by one such plan drawn up for the wider county of Cheshire. Its formal aims are to bring together 'all partners from public, private and third sectors, with an interest in the Visitor Economy', so that they are able 'to work together effectively to improve and develop the visitor product over the next five years', and to agree 'the basis for future priority actions and resource allocation' (Marketing Cheshire, 2012). For *Visit York*, the planning framework is set by a rolling three-year marketing strategy within which an annual business plan is prepared. Work on the latter starts in the autumn of every year, with final sign-off by governance in February. The plan itself is made up of three elements; in the words of the former CEO of *Visit York*:

> First there is the marketing and PR strategy, which is quite tight, with the conference stuff in it; then the membership strategy, and finally the

visitor information plan which is really about the tourist information centre; how we are going to run it and get more income and support. When you put the three bits together, you've got the business plan. Hand on heart, if you had a look at it, you would see it's very financially orientated. (Cruddas, 2014)

The significance of *Visit York's* three-year strategic framework is that it affords the DMO an opportunity to address planning and development issues and to modify, and to otherwise change direction in respect of the urban destination marketing activities it undertakes:

On one level, a tourism strategy may be merely a high level conversation which in practice carries little weight and is of no practical value. But it can be much more than that. The way I look at it is this; within a destination, there is never any shortage of ideas and aspirations as to the 'way forward' on how the destination should be marketed and developed. Everybody, quite rightly, has a view. So developing a tourism strategy is a way of checking ideas against reality. Whenever we were developing a strategy, I would always say: 'yes, that's a great idea, but let's park the creative thinking for a moment and consider exactly how we are going to deliver this'; and that's when you get into matters people are less keen to discuss, especially resourcing. If you can take things forward by dialoguing in this way, then a strategy is really important because it prevents the DMO from falling into the black hole of just doing the same thing year-in year-out. In other words, as the DMO you do more of the same, because that is what you are comfortable with. (Cruddas, 2014)

3.8 Performance Management and Appraisal: The DMO Measurement Toolkit

The final piece in the jigsaw which is the practice of destination marketing operations is how urban DMOs measure themselves in terms of inputs, outputs and outcomes. On the face of it, the rationale for measurement is to provide intelligence on which to appraise past performance and to inform future strategy and operations. At less 'pure' and murkier levels, however, there are generally ulterior motives, as executive, governance and third parties use measurement as a way of 'wielding power and control' (Peters, 2014). From his practitioner days as the executive head of Nottingham's DMO, the author recalls how the receipt of much-needed central government funding (channelled through a regional development agency) was conditional upon satisfactory completion of a tortuously

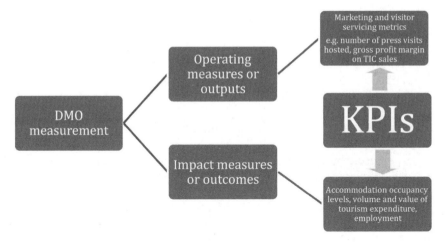

Figure 3.2 The DMO measurement toolkit

bureaucratic and frustrating paper chase. On behalf of my DMO, I was obliged to report upon outputs (e.g. number of brochures produced, partner income raised, press trips hosted, unique website visits registered) which were deemed to be 'proxy indicators' of key outcomes, when in fact they were no such thing. Meaningless as the paper chase itself was, the process established authoritarian relationships, enabling the regional development agency to exercise a large measure of control over an otherwise independently constituted PPP.

However imperfect and 'political' measurement may turn out to be in practice, it is nonetheless a fundamental aspect of the DMO world, and the principal dimensions are summarised in Figure 3.2, which I have entitled the DMO measurement toolkit. This exemplifies typical output and outcome measures; *operating measures* relate to DMO outputs (e.g. number of brochures produced, partner income raised, press trips hosted, unique website visits) and are routinely collected as the activities themselves are discharged. By way of contrast, *impact measures* pertain to outcomes and are derived from bespoke studies and surveys which are normally undertaken by independent, third-party research agencies and consultancies. Through these studies, DMOs are able to produce data indicative of two broad sets of outcomes; *volume* in terms of accommodation occupancy levels (utilisation) and the number of tourist trips and overnights spent in commercial accommodation and other outlets, and *value* and *employment* in respect of the associated expenditure and FTE jobs generated. For instance, by drawing on the findings of four separate studies (viz. the International Passenger Survey 2010; UK Tourism Survey 2010; Visit Scotland Tourism in Western Scotland 2010; and LJ Forecaster monthly accommodation occupancy), GCMB were able at the beginning of 2013 to cite the following headline volume and impact indicators for the 2010 tourism year:

- 2.3 million overnight trips, of which 1.75 million (76%) were from the UK;
- average hotel occupancy for the year of 75.4%;
- 30,000 FTE jobs generated by tourism spending.

As far as value was concerned, the headline statistics were:

- expenditure by domestic UK tourists totalling £365 million;
- spending by overseas tourists amounting to £230 million.

The studies, of course, contain a wealth of data over and above the headline statistics reproduced above so that, for instance, we 'know' that in 2010 four countries (i.e. USA/France/Germany/Spain) accounted for 41.5% of all overseas tourist spending in Glasgow.

As Figure 3.2 shows, the 'glue' which binds together operating and impact measures comes in the form of the key performance indicators (KPIs) on which DMO senior management teams periodically report to their respective governances. By way of illustration, Table 3.1 sets out the 14 KPIs used to assess and otherwise monitor GCMB operations during the 2011/2012 year, indicating actual performance against the targets originally set at the three-quarter point in the year. It can be seen from this that there is an equal mix of output and outcome measures, each of which conforms to SMART criterion inasmuch as they are specific, measurable, assignable, realistic and time based. It should be noted that KPIs, as these are routinely applied in the DMO world, represent somewhat imperfect measurement instruments. For instance, the KPI 8 in Table 3.1 shows that the membership fee income target of £165,000 was achieved (just!) in the 2011/2012 year, but this begs the question of how meaningful a measure this is of the health or otherwise of a commercial membership scheme. Arguably, membership recruitment and retention would serve as a far more sensitive and revealing indicator of performance. KPI 2 in Table 3.1 (so-called brand saliency level) has major shortcomings, as explained by the Bureau's Head of Communications and Marketing:

> We utilise a UK consumer panel in order to measure brand saliency; panel members are asked questions relating to their perceptions of Glasgow, and that includes respondents who have visited Glasgow recently and those who haven't. We ask them why they aren't choosing Glasgow and to identify the barriers. The brand saliency figure was a bit down on what we had hoped, but actually it is a bit of a misnomer because what is actually being measured are perceptions of Glasgow as opposed to perceptions of the 'Glasgow: Scotland with Style' city brand. (Rice, 2013)

Table 3.1 Key performance indicators for *Glasgow City Marketing Bureau*, 2011/2012

		KPI target	KPI performance as at 31 December 2012
(1)	Maintenance of city occupancy levels	75%	75%
(2)	City brand *Glasgow: Scotland with Style* saliency level	+1%	−3%
(3)	Unique visitors to see glasgow.com and associated websites	1.9 million	1.6 million
(4)	Consumer media coverage as measured by opportunities-to-see (OTS) metrics	205 million	487 million
(5)	Corporate media coverage as measured by opportunities-to-see (OTS) metrics	30 million	58 million
(6)	Conventions won by Bureau – delegate days	350,000	411,000
(7)	Conventions won by Bureau – delegate spend	£100–£130 million	£120 million
(8)	Convention Bureau commercial membership fees	£165,000	£164,655
(9)	Convention Bureau in-kind support	£30,000	£43,000
(10)	Convention Bureau accommodation booking revenue	£155,000	£118,000
(11)	Convention Bureau active conference ambassadors	1,400	1,485
(12)	Unique visitors to events financially supported by the Bureau	180,000	217,000
(13)	Attendees at events financially supported by the Bureau	400,000	466,000
(14)	Economic impact target for events financially supported by the Bureau	£31 million	£24 million

Source: Glasgow City Marketing Bureau.

Ultimately the robustness and validity of KPI metrics lie in the extent to which: (a) they are a meaningful measure; and (b) they actually quantify the activity they are purporting to measure. Arguably, they should be used as reference points for evaluation rather than as definitive measures of performance. Certainly, individual KPIs nearly always invite more questions than they answer, as this DMO chief remarked in respect of an almost omnipresent KPI for visitor servicing, viz. 'footfall' or number of personal callers at the TIC:

> One thing I would like to know is how people use the Tourist Information Centre. I know how many people go in there because we have a footfall indicator – so it's about 280,000 a year – but that doesn't really tell me

very much. I want to know what they think about it, whether they had a meaningful interaction. I would like to know how many of our visitors don't use the TIC. It's an expensive operation (the TIC) that we really need to think about. (Michel, 2014b)

For outcome metrics in particular, questions should always be asked as to how far the DMO can realistically influence matters in this field of activity. In the case of KPI 1 in Table 3.1, for instance, is GCMB capable of maintaining overall hotel occupancy levels within the city, when so many factors over and above DMO marketing are shaping the demand for such accommodation? Across all the key outcome measures, it must be recognised that there are many 'influencing' factors at work other than that of the marketing of the DMO. A combination of cost and methodological reasons prohibits DMOs from routinely undertaking marketing evaluation studies in order to estimate 'conversion' from the leisure tourism marketing activities it undertakes, and the associated ROI as measured by the tourist trips, spend and employment generated (Heeley, 2011: 33–36). The Head of Marketing and Communications at GCMB hints at the measurement imponderables and limitations:

We do measure by campaign. We've just done a campaign, for instance, in Northern Ireland working with Stenna, the Charles Rennie Mackintosh Society, and Glasgow's leading attractions, so over a period we can look at Stenna's passenger numbers and code the promotions in the visitor research we carry out at the attractions. It's a basket of measurements. It's an imperfect science, to be honest, when we try and disaggregate what we do in the context of the wider city. We try and make it as robust as we possibly can, so if we're doing something with Virgin or Ryan Air we get a carrier's metric, a hotel metric, a visitor attraction metric, and we utilise PR codes wherever we can. So we put together a basket of measurement indicators. Sometimes we can arrive at a ROI figure, but normally it isn't possible to do that. We don't want to fudge the figures. It's hard to disaggregate. (Rice, 2013)

As we can see from the above, it is extremely difficult (in the author's view more or less impossible) to disentangle and then gauge the relative effects of the various marketing influences so as to accurately estimate DMO 'share'.

Moreover, as we have argued in the Preface, the net impact of DMO leisure tourism marketing operations is likely at best to be marginal. As a consultant frankly and succinctly put it at a conference attended by the author nearly 30 years ago:

People's perceptions of a destination come from a whole hodgepodge of sources, and this is what makes tourism marketing very difficult. ... Having created this or that image for a city, or having marketed this or that product, some claim responsibility for 'X' number thousand visitors who come. In reality that is almost impossible to measure. ... The influence of marketing is not the primary influence on motivation to travel or the selection of a destination ... there is no reliable and generally applicable method of proving a direct causal relationship between it and tourism revenue. ... For instance, advertising is only noted by about 4–5% of people as an influence in the choice of destination. The main single influence is recommendations from friends or relatives. (Sweeney, 1988: 45–46)

Motivational researches support the thesis that DMO marketing influences are likely to be relatively unimportant influences. For instance, the 2013 York Visitor Survey (Visit York, 2014: 4) indicated that the main reasons for visiting were the city's 'ambience' (46%), specific attractions such as York Minster and the National Railway Museum (22%), the advice of friends and relatives (10%), events and festivals (8%) and retail opportunities (4%). As an aid to planning their trip, only 14% and 3% of survey respondents used the DMO website and visitor guide, respectively, while during their stay just 1% visited the TIC (Visit York, 2014: 4).

Whereas marginality of influence and/or an inability reliably to ascertain DMO 'share' is openly acknowledged by some DMOs, others (arguably the majority) appear less inclined to do this, 'passing off' the key outcomes as being wholly or substantially attributable to their marketing and sales activities. They may do this implicitly or explicitly, unintentionally or deliberately. In the case of *Visit York* below, the imputation is surely implicit and unintentional, hinging on how the phrases 'helped boost' and 'has worked to increase' are construed:

> The organisation has helped boost annual visitor numbers to the city from 2.1 million visitors in 1987 to seven million today and it has worked to increase the value of tourism to the local economy from £55 million to a record breaking £443 million. (Visit York, 2013)

In the case of the Tourism Manager at *Visit Bradford*, credit is being claimed in a more conscious manner:

> Our latest figures show tourism is worth £538 million to the area. Since I came into post four years ago, that's a growth of £47.5 million, so we [Visit Bradford] must be doing something right. (Tillotson, 2014)

In this extract from a newspaper report announcing my arrival in Nottingham as the city's newly appointed tourism chief, the imputation or 'passing off' comes direct from the journalist writing the piece:

> Tourism in Nottingham will be worth at least £600 million within ten years – an increase in 40%. That is the pledge of John Heeley, the man

charged with making it happen. ... Nottingham (currently) attracts 2.5 million staying visitors each year, who spend £434 million. (Nottingham Evening Post, 2003)

Here, it is suggested that the DMO I was about to set up (*Experience Nottingham*) would be more or less wholly responsible for securing a 40% increase in the volume of tourism to the city – an increase that was probably as unachievable on the part of *Experience Nottingham* as it was unquantifiable, although I wasn't minded to object!

A final, 'cheesy' example of 'passing off' is the script of a professional advocacy video produced in August 2013 by the trade body for North America's visitor and convention bureaux, the *Destination Marketing Association International*:

They're the people who create life long memories. ... They create great jobs. One in eleven jobs on the planet are supported by travel and tourism. ... Their passion, commitment and partnership fuels tourism and travel spending which now totals 6.6 trillion dollars globally. For the first time in history more than 1 billion people travel to places marketed by these extraordinary organisations and people. They are called official destination marketing organisations. ... They are powered by real people. (Destination Marketing Association International, 2013)

Above, the clear inference is that DMOs lie at back of one billion trips and $6.6 trillion expenditure, and no less than one out of every 11 jobs 'on the planet'.

The diametrically opposing 'reality' – that DMOs are unable to measure the effectiveness of their marketing activities and demonstrate 'share' in aggregate volume and value outcome terms – is captured in the following comments made by selected DMO chiefs and directors, beginning with the Chief Executive of *Leicester Shire Promotions*:

We are always careful never, ever to claim that we alone as the DMO are the sole influence on the major volume and value outcomes. (Peters, 2014)

He goes on to say:

We have a five year strategy and that brings cohesion to it all. It doesn't shape the approach of organisations other than ourselves as much as it could, but it is there, and it does iterate that we need to grow overnight stays, it does explain the rationale behind that, and it does talk about the ways partners – public and private – need to work together to achieve that end. It also makes clear that the DMO in isolation cannot pull it all off. It's very dangerous for a DMO to claim entire responsibility for the volume and value of tourism to a destination, because there is so much outside of its control. So the figures can move upwards and downwards, without the DMO being involved one way or the other. And the problem is, if you claim the glory when the figures go up, how do you explain your way out of it when they go down. (Peters, 2014)

The Chief Executive of *Marketing Cheshire* points to an inability to conduct survey-based research of the kind that might enable rigorous quantification of DMO 'share':

> We have a figure for the value of tourism to Chester, but it's impossible to know how much of that we are responsible for, especially as so little money is available to do broad survey work. (Michel, 2014b)

A representative of VTB points out that his organisation is unable to estimate market 'share' for which his organisation is likely to be responsible:

> We have precise bednight figures; by law every commercial accommodation establishment in Vienna must report this data to the government on a monthly basis, split into overnights, arrivals, revenue and nationality. But to be honest, we are unable to quantify the VTB share. I wish we could because I think our share is a good one. We work hard to publicise the annual volume and value counts, and in the recent past there has been good year-on growth. However, there is a saying: 'success has many fathers, failure is an orphan'. And this is very much true for us; if the results are favourable, it is the whole destination and all our partners who are successful – it is everybody's hard work. If the results are not so good, then it is down to us. We have to live with this, I'm afraid, but we live with it very well. (Penz, 2013)

The inability of urban DMOs accurately to pinpoint their 'share' of the main volume and value outcomes, allied to the related logic and evidence suggesting that any such 'share' is likely to be marginal, is arguably their Achilles' heel, and it sets in motion the most fundamental of paradoxes. Inasmuch as their core purpose is 'bringing in the business' (see Section 2.3 of the previous chapter), individual DMOs find themselves in the unenviable position of being unable to assess or otherwise quantify the extent to which they realise their core purpose. Put another way, they cannot scientifically and objectively demonstrate to stakeholders, customers and the wider public at large that they are actually 'doing the business'. In its turn, this leads to a situation where – sometimes publicly, but more often than not privately – local politicians and business leaders choose to regard the DMO as a 'woolly' marketing organisation (Heeley, 2011: 97), the point at which we closed the last chapter. In the light of this paradox – this DMO Achilles' heel – the former Chief Executive of *Visit York* pithily and diplomatically remarks: 'if you were a private company, you would have a much tighter performance management regime' (Cruddas, 2014).

3.9 Conclusions to Part 1

> *... like a dog's walking on its hinder legs. It is not done well;*
> *but you are surprised to find it done at all.*
> Samuel Johnson, Saturday 30 July 1763, as recorded in
> Boswell's *The Life of Samuel Johnson*

We began this chapter with two quotes, both of them mirroring what we styled in the Preface and Chapter 1 as the 'theory of marketing competitive advantage'. In that theory, DMOs celebrate what is different and appealing about their towns and cities in the form of competitive advantage. In a world of urban 'sameness', this perforce means DMOs focusing on Johnson's 'minute diversities in everything' which, in their turn, are 'wonderful' to the visitor or tourist. In 'Ogilvy-speak', this is the urban destination marketer promoting and costing a consumer 'dream' in which superlatives inevitably abound: 'the most wonderful cathedrals, the most delightful architecture', and so on and so forth. Destination marketing has gained a foothold on the urban policy agenda precisely because it seeks to capitalise on this consumer 'dream', holding out a threefold 'promise' for towns and cities of:

(1) differentiation and economic gain in an increasingly homogenised world;
(2) a coordinated marketing of 'sense of place', with penetration of one of the world's largest and fastest growing industries to yield local economic benefit in respect of business turnover, employment and prosperity generally;
(3) a rare apolitical platform on which a town or city can 'come together' to celebrate what is special about it.

Our empirically based review of urban tourism marketing in Chapters 2 and 3 appears to be congruent with both this consumer 'dream' and the urban 'promise'. Intuitively, when set against 'dream' and 'promise', there is logic and force to the six organisational parameters discussed in Chapter 2, that is nomenclature, core purpose, status, structure, finance and partnering. The same is true of the marketing template portrayed in Figure 3.1 and the associated brand, planning and performance management frameworks, as discussed and exemplified in Sections 3.2–3.8 above. The five DMO activity areas – media and travel trade relations, advertising and promotions, conventions, sporting and cultural events, and print, web/digital and visitor servicing – are relevant to the task in hand, which is ostensibly to 'bring in the business'. Moreover, across all five activity areas and the brand, planning and performance management frameworks within which they are cocooned, there is undoubtedly much good work, honest intent and fulsome achievement.

Having said that, 'scratch beneath the surface' – as we have attempted to do in Chapters 2 and 3 – and a different picture begins to emerge, and serious doubts begin to be cast as to whether or not urban destination marketing is presently being discharged coherently and effectively by Europe's now more or less ubiquitous urban DMOs. Having, so as to speak, lifted up the bonnet and taken a good look around, there is an overriding sense in which we are a long way away from realising the 'dream' and 'promise' underpinning contemporary urban destination marketing. Indeed, for the author this review of the DMO practitioners and their urban marketing operations brings to mind Johnson's dog walking on its hind legs, as per the above quote. Bearing in mind the financial and reputational deficiencies we spotlighted in Chapter 2, it is hardly surprising to find that the marketing operations discussed in this chapter are not in the main being discharged 'well'. To be sure, we discovered in the previous chapter that the platforms on which DMOs operate are nearly always riddled with constraints and imponderables. There is a widespread absence of clarity as to nomenclature and core purpose. Local government based DMO arrangements have inherent weaknesses, while among PPP-based DMOs there is a growing and dangerous overreliance on earned sources of private sector and trading income. Among PPPs, there is fitful application of corporate partnering alongside widespread adoption of problematic commercial membership schemes. For virtually all urban DMOs – public sector or PPP – there is paucity of operating budget, especially when measured against the 'dream' and the 'promise' referred to above. While finance (or the lack of it) preoccupies DMOs, corporate public relations activity designed to inform and mould external reputation is conspicuous more or less by its absence, so that this ubiquitous organisational genre remains quintessentially misunderstood, undernourished and under-loved.

Because the foundations on which they operate are generally weak and constrained, it follows therefore that the DMO marketing operations considered in this chapter are not in the main 'done well'. Nor, as we have discovered in this chapter, are these self-same operations measured well. To be sure, there are KPI schedules which are SMART, but these major on metrics which are often less than meaningful such as TIC footfall, commercial membership fee income and brand saliency; other metrics are measured inconsistently and misleadingly (e.g. value of conference and short-break bookings), while some (notably AEV) are 'simplistic' to the point where they ought not to be employed (Pike & Page, 2014: 213). Alongside this, there is a fundamental inability on the part of DMOs accurately to measure tourism impact and rate of return on their marketing investments, and to pinpoint resultant market 'share'. In turn, this means DMOs cannot in all honesty appraise their performance against their stated core purpose – an Achilles' heel of momentous significance because it means that DMOs *are* literally 'woolly marketing organisations' (see the very end of Chapter 2). As a consequence, DMOs and the urban destination marketing they undertake are rarely afforded a priority, with stakeholders being characteristically lukewarm and taciturn. An inability convincingly to measure core purpose translates itself into all-round vulnerability. DMOs lay themselves open to 'cuts' and exclusion from the 'top table', and their work receives inconsequential media coverage and is consigned to the periphery of urban life and governance. Perhaps in this sense it is not too fanciful to liken the current state-of-the-art in respect of urban destination marketing to Ghandi's magical (but probably mythical) quip about Western civilisation, to the effect that it would be 'a good idea'. Looked at in this way, urban destination marketing is an ideal to which all towns and cities might well aspire, but one which presently, for the most part, represents 'work in progress'. As such, the practice of urban destination marketing as we have reviewed it in Chapters 2 and 3 is replete with good ambition and intent, but is more or less flawed in its subsequent organisation, delivery and appraisal.

A state-of-the-art review with a 'not done well' conclusion will appear as harsh, unyielding and overly critical to some, and doubtless these matters will be contested and there will be many points of disagreement. It goes without saying that in the author's view the evaluation being made here is justified on the basis of the evidential materials supplied and the arguments applied. In a more positive vein, and as already hinted at, we will demonstrate in Part 2 how a small band of DMO 'leaders of the pack' and other 'exemplars' have begun to achieve levels of excellence in their urban destination marketing sufficient to set themselves apart from the overall 'not done well' assessment with which I have concluded this review. However, before we can properly contextualise and assess such exceptional performance (and the 'not done well' operations of the rest), it is necessary first to address the gap which exists between the theory of urban destination marketing, as per the current academic and practitioner paradigm (which we have termed the 'theory of marketing competitive advantage'), and the manner in which we have depicted practice actually taking place in Chapters 2 and 3. That leads us directly on to Part 2 and the next two chapters, in which (among many other things) we will suggest that the main reason why DMOs are in the main struggling to perform well is that they are tasked with an all but impossible mission of 'bringing in the business'. To keep up our analogy, dogs do many things well on four legs, but if the criteria with which we assess them is their abilities to walk on two, then they will inevitably always be found wanting. Similarly, task DMOs with 'bringing in the business' as the be-all and end-all of their existence, and they are more or less doomed to failure. Task them differently and more appropriately, and the end-result may well be an altogether more purposeful and impactful set of DMO marketing operations. On that altogether more optimistic note, we move on to Part 2.

Part 2
Theory

4 A Critique of the Theory of Marketing Competitive Advantage

> *Discovery commences with the awareness of anomaly, i.e. with the recognition that nature has somehow violated the paradigm-induced expectations that govern normal science. It then continues with a more or less extended exploration of the area of anomaly. And it closes only when the paradigm theory has been adjusted so that the anomalous has become the expected.*
>
> Thomas S. Kuhn (1962) *The Structure of Scientific Revolutions*

This chapter divides into six sections. The first begins by summarising the three-stage 'theory of marketing competitive advantage', and then – based on a selective literature review – it goes on to trace the origins and evolution of this theory, as it took root towards the end of the last century to become in the new millennium a prevailing orthodoxy-cum-mantra. The review is selective inasmuch as it highlights key articles, texts and other items which exemplify the fundamental principles, tenets and axioms of the paradigm as it has evolved over a 40-year period to become a 'collective mind-set' (Vargo & Lusch, 2004: 2). During these years, great and fundamental changes have taken place in the external environment facing DMOs (Heeley, 2011), numbered among which are low-cost air travel, globalisation, the web and internet, social media, self-packaging and the threat of disintermediation, user-generated content, sustainability, public–private partnerships (PPPs), privatisation, the demise of the Soviet Union, the sovereign debt crisis – the list is almost endless. As a result, destination marketing has undergone often profound change, to the point where the DMO world of the 1980s is substantially different in form and content from that which exists nowadays (Heeley, 2011). Nonetheless, we will discover in this chapter that the guiding tenets of the 'theory of marketing competitive advantage' – Pike and Page's '4Ps marketing paradigm' – remain more or less unscathed and unchallenged, as pure and pristine as ever. The 'less' here is a reference to the emergence of a new and wider paradigm for marketing – Vargo and Lush's 'dominant logic for service sector marketing' – which 'disposes of the limitations of thinking of marketing in terms of goods taken to market', pointing instead to 'opportunities for expanding the market by assisting the consumer in the process of specialisation and value creation' (Vargo & Lusch, 2004: 12). The implications of this for the tourism sector are only beginning to be worked through (e.g. Shaw *et al.*, 2011), but for destination marketing this emergent paradigm shifts the emphasis away from the products brought by the DMO to market to the process of creating that exchange. In so doing, attention is drawn to the ways in which DMOs can proactively engage with their customers through co-creation and co-production (Pike & Page, 2014: 203).

Notwithstanding the application of 'service sector dominant logic' to destination marketing, the 'theory of marketing competitive advantage' remains dominant and more or less inviolate as the paradigm with which academics and practitioners explain or otherwise account for urban destination marketing. That said, we discover in Section 4.2 of this chapter that contained within the academic literature there has always been a strand of discordant findings and comments. Although ultimately querying some of the paradigm's central tenets and generalisations, these findings and comments have occurred unevenly and in an isolated fashion, never at any point having a collective momentum with which to question the validity and relevance of 'the theory of marketing competitive advantage'. The third section of this chapter presents just such a challenge, comparing the 'theory of marketing competitive advantage' with practice. In doing so, it refers to the empirically based findings on practice contained in Chapters 2 and 3, as well as drawing on new evidential materials derived from the various surveys referred to in Chapter 1. Utilising terminology employed by Kuhn himself, 'anomalies' are encountered at each stage of the theory, forming 'counter-instances' which cannot readily be assimilated into the existing paradigm. In particular, it is suggested that mainstream DMO operations revolve around a 'marketing of everything' approach, as opposed to one based on a marketing of competitive advantage. By dint of the various anomalies, fundamental doubt is cast on the appropriateness and correctness of the core generalisations contained within the 'theory of marketing competitive advantage'. Section 4.4 documents how the *Vienna Tourist Board* (VTB) and *Innsbruck Tourism* stand outside the 'marketing of everything' approach employed by virtually all the other DMOs in Europe. By 'marketing the difference', they form interesting and notable exceptions that nonetheless 'prove the rule' in respect of 'marketing of everything' approaches being mainstream. In the case of VTB, we discover that 'marketing the difference' is done consciously and systematically, using the Board's destination branding framework to achieve a genuine differentiation of place. In this way, marketing content and imagery highlight and celebrate what is truly distinctive about the Austrian capital. Penultimately, Section 4.5 of this chapter suggests that 'marketing of everything' approaches translate into a monolithic 'theming of urban sameness', reflecting and contributing to globalisation and the standardisation of 21st-century urban landscapes and society with which it is associated. Section 4.6 concludes that 'the theory of marketing competitive advantage', as it has been applied to urban destination marketing, is no longer fit for purpose and, as such, the existing paradigm requires substantial reworking and adjustment.

4.1 The Evolution of a Paradigm: The Theory of Marketing Competitive Advantage, 1980–2014

Urban destination marketing as per 'the theory of marketing competitive advantage' may be summarised as a three-stage model, as depicted in Figure 4.1. The theory runs like this:

- On the product/supply side, *a town or city identifies and/or creates unique selling propositions (USPs) with which it can differentiate itself* in the tourist marketplace. Uniqueness and differentiation therefore lie at the heart of the 'theory of marketing competitive advantage', forming the 'what' of urban destination marketing – Stage 1 of Figure 4.1.
- On the basis of this uniqueness and differentiation, a DMO then positions, promotes and distributes the tourist 'offer' of the town or city, as per the DMO marketing template described in Chapter 3, facilitating the customer in his/her decision to purchase products ahead of and/or during his/her visit. In this way, *the DMO takes its differentiated product to market*. These activities constitute the 'how' of urban destination marketing as per Stage 2 of Figure 4.1.
- The audiences thus targeted then respond to the 'offer', with *the DMO and the tourist industries it serves 'converting' and otherwise 'fulfilling'* these responses so as to generate visits. The resultant spending and its associated economic impact, as measured by income, employment and turnover gains, represent the 'outcomes' of urban destination marketing. In turn, these outcomes answer the fundamental 'why' of urban destination marketing. As we saw in Chapter 2, DMO core purpose is premised on securing these very outcomes.

In short, competitive advantage is identified as a means of differentiation, whereupon the DMO takes its differentiated product to market and then – working with its industry partners – it subsequently converts and fulfils the demands thus generated. Figure 4.1 in effect represents the disciplines of economics and marketing applied to urban tourism: packaging, promoting and otherwise 'commodifying' the latter – as if it were a tube of toothpaste, a packet of cornflakes or a television set. Looked at another way, it is destination marketing's version of the 'four Ps' and the 'marketing mix'.

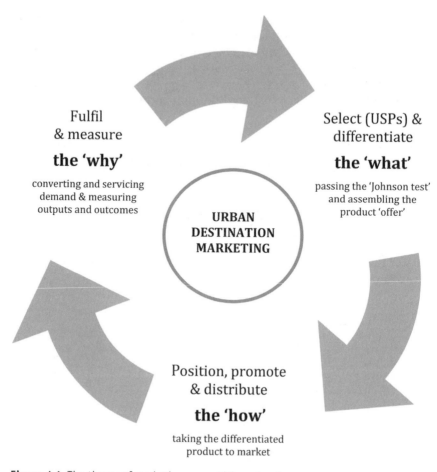

**Fulfil
& measure**

the 'why'

converting and servicing
demand & measuring
outputs and outcomes

**URBAN
DESTINATION
MARKETING**

**Select (USPs) &
differentiate**

the 'what'

passing the 'Johnson test'
and assembling the
product 'offer'

**Position, promote
& distribute**

the 'how'

taking the differentiated
product to market

Figure 4.1 The theory of marketing competitive advantage

As such, the 'theory of marketing competitive advantage' is as readily understandable as it is gloriously and sublimely logical, so much so that it appears unproblematic, obvious and required. Not without trepidation, therefore, is the author now mounting a critique of the theory, and as good a starting point as any is history.

The origins of the 'theory of marketing competitive advantage' as related to tourism doubtless stretch well back in time, but we can usefully, if somewhat arbitrarily, commence with a conversation which took place on Tuesday 12 October 1779, as recorded in James Boswell's *The Life of Samuel Johnson*. Asked by Boswell whether or not he wished to go with him on a tour of Ireland, Johnson replied that this island was 'the last place' on earth to which he would 'wish to travel', prompting the following question and answer:

BOSWELL: Is not the Giant's-Causeway [a striking coastal rock formation on the northern tip of Ireland] worth seeing?

JOHNSON: Worth seeing? yes; but not worth going to see. (Boswell, 2008: 744).

The gist of the paradigm we have termed the 'theory of marketing competitive advantage' is here for all to see. Tourism to and within a destination is viewed as conditional upon the existence of USPs. If a place has these, and people are made aware of their existence, then tourism follows just as day follows night. In this particular case, Johnson is conceding that one such potential USP – the Giant's Causeway – has some touristic merit, but from his standpoint this is insufficiently compelling to warrant a visit, presumably when set against other comparable attractions, and alongside the cost and inconvenience to which a visit would also give rise. The Giant's Causeway is, in Johnson's opinion, 'worth seeing but not worth going to see'; in other words, it is an attraction, but not a USP capable of motivating a trip in its own right. In this sense, it can be seen that the 'theory of marketing competitive advantage' hinges on destinations possessing a genuine, critical mass of competitive advantage in the form of USP attractors. As Johnson's riposte establishes, from the point of view of the destination, the possession of such attractors is to say the least an exacting requirement (a 'big ask' in modern parlance), and I will refer to it subsequently as the 'Johnson test'. Within any one destination, there is nearly always an abundance of items 'worth seeing' but few (if any) are 'worth going to see'. Precisely because the 'Johnson test' is so difficult to pass, we begin to see already how the 'theory of marketing competitive advantage' does not always work well in practice, but much more about that later on in this chapter.

As far as the author can establish, the 'theory of marketing competitive advantage', as a paradigm within which to account for urban destination marketing, surfaces within academe and practice during the 1980s. A practitioner example is a study of Glasgow's tourism potential completed in 1983 by the consultants Pannell Kerr Forster (PKF). It concluded that at that particular point in time the city's 'product profile did not meet the requirements of Scotland's "traditional tourist"' who instead were making a beeline for the attractions of Edinburgh and the Highlands and Islands (Friel, 1989: 76). In other words, Glasgow at that time lacked USPs and therefore competitive advantage. In the light of this assessment, PKF's report recommended that Glasgow establish a trio of 'flagship' visitor attractions at an estimated cost of £47 million: an aquarium, a science centre and a folk heritage museum (Heeley, 1988: 13–15). The PKF report in effect equipped the newly formed DMO for Glasgow (the *Greater Glasgow Tourist Board*) with a strategy; in the short-to-medium term it was enjoined to attract 'footloose' cultural events (the city subsequently staged the 1988 Glasgow Garden Festival and, two years later, became European Capital of Culture), while encouraging over the longer term a sustained development of competitive advantage in respect of new visitor attractions, as well as the refurbishment of existing museums and galleries (Heeley, 2011: 39–44). Contemporaneous examples of the 'theory of marketing competitive advantage' as it was crystallising in academic minds, are evidenced in a tourism marketing and management handbook published towards the end of the 1980s (Witt & Moutinho, 1989). In this text, Pearlman emphasised the need for destinations to concentrate on 'those products which have unique appeal' (Pearlman, 1989: 11), while Middleton defined 'destination attractions' as 'the elements within the destination's environment which, individually and combined, serve as the primary motivation for tourist visits' (Middleton, 1989: 573).

During the 1990s, the 'theory of marketing competitive advantage' gathered significant momentum as both an academic and practitioner perspective. In *The Tourist Gaze*, for instance, John Urry argued that tourists seek out differences, directing their attention to more or less unique features of culture, heritage and landscape which are divorced from their own everyday experience. Places, he opined, were for the most part relatively substitutable, so that in competing for customers it was imperative that destinations should major on images grounded in uniqueness and therefore competitive advantage (Urry, 1990). In the same year as *The Tourist Gaze* was published, Gilbert drew on marketing principles to suggest that countries and their national tourist organisations should differentiate themselves in their market positioning on the basis of USPs (Gilbert, 1990). Meanwhile, in *Selling Tourism Places*, Goodall advanced the view that tourist destinations could be branded, distributed and sold in much the same way as any commercial commodity (Ashworth & Goodall, 1990). The tourist, he said, purchases a resort because it represents value for money in the form of 'superior place product' (Ashworth & Goodall, 1990: 259). The trick, according to Goodall, was successfully to link together 'place product marketing and the tourist's holiday choice process' (Ashworth & Goodall, 1990: 261). In a similar vein, another text saw the twin challenge of destination marketing as identifying 'the resort's special advantages' and, on that basis, understanding 'how to entice those visitors which the destination hopes to attract' (Laws, 1995: 113). Writing specifically about towns and cities, Page depicted destination marketing as 'promoting the place's values so that potential users are fully aware of the place's distinctive advantages' (Page, 1995: 208).

Arguably the seminal statement of the 'theory of marketing competitive advantage' as applied to urban destinations in the 1990s was Kotler's *Marketing Places: Attracting Investment, Industry, and Tourism to Cities, States and Nations*. Its core idea was that towns and cities were increasingly competing with each other 'to attract their share of tourists, businesses, and investment' (Kotler et al., 1993: 21). DMOs were tasked with undertaking a comprehensive 'place audit' in which strengths, weaknesses, opportunities and threats (SWOT) could be identified (Kotler et al., 1993: 81). The audit enabled a destination to assess 'economic/demographic characteristics' and 'sort them into competitive strengths and weaknesses'. Having completed such an audit, the DMO was tasked with undertaking the actual marketing of 'place advantage' (Kotler *et al.*, 1993: 81, 215). In this and later texts (e.g. Kotler, 1997), Kotler's direct and easy-to-understand commands were 'identify', 'choose' and 'communicate', viz. identify a set of possible competitive advantages, choose one, and then effectively communicate it to target audiences. His work was to prove most influential in shaping the thinking of academics and practitioners alike.

These early, pioneering writings on the 'theory of marketing competitive advantage' were all published in the last two decades of the 20th century, corresponding to a period when tourism itself had become an academic growth industry (Heeley, 1982) as well as something to which towns and cities in Europe were increasingly turning their attention in policy and administrative terms (Heeley, 2011: Chapter 1). In particular, former industrial centres were seeking to boost and regenerate their flagging economies (Law, 1992), while in so-called 'heritage towns' and capital cities there was a growing recognition that purposeful urban management required a more holistic and resident-centred treatment of tourism, so as to minimise and otherwise 'manage' disbenefits, while at the same time maximising employment and turnover gains (Heeley, 1987). In a UK context, and as highlighted in the Preface to this book, the urban tourism marketing 'success stories' of Glasgow and Bradford attracted an almost messiah-like following, providing role models at back of which lay the 'theory of marketing competitive advantage' and three-stage model depicted in Figure 4.1.

Into the new millennium, academic and practitioner perspectives on urban destination marketing coalesced around the 'theory of marketing competitive advantage' and the marketing processes and techniques with which it was associated, notably destination audit/SWOT analyses, differentiation, segmentation, destination competitiveness and branding, and promotion/distribution. In 2000, for instance, Buhalis exhorted destinations to differentiate their products by emphasising their uniqueness (Buhalis, 2000). Pointing to the latest internet and web-based technologies, he suggested that DMOs now had greatly enhanced capabilities with which to deliver differentiated tourism products. A paper by Kavaratzis and Ashworth on city branding conceptualised the process as a differentiation of both product and consumer (Kavaratzis & Ashworth, 2005), while Anholt proselytised the wider notion of destination branding, depicting success in this field as a process of exploiting 'competitive identity' (Anholt, 2007). In a book bearing that title, Anholt singled out tourism as the single most important way – the most powerful of six 'booster rockets' – with which a nation or locality could market itself to become 'known' and hence prosper (Anholt, 2007: 88–91).

Kolb (2006), in *Tourism Marketing for Cities and Towns*, sets out the process of urban destination marketing in manual form. Strategically, this begins with identification of the 'unique characteristics' of a town or city, followed by the packaging of these so as to effectively market the place as 'truly unique' (Kolb, 2006: 14). Tactically, an urban destination had to segment the market, brand the destination, and then position its product (Kolb, 2006: 16–23, 228–229). Segmentation, Kolb said, profiled the potential consumer, whereas branding involved 'promoting the unique benefits that the tourist will experience' (Kolb, 2006: 18). As such, the brand should be 'incorporated into all the promotional material created by the city' (Kolb, 2006: 23). Working along the grain of the destination brand, positioning referred to 'how the consumer differentiates between similar products' and, as such, 'answers the consumer's question of why the city is unique' (Kolb, 2006: 228). Positioning, in turn, was based on the 'core product' or USP(s) identified in the destination audit or SWOT analyses. For a town or city, USPs could range from a 'unique botanical garden' to a hallmarking sporting or cultural event, through to its 'fall foliage' or the 'superior quality' of its customer service (Kolb, 2006: 228–229).

Classic 21st-century statements of the 'theory of marketing competitive advantage' in respect of destination marketing are to be found in the works of Pike, Ritchie and Crouch, Morgan and Pritchard, and Morrison, and we shall briefly consider each in turn. In *Destination Marketing: An Integrated Marketing Communications Approach*, Pike's starting point is the competitive tourism marketplace which 'forces DMOs at all levels to develop effective differentiation strategies' (Pike, 2008: 116). In such a context, the DNA of the DMO may be seen to be reducible to competitive advantage:

> A successful strategy achieves a point of difference against competitors on an attribute deemed important by the market. A DMO's resources consist of sources of comparative and competitive advantage. (Pike, 2008: 132)

In their book, *The Competitive Destination: A Sustainable Tourism Perspective*, Ritchie and Crouch assemble a model of destination competitiveness, identifying the key contextual variables (Ritchie & Crouch, 2003). The model itself had been developed by the authors 'in a number of papers from the early 1990s', with their 2003 text providing the platform for 'its most complete presentation and explanation' (Crouch, 2012: 4). As such, this text is arguably the definitive representation of what we are here styling the 'theory of competitive advantage' (Ritchie & Crouch, 2003: 105). For the authors, the building blocks of competitiveness on the product side of the equation are the 'core resources and attractors' which form 'the primary elements of destination appeal' (Ritchie & Crouch, 2003: 69). Chapter 6 of *The Competitive Destination* is given over to an exhaustive enumeration of such USPs – instancing among many others the Alps, the Quebec Winter Carnival, the Leaning Tower of Pisa, the River Kwai bridge, Disney World, Munich's *Oktoberfest*, papal visits and vineyard tours (Ritchie & Crouch, 2003: 110–129). In a recent paper, Crouch refers to 'sports events like the Olympic Games, Formula 1 race tracks ... the football World Cup, or cultural facilities like the Guggenheim Museum in Bilbao, Spain or the Millennium Dome in London' (Crouch, 2012: 2). For Ritchie and Crouch, USPs such as these form the indispensable foundation upon which a destination, through its DMO, can differentiate itself from competitors and position itself in a highly competitive tourism marketplace. The framework for DMO marketing activities is provided by the destination brand which captures and conveys the essence of 'the destination experience', distilled as it is from the raw material of its core attractors and resources (Ritchie & Crouch, 2003: 198). DMO marketing activities must surpass those of rival destinations, ensuring that the destination's 'market positioning is congruent with the competitive strategies adopted by the competition and the strengths and weaknesses they are able to bring to bear on their chosen markets as well' (Crouch, 2012: 4).

Morgan and Pritchard, in *Destination Branding: Creating the Unique Destination Proposition*, suggest that nowadays nearly all destinations could lay claim to having 'a unique culture, landscape and heritage', 'high standards of customer service and facilities' and 'the friendliest people' (Morgan *et al.*, 2008: 60). In this way, it becomes 'more critical than ever' for destinations 'to create a new identity – to differentiate themselves from their competitors' (Morgan *et al.*, 2008: 60). Other contributors to this text echo the need to create 'superior' destination brands which competitors cannot then emulate, presenting case studies in which fine-tuned differentiation is exemplified. For example, a chapter by the then Marketing Director of the *Wales Tourism Board* (Roger Pride) applauds 'the quest for true differentiation', belittling 'imitation and copycat strategies' (Morgan *et al.*, 2008: 161). The 'Golf as it Should Be' campaign which Pride uses as his case study shows how this sport was being differentiated by reference to fun (Wales), seriousness (Scotland), corporateness (England) and booziness (Ireland).

Finally, a text by Morrison views the 'major outcome' of three separate lines of research, relating to destination image, resident attitudes and current DMO marketing plans, respectively, as being:

> ... a clearer understanding of how the destination is different from its competitors, and how this will be reflected in the marketing strategy ... competitive strategy is about being different and the DMO must identify these differences early in its marketing planning. Sometimes these differences are referred to as USPs (unique selling points or propositions), sustainable competitive advantage (SCAs) or differential-distinct competitive advantage. (Morrison, 2013: 84–85)

In this respect, visitor attractions and events play the 'key role in the destination mix, representing the unique assets that draw people to the destination'

(Morrison, 2013: 94), while market positioning through the vehicle of the destination brand adopted by the DMO is central to making the place 'unique among competing destinations from the tourist's perspective' (Morrison, 2013: 289). In this way, destinations differentiate themselves on the basis of USP parameters and values as diverse as love ('Virginia is for Lovers'), exploration ('Canada: Keep Exploring'), yellow rice wine ('Vintage Shaoxing'), islands and beaches ('Queensland: Where Australia Shines') and so on and so forth (Morrison, 2013: 295–303).

Tourism journal articles are nowadays redolent with the 'theory of marketing competitive advantage' as the basis of destination marketing. Although ostensibly 'redefining tourism promotion', one such piece turns out to be a mere restatement of the fundamental generalisations contained within this paradigm. It sets the familiar context ('the flooded market of locations and destinations'), with the equally predictable prescription to differentiate on the basis of uniqueness:

> To be a success ... a city brand needs to be a unique and identifying symbol, a trademark that serves to differentiate competing products, services and places. (Paskaleva-Shapira, 2007: 112)

Another journal article defines and geographically delineates the tourist destination on the basis of the 'theory of marketing competitive advantage':

> ... it is conceptually and managerially more effective to view a destination as that geographical region which contains a sufficiently critical mass or cluster of attractions so as to be capable of providing tourists with visitation experiences that attract them to the destination for tourism purposes – an oft-cited example being the Alps in Western Europe. (Bornhorst et al., 2010: 572)

A final journal contribution, this time on best practice in regional-scale destination marketing, reiterates what Kotler had posited nearly 20 years previously, viz. that destination marketing must be grounded in the articulation of a 'region's unique points' which serve to 'set the region apart from its competitors' (Cox & Wray, 2011: 531, 528). This, in turn, is 'central to the entire framework of best marketing practices for a regional destination' (Cox & Wray, 2011: 534). The 'ultimate requirements of a successful destination marketing strategy are for the region to be able to present a unique identity to potential visitors' (Cox & Wray, 2011: 528).

As in academe, the dominant practitioner perspective on urban destination marketing remains the 'theory of marketing competitive advantage'. Here, much of the time, it lies implicit in action and activity, as discussed in Chapter 1. Nonetheless, over the past decade and a half there has been a slow drip of documented expressions of the 'theory of marketing competitive advantage'. For instance, the former CEO of the *British Travel Association/ British Tourist Authority* (now *Visit Britain*) posited in an introductory tourism text that SWOT analyses were fundamental to successful destination marketing, because they isolated competitive advantage in a comprehensive and objective manner, so that 'once clearly identified, these strengths will be strongly promoted ... in a competitive situation where switching brands or products is a real possibility' (Lickorish & Jenkins, 1977: 155). Drawing on his long tenure as the executive head of Britain's national tourist organisation, Lickorish went on to itemise as key USPs the Royal Family, the Heathrow 'international gateway', and the 'unique appeal of the British countryside' (Lickorish & Jenkins, 1977: 155). Another example, drawn from an edition of the e-newsletter *DMO World*, is a master class on destination marketing, with its central message of 'competitive superiority through differentiation' (DMO World, 2005). It cited the small town of Barrie in Ontario as successfully differentiating itself on the back of a shopping mall majoring on brand name discounting. In an account of the celebrated 'Incredible India' destination marketing campaign, the then head of India's national tourist organisation (Amitabh Kant) acknowledges the pioneering writings of Kotler, while lauding the campaign for its having 'differentiated India as a tourism destination based on its inherent strengths', using USP icons as diverse as curry, tigers and elephants, and the Taj Mahal (Kant, 2009). Finally, a pristine and succinct practitioner statement of marketing competitive advantage appeared in a handbook published in 2005 by the *International Association of Convention and Visitor Bureaux* (now *Destination Marketing Association International*). Put simply, the guiding principles of successful destination marketing were to 'sell your strengths' and 'focus on amenities not found in competing destinations' (IACVB, 2005: 31).

Similarly, the practitioner interviews undertaken for the purposes of this book reflect what amounts to a deep-seated practitioner belief in 'marketing the difference' based upon competitive advantage. For instance, on the subject of *Visit York*'s promotional and advertising campaigns, the organisation's former Chief Executive asks herself:

> What is different about York? Everywhere says they have nice shopping, friendly people and pleasant attractions, so you need to think about what's different. (Cruddas, 2014)

Reflecting on Liverpool, a DMO executive adumbrated the city's USP's as 'football, the Beatles and maritime heritage', going on to say about urban destination marketing:

> So our business is very competitive. It's not just about other destinations. It's about disposable income and what people have to spend on things.

So, what are your unique selling points? That's what you have to get across to your visitors. (Wilkinson, 2014)

4.2 Discordant Voices

As exemplified above, the 'theory of marketing competitive advantage', as an academic and practitioner perspective within which to explain and otherwise account for urban destination marketing, now occupies centre stage. While its mainstream, hegemonic position has never to the best of my knowledge been challenged explicitly, from around the midpoint of the 1990s onwards a handful of mainly academic commentaries nonetheless picked up on issues and themes which hinted that the practice of marketing urban destinations might be at odds with the 'theory of marketing competitive advantage'. For example, Judd's survey of US cities remarked upon the difficulties faced by them in constructing appropriate destination imagery, observing how few places possessed iconic USP attractors such as the Eiffel Tower (Judd, 1995). Cities 'that lack image cannot easily be promoted to tourists', he said, observing that typically urban DMO promotions were obliged to major on the attractiveness of their rural backdrop and/or on a rather fluffy and nebulous set of imagery he characterised as the 'nostalgic city of the past' (Judd, 1995: 117). In a detailed content analysis of the destination marketing materials produced by four provincial cities in England (i.e. Birmingham, Manchester, Sheffield and Stoke-on-Trent), Bramwell and Rawding noted that, while there were some points of contrast in the imagery contained within guides and brochures, any such differentiation had strict limits (Bramwell & Rawding, 1996). The authors highlighted repeatedly used messages evident across all four cities: they 'all used the big city imagery of exciting, lively, and cosmopolitan ... with lots to see and do, together with upbeat, confident messages that they are dynamic and culturally enlivened' (Bramwell & Rawding, 1996: 208).

At the turn of the new millennium, Swarbrooke suggested that urban authorities had often utilised tourism as a tool of economic and social regeneration 'almost as a last resort', accusing them of taking an 'uncritical view' of tourism's alleged economic benefits (Swarbrooke, 2000: 271, 277). At the back of this, Swarbrooke pointed to a failure rigorously to assess whether or not a town or city had a foundation of genuine competitive advantage on which to market itself effectively as an urban tourist destination:

> Many towns have spent money on trying – unsuccessfully and unrealistically – to establish themselves as tourist destinations ... there is a need for realism, a need by decision-makers to realise when tourism is not a viable option for a town or city. (Swarbrooke, 2000: 278, 282)

In a similar vein, Ashworth suggested destination audit exercises were, in practice, of limited efficacy. Because of their natural and self-interested commitment to place, he points out that local politicians and DMO officials 'are in a poor position to evaluate the place product effectively', while the ostensibly 'independent' consultants hired by them are all too 'likely to concur' with the view that the town or city in question has 'got what it takes' to be a significant urban tourism player (Ashworth, 2011).

A text by Christopher Law, *Urban Tourism: The Visitor Economy and the Growth of Large Cities*, queried whether urban destinations could successfully be branded in the same way as ordinary commodities (Law, 2002). Echoing Law, some commentators (the author included) are lately emphasising the problematic nature of the city branding projects briefly referred to in Section 1.5 of Chapter 1. Indeed, the editors of *City Tourism: National Capital Perspectives* state flatly that urban fragmentation 'inhibits developing a cohesive and unique brand' (Maitland & Ritchie, 2009: 268). Case studies in this volume of Brussels and Budapest amply demonstrate the point being made (Maitland & Ritchie, 2009: 142–158, 201–212). In the light of the inevitably complex and multi-faceted nature of towns and cities, it is difficult successfully to reduce their branding 'narratives' to a handful of competitive advantages with which to then differentiate one place from the next. In addition, the process of devising and implementing such brands is a tortuous and much misunderstood one, aggravated by adoption techniques which are typically weak and constrained (Heeley, 2011: Chapters 7 and 8).

In relation specifically to the content and imagery of destination marketing, Law has made the quite striking observation that this is rarely determined by a systematic and rational assessment of competitive advantage, claiming instead that a 'package of elements is put together by promotion agencies ... on the basis of intuition rather than market research' (Law, 2002: 54) – striking, that is, from within a perspective informed by the 'theory of marketing competitive advantage'. Wang, in his study of North American visitor and convention bureaux, instances the practical difficulties faced by such organisations in emphasising USPs (Wang, 2008). In a case study, Wang shows how tourist industry stakeholders resisted the notion that the convention bureau in question should focus its marketing on the distinctive way of life of the resident Amish community. Stakeholders desired the bureau to market the attractions of the destination as a whole, criticising it for concentrating 'too much on Amish related products and not fully marketing the area to its maximum capacity' (Wang, 2008: 201). Gilbert, writing on destination marketing in a student handbook entitled *Tourism: Principles and Practice*, suggests DMOs 'have to be even-handed in their support for businesses' because 'it is difficult politically for them to back product winners' (Cooper *et al.*, 2008: 612). In the previously mentioned account of the 'Golf as it Should Be' marketing campaign, the author (Roger Pride) concedes that 'the majority of destinations still struggle to differentiate their offer from the competition' (Morgan

et al., 2008: 160). Indeed, in a recent journal article reporting on the findings of a content analysis of urban destination marketing materials, the author expresses his surprise at the uniform content of destination marketing: 'Given the difference of cities, it is astonishing to discover that cities' tourism promotion materials repetitively use similar slogans, phrases and expressions' (Uysal, 2013: 17) – 'astonishing', that is, when viewed from within the 'theory of marketing competitive advantage' where uniformity of content can have no place whatsoever. In this connection, it may be observed that Uysal's comments mirror those of the destination branding consultant, Bruce Turkell, reproduced below, as he gently chides the chief executives and senior directors of North America's visitor convention bureaux at a recent conference of the *Destination Marketing Association International*:

> I got to talk honest … we have a big problem. … We did an experiment in our offices a couple of weeks ago. … We cut out the ads for every single North American destination we could find … and you know what? You can't tell the difference between one and the other. … All of the ads are exactly the same … every destination shows the same thing – the United States of Generica. We are becoming so much like our neighbours there's no reason to travel. (Turkell, 2012)

Finally, in respect of the outcomes of DMO marketing, Pike points out that 'quantifying a DMOs contribution … is currently an impossible task … the success of a destination will be as a result of a combination of factors, many of which will be exogenous to the DMO' (Pike, 2008: 369). Gilbert casts further doubt on the efficacy of DMO marketing operations when he cryptically remarks that much the greater part of DMO marketing has hitherto been 'elementary' (Cooper *et al.*, 2008: 613).

From Judd onwards, discordant notes have therefore been struck in respect of the 'theory of marketing competitive advantage' as it has been applied to urban tourist destinations. Clearly, urban destination marketing as per this theory is at odds with a world in which most urban destinations lack genuine competitive advantage, where the content of marketing materials is strikingly similar, where political even-handedness precludes 'backing winners', where rigorous audits and SWOT analyses are by and large absent, where city branding is problematic, and where by implication public as well as private industry monies are being wasted on unmeasurable and/or ineffective marketing operations. Valid and thought-provoking as these discordant voices are, it is worth reiterating that the observations of Judd *et al.* have at no point challenged the 'theory of marketing competitive advantage' as a dominant paradigm within which to account for and otherwise explain urban destination marketing. In a recently published review however, two academics have hinted that such a challenge may one day be mounted to what they refer to as the 'dominant 4Ps paradigm':

> As yet, there is no accepted alternative to the dominant 4Ps paradigm for destination marketing. ... As the thinking around DMO roles matures, it would not be inconceivable to see research considering the development of an alternative to the 4Ps marketing paradigm for DMOs. (Pike & Page, 2014: 217)

Just such an alternative is developed by the author in the next chapter. As far as Judd *et al.* are concerned, the 'theory of marketing competitive advantage' is as omnipresent in their writings as it is in the rest of the academic literature. As such, their 'discordant voices' are best viewed as providing groundwork for the development of a systematic critique of the 'theory of marketing competitive advantage', and it is to this that we now turn in the remainder of this chapter.

4.3 'Mind the Gap': Marketing Everything Rules OK

Put bluntly, the 'theory of marketing competitive advantage' bears only a slight and fitful relationship to practice 'out there' in the real world of urban destination marketing. There is a wide and chronic gap between theory and practice. As intimated in the 'discordant voices' exemplified in the section above, at each stage of the model depicted in Figure 4.1 there is evidence and comment contradicting what we would expect to be the case were the 'theory of marketing competitive advantage' to apply. Using Kuhn's terminology, these contradictory occurrences are 'anomalies' which, in turn, represent 'counter-instances' of the theory in question – in our case, the dominant academic and practitioner paradigm we have styled as the 'theory of marketing competitive advantage' (Kuhn, 1970: 52–82). Referring specifically and explicitly to anomalies and counter-instances, we can now systematically critique the 'theory of marketing competitive advantage' on the basis that it more or less fails in practice to 'tell it like it is'.

Our starting point is that the 'theory of marketing competitive advantage' takes as read that towns and cities have or can create USPs capable in their own right of being the 'primary motivation' for tourist travel (Middleton, 1989: 573). As we showed in our review of the academic literature, unearthing USPs is a prime outcome of the SWOT, product evaluation and other destination audit techniques which are so central to the principal academic treatises and text books relating to urban destination marketing. The assumption is made in the academic literature that just about every town and city can identify and then select such USPs, so that these may then be 'offered up' in the tourist marketplace. In reality, we have already posited that few destinations pass the 'Johnson test' in that they do *not* possess the USP attractors which make them not only 'worth seeing' but – crucially – 'worth going to see'. As far back as 1995, we noted in the previous section how one commentator counselled that few towns and cities in reality possessed USPs like Paris with its Eiffel Tower (Judd, 1995). Even in the case of this celebrated Paris icon, it is questionable whether or not it serves as a 'primary motivator' of tourist visits. For sure, it is often a 'must see' on a person's first visit to Paris, but in how many cases does it actually generate or motivate that trip?

In assuming explicitly or implicitly that nearly all places have or can create such USP attractors, the 'theory of marketing competitive advantage' begins to fall down, as it were, at the very first hurdle. It is worth our while halting here to note a consequent anomaly. On the one hand, DMO practitioners nearly always subscribe to the existence and importance of USPs as a basis for their organisation 'marketing the difference'. On the other hand, those self-same practitioners nowadays typically describe their marketing approach as being a 'thematic' one, which is more or less the antithesis of 'marketing the difference' based on specific aspects of competitive advantage! Indeed, as we shall amply demonstrate in this section, urban destination marketing content and imagery is rarely determined by reference to USP attractors, even when these are available. Instead, it is approached thematically, by opportunistically and pragmatically taking advantage of the sum total of available products within a defined geographical area (the latter usually delineated by reference to local government boundaries). To cite just one example at this stage in our argument, consider the comments below by the former Chief Executive of *Destination Humberside*:

Clearly you're looking at your product offer. We were Humberside, within which Hull was a dominant player. What you had there was a city with a very long maritime heritage. There was the William Wilberforce connection (a native of Hull and leading abolitionist in respect of the UK slave trade). To be truthful, people didn't really understand Hull. It was the end of a railway line, and hotel capacity was limited. Actually, when you get to Hull, it is quite a charming place. It has a lot of character. So Hull was a city offer. Maybe it couldn't match Manchester and Leeds or even Sheffield, but it was a city offer. Also in Humberside, there was the historic town of Beverley, 'traditional' seaside at Bridlington, and the Wolds – a countryside offer which was all about peace and tranquillity. So you package that – you've got a maritime city, historic town, traditional seaside resort, and a rural offer. So you're basically theming heritage of one sort or another. Those were the strengths we marketed. Over the other side of the Humber, you had Scunthorpe and Grimsby to work with; both had seen better days, and in terms of attracting visitors I must say those two places were a real challenge. We theoretically did have one USP in Humberside, and that was the Humber Bridge – at that time it was the world's longest single-span suspension bridge. But there was not an awful lot to see there, just a bridge and country park, and the market for that was limited. (Wilkinson, 2014)

The broadly thematic determination of marketing content and imagery instanced above, in which opportunistic and pragmatic considerations are uppermost, and in which more or less everything 'worth seeing' is embraced, is confirmed by researches undertaken for this book, in which 62 European cities were appraised in respect of: (1) whether or not they possess competitive advantage in tourism; (2) the intensity of DMO leisure tourism marketing; and (3) the mainstream DMO approach to determining marketing content and imagery, as evidenced by the visual and other downloadable materials available on their destination websites. The results are summarised in Figure 4.2. Contrary to what one would expect to happen according to 'the theory of marketing competitive advantage', where DMOs would always 'market the difference', the vast bulk of cities and towns (58 out of 62) were in fact promoting a remarkably standardised set of messages and imagery in which virtually everything which was remotely pleasant about their respective places was included. Figure 4.2 labels this dominant, mainstream approach as the 'marketing of everything'.

While manifestly at odds with what one would expect to happen under the 'theory of marketing competitive advantage', a 'marketing of everything' approach is in fact a logical outcome of DMO *realpolitik*. Destination marketing, as we have seen in Chapter 2, is a collaborative, partnership exercise, a bringing together of multiple public and private sector stakeholders across governance, strategy and operation. In such an organisational setting, DMO marketing content nearly always gravitates away from what is considered unique or different to reflect instead the diverse interests and 'payback' requirements of *all* the stakeholders (Heeley, 2011: Chapter 5). Guides, brochures, advertisements and videos become all-embracing and lowest common denominator, as opposed to concentrating on a single or small number of USP attractors. This is underscored by financial realities of the 'he who pays the piper calls the tune' variety. With urban DMOs increasingly obliged to exploit earned and private sector funding streams, mainly through commercial and corporate membership schemes (see Chapter 2), it self-evidently becomes ever more difficult for DMO marketing to be shaped by USPs and a policy of 'backing winners'. On the contrary, what the DMO markets is shaped by the diverse and sometimes conflicting interests of its various members. *Visit York's* former Chief Executive recalls the tensions and pressures involved:

York's competitive advantage is its 2000 years of history, evident as you walk around the city. However, when we did focus group research with potential visitors who hadn't been to York, we found that 'history', as

DMO marketing content	Destination _does_ have competitive advantage	Destination _does not_ have competitive advantage	Intensity of DMO marketing
Focus on competitive advantage	Vienna Innsbruck	Gothenburg	Very strong
Focus on everything	Amsterdam Barcelona Belfast Berlin Brussels Bilbao Cannes Helsinki London Nice Paris Stockholm	Antwerp Birmingham Glasgow Hamburg Lyon Manchester Newcastle Rotterdam	Strong
Focus on everything	Bath Cardiff Chester Cracow Dublin Dubrovnic Ghent Milan Pisa Prague York	Belgrade Bremen Dijon Gratz Hanover Leicester Leeds Munich Nottingham Sofia Turku Turin Uppsala Utrecht Zagreb	Medium
Focus on everything	Florence St Petersburg	Bolton Bradford Bratislava Bristol Coventry Derby Lviv Sheffield Warsaw	Low
Focus on nothing	Rome Venice		Absent

Figure 4.2 Destination marketing in 62 European towns and cities by reference to competitive advantage, marketing content and intensity of DMO marketing

such, was actually putting them off. Unlike Glasgow, Manchester and Leeds, York was not seen as 'modern', 'cultural' and 'dynamic', and as having something a bit new and different on offer. So we moved away a bit from history, to promote themes like 'shop in the city', and to emphasise festivals and events. While this pleased our retailers and some of the other members, the historic attractions and bodies like the Civic Trust were up in arms. 'Why are you ignoring our USP', they said? But looking back, we could have done more with our competitive advantage, but it is difficult when you are driven by members, and by visitors and journalists who are always looking for something fresh and new. (Cruddas, 2014)

Another illuminating example of a destination having demonstrable competitive advantage but nonetheless pursuing a 'marketing of everything' approach is the Spanish city of Bilbao. The principal reference point here is what has become known as the 'Guggenheim effect' (Plaza, 2006). In a nutshell, the latter refers to how the £145 million Guggenheim modern art museum (opened in 1997) is deemed to have spearheaded the economic and social revival of the city. Over the period 1994–2011, overnight stays in Bilbao's hotels rose from 442,000 to 1.3 million, much of the increase attributable to the desire to 'do' the 'must see' Guggenheim (Robles, 2013). From the late 1990s onwards, several towns and cities sought to emulate the 'Guggenheim effect', notably Sheffield and Valencia (Heeley, 2011: 13, 79, 126), as well as Helsinki, Milwaukee, Antwerp, Seattle and Denver (Santamaria, 2013). Few can lay claim to outright success (e.g. Valencia's City of Arts and Science), some have failed (e.g. Sheffield's National Centre for Popular Music), while the achievements of the majority have been considerably less than anticipated (e.g. Seattle's Experience Music Project, Antwerp's MAS and Helsinki's Kiasma). Bilbao's Guggenheim, it should be noted, was part of an integrated plan with heavy investments in transport, drainage, street furniture, squares, walkways, business and technology parks, and conferencing facilities. Supported by these investments, the Guggenheim complex undoubtedly provides Bilbao with a compelling USP, making the city in Johnsonian terms 'worth seeing and worth going to see'. Even here, however, in arguably *the* classic example of an urban destination fashioning 'from scratch' a genuine competitive advantage, the DMO – *Bilbao Tourism* – steadfastly pursues a 'marketing of everything' approach. As a Bilbao politician (Councillor Asier Abaunza Robles) explains:

The Guggenheim is the cherry on the cake. At first we concentrated on it. Now we promote everything, for example, the opera, wine, and dining. (Robles, 2013)

A 'marketing of everything' approach therefore typifies cities and towns blessed with competitive advantage and those in which it is deficient. Of the

62 European cities and towns enumerated in Figure 4.2, just two are 'marketing the difference' in respect of leisure tourism (viz. Innsbruck and Vienna), with content in the bulk of the remainder (58) embodying a 'marketing of everything' approach. The final two, Venice and Rome, I have labelled as 'marketing nothing' inasmuch as the DMO organisational infrastructure in both of these Italian cities is non-existent.

The city of York's DMO – *Visit York* – exemplifies the way in which a 'marketing of everything' approach imbues campaign and other promotional activities. The Head of Marketing for *Visit York* summed up the content of what her organisation marketed as being the 'sum total of the York product', going on to make the following observations:

> Heritage cities throughout the UK have the same vibrant, historic city kind of line. We are all saying the same thing and promoting the same kind of messages. In academic marketing terms, the obvious logic is to identify USPs and then promote them. The reality of the situation is that the USPs of York – 2000 years of history, cobbled streets, cathedral and city walls – are replicated in other places like Bath, Chester, Durham, Salisbury and so on. In our marketing there are nuances and angles which are more or less unique – for instance no other city can promote the Vikings as well as we do – but, with the exception of Stratford and its truly unique Shakespearian association, essentially we all have the same core product. None of us have that absolute, unique USP. So we are pragmatic about what we market and how we market. (McMullen, 2014)

In this way, the product identified by destinations and the one taken to market by DMOs – Stages 1 and 2 of Figure 4.1 – become reducible in practice to the most universal and, at the same time, fine-tuned of parameters:

> So much of our marketing is done through imagery. The visitor is buying into the experience of a historic destination. So I am actually one for maximising our photography, our imagery, the quality of the experience and the welcome afforded to the visitor. (McMullen, 2014)

Manchester provides a contrasting urban context which nonetheless yields a similar 'marketing of everything' approach. Here, as confirmed by the Chief Executive of *Visit Manchester*, a football club (Manchester United) 'underpins the visitor economy' (Simpson, 2014), prompting the basic query as to how in any practical or meaningful sense the DMO could gear its destination marketing to this particular competitive advantage, bearing in mind that 'brand Manchester United' is a global icon, massively and relentlessly promoted by betting, media, sportswear and other interests. So it is that *Marketing Manchester* adopts a 'marketing of everything' approach.

The sense in which in practice Europe's DMOs typically take an undifferentiated product to market – Stage 2 of Figure 4.1 – is confirmed by examining how DMOs utilise the brand frameworks within which marketing content and imagery is located (see Section 3.7 of Chapter 3). Under the 'theory of marketing competitive advantage', the destination brand is critical to 'survival in a globally competitive marketplace' precisely because it enables DMOs to 'create a product image consistent with the perceived self-image of the targeted consumer segment' (Morgan et al., 2008: 60–61). In other words, the brand operates like a sieve; it enables the DMO to spotlight USPs/competitive advantage in the marketing it undertakes, while at the same time 'weeding out' any inconsistent imagery and content. Contrary to the theory, urban DMOs do not (seemingly with the sole exception of VTB) use their brand platforms in this sieve-like fashion so as to ensure that competitive 'difference' is the focus of what is actually marketed. So noteworthy is the VTB exception that we devote most of the next section to documenting the singular way in which it utilises its brand platform.

When theory is compared with practice, a further set of anomalies arise at Stage 2 of Figure 4.1. Under the 'theory of marketing competitive advantage', market positioning and the segmentation techniques with which it is associated is inevitably afforded considerable prominence as the means by which DMOs can identify and reach their target audiences in a scientific and researched manner. Pike, for instance, devotes an entire chapter to this subject (Pike, 2008: Chapter 13). However, contrary to what is stated or implied in the theory and the text books, DMOs rarely use these techniques in the execution of campaign and sales activities. This is reflected in the 'broad-brush' and scatter-gun approaches employed in so much DMO marketing (as exemplified in Chapter 3), associated with which are non-existent or at best fairly 'crude' consumer databases. This situation, in turn, mirrors the limited amounts of budget generally available for advertising and promotional activities, as again exemplified in Chapter 3. The following comments on market positioning and segmentation techniques were made by one of our DMO chief executives:

> So we're very conscious of the need to target our audiences, but the problem is we don't have the fire power to be able to go and buy the databases and do direct mailings. We only target our audiences in a fairly basic way. For instance, a theme next year is cycling so we'll be going for a slightly younger group; people probably in their thirties who are a bit more active. Our tag line will be 'A world away which is not far away'. This is pure marketing in one sense – identify your target audience, and tell them what you've got that's different. The difficulty we have is how to distribute our offer effectively. We don't have the budget to buy into the data bases. The even bigger problem in marketing terms is that we don't communicate with people post-visit. We are appalling at this. We have

> 5 million overnight stays a year, but we don't have the resources or capability to contact them and say 'how was it? Did we meet your expectations? Would you come again? Would you recommend us? Where did you go?' If you are, say, an Alton Towers, you actually track the people who flow through the attraction. We have no real idea about who our visitors are. (James, 2013)

The databases held by DMOs are typically built up over time and are not bespoke to particular positioning techniques or campaigns. As one DMO chief put it:

> So we developed our destination management system to collect data to the point where we had a 40,000 database of people who had expressed some or other interest in visiting the area. We would simply use that as the audience for our campaigns – sometimes we used email addresses, other times we did direct mail. (Wilkinson, 2014)

At Stage 3 of Figure 4.1 – the consumer end of the equation – the gap between the 'theory of marketing competitive advantage' and practice becomes ever starker. The outcomes of urban destination marketing in practice fall well short of those envisaged or implied within the 'theory of marketing competitive advantage'. Fundamentally, prospective tourists do not respond in a simple 'itch: scratch' way to the promotional and sales campaigns which are the basis of urban destination marketing. As market intelligence and surveys of the tourist's social psychological motivation to visit a place consistently indicate, DMO marketing influences lie at the margins of consumer choice and motivation – as we have illustrated in the previous chapter. Far more important are the influences of friends and relatives, prior knowledge and experience of a town or city, and perceptions (often dated and chaotically random) of a place's generic reputation or image. The critical (and as a former DMO practitioner, heretical) implication is that in the vast majority of instances the numerical level of 'conversion' from urban destination marketing is slight, as are the resultant values attributable to that marketing in terms of volume, value and impact. In this respect (and as discussed in Section 3.8 of Chapter 3), it is worth noting that the definitions and data used in tourism impact and marketing evaluation studies, as well as the models and methods employed, are suspect to the point where the measurements arrived at are subject to large amount of error and misinterpretation (a concrete example is given in the Preface). In the author's view, the findings of campaign evaluation studies are especially spurious due to the difficulty of establishing a reliable congruence between the statistical population being targeted under the campaign, and the sample from which interviewees are drawn so as to assess conversion levels from that population. Despite this, findings from such studies (as from those measuring tourism demand and impact generally) are nearly always accepted at face value. Tellingly, few DMO practitioners understand the methodologies, as one former DMO chief candidly remarked:

> We got a company to come in after each campaign to measure effective-ness, so that we were able to go back to the local authorities and the private sector who helped fund these campaigns and say: 'look, that cam-paign brought in £1.8 million of visitor spending, and for every £1 invested we got £37 back'. The company interviewed people who had been targeted. Trying to measure marketing and advertising effectiveness is not easy. I'm not a research specialist, and I don't pretend to under-stand the methodology employed. All I know is that the company would translate our marketing activities into a ROI value, and it wasn't that expensive – £2000 or something like that per campaign wasn't a lot. But it was worth it as a great way of reassuring our funders. (Wilkinson, 2014)

What remains in this section is to pull together the key arguments which have been advanced so far in order to demonstrate that the 'theory of mar-keting competitive advantage' demonstrably fails to 'tell it like it is' at each of its three stages as per Figure 4.1. At Stage 1, we are proposing that the majority of towns and cities do not have a critical mass of competitive advan-tage. An inherited base of attractiveness compelling enough to pass the 'Johnson test' either does not exist and/or has not yet been created. Moreover, even in those cities and towns possessing a critical mass of competitive advantage, few DMOs 'gear up' their destination marketing towards its exploitation. As evidenced in this section, DMOs nearly always adopt an unselective 'marketing of everything' approach, irrespective of whether or not the destinations they represent possess competitive advantage in tour-ism. Overwhelmingly, at Stage 2 of Figure 4.1, DMOs therefore take an undifferentiated product to market, to the point where *Innsbruck Tourism* by default, and VTB by design, become the 'ones that get away', as we shall see in the section to follow. The main reasons for 'marketing of everything' approaches might best be summed up as DMO *realpolitik* or the politics of destination marketing organisations. The latter may be viewed as a rather neglected aspect of study (Elliott, 1997). As a former practitioner, I know from first-hand experience how hard it is to be selective in what you promote as a DMO. As exemplified above, in organisational settings which emphasise PPP, increasing use of networks, and reliance on sponsorship and member-ship fees, the dangers of being seen to be favouring something or somebody are all too real and omnipresent.

Finally, at Stage 3 of Figure 4.1, there is travel motivation. To reiterate what is a self-evident truth, the prospective visitor does not respond in a naive, automaton-like fashion to DMO marketing. One obvious reason for this is that the consumer may well choose to use destination marketing channels other than those of the DMO. The CEO of *Marketing Cheshire* asks herself this question:

> Does a person really need a DMO? Taken from the consumer point of view, they can probably get by using TripAdvisor and Late Rooms and those other third party booking agencies. That will probably do for them. (Michel, 2014b)

In truth, the motivation to visit a destination for leisure and business purposes is complex, involving a multi-layered interplay of physical, psychological, economic and sociocultural forces which, in turn, are mediated in an opaque and deeply personalised manner by the individual. As Pearce says, the 'underlying reasons for travel are covert in that they reflect an individual's private needs and wants' (Pearce, 2005: 51). In such a setting, the urban DMO and agencies such as TripAdvisor and Late Rooms are clearly just one of a set of 'multiple information pathways' shaping an individual's choice of destination (Pearce, 2005: 91). Heretical as this will doubtless appear to former practitioner colleagues, DMO marketing for the most part lies at the edge of the consumer decision-making process in tourism, to which the inevitable concomitant is failure on the part of DMOs to yield significant levels of return from their marketing in terms of urban economy or profile.

In relation to the gulf between theory and practice, a final point to take into account is that the 'theory of marketing competitive advantage' as set out above has had DMO leisure tourism marketing as its central point of reference – in other words, the media and travel trade relations, advertising and promotions, and print, web/digital and visitor-servicing activity areas depicted in Figure 3.1. It is noteworthy how the remaining two event-based activity areas which feature in the DMO marketing template (viz. attracting conventions and sporting championships/festivals) are afforded only cursory treatment within the academic literature which pertains to the 'theory of marketing competitive advantage'. Intuitively, they 'sit' rather uneasily within this theory because the primary focus of the DMO marketing with which they are associated is less the destination and more the event in question. As we have seen in Chapter 3, the visits of the conference delegate or the 'sports and cultural tourist' are premised on the event rather than the place in which it takes place, and the promotional and sales work of the DMO is centred on the event organiser as opposed to the consumer or intermediary wishing to 'buy into' a destination. Unsurprisingly, therefore, the standard texts on *destination* marketing afford relatively little space to the DMO convention and other event-based marketing we have appraised in Sections 3.4 and 3.5 of Chapter 3. 'Stimulating events' of a sporting and cultural kind, for instance, merit just a page and a half in Pike (2008: 111–112). Reflecting this partial vacuum, specialised texts have arisen which provide more or less comprehensive overviews of business and other aspects of events tourism (notably, Richards & Palmer, 2010; Rodgers, 2013). Even in such texts, the event bidding or procurement role – the essence of DMO involvement in the conventions and sporting/cultural events fields – is dealt with *en passant* or as part of a specific chapter or section of such a chapter (e.g. Rodgers, 2013: Chapter 3).

4.4 Exceptions that Prove the Rule: Innsbruck and Vienna

As Figure 4.2 shows, the DMOs for Innsbruck and Vienna are exceptional because they actually 'market the difference', and this merits our serious consideration inasmuch as this is precisely how we would expect things to happen within the 'theory of marketing competitive advantage'! *Innsbruck Tourism* in their marketing repeatedly give prominence to the city's wonderful mountain setting (and attendant recreational opportunities) as well as its special historic heritage. The CEO of *Innsbruck Tourism* comments as follows:

> The competitive advantage of Innsbruck is that we always try marketing-wise to underline a unique combination. The first part is Innsbruck as historical and cultural, emphasising the great role it played being the fourth capital city of the Hapsburg Empire. Gratz and Salzburg cannot claim this. The other part is the important role Innsbruck plays as a leisure city, a city of mountain sports – skiing especially, biking and walking also. This unique combination is the driver in our general touristic marketing, making Innsbruck special, differentiating it from the others. That is why our motto is 'Innsbruck: capital of the Alps'. This is why we try always picture-wise to position the city with the mountains in the background. What else would we promote? (Kraft, 2013)

The last sentence indicates the sense in which Innsbruck markets the difference less as the end-product of a conscious and controlled process, and more by default – as an inevitable and 'obvious' thing to do in the light of the city having such a compelling set of natural and historic assets. In contrast, 'marketing the difference' is achieved in the case of VTB by strict adherence to a *Vienna: Now or Never* brand manual in which there is a clear delineation of five competitive advantages or 'brand modules', of which 'imperial heritage' is the mainstay, with 'music and culture' and 'savoir-vivre' (essentially food/drink) also being important. Further specificity in respect of marketing content is achieved through the enumeration of a handful of quintessentially Viennese 'brand drivers', each of which pertains to a specific module (e.g. Schonbrunn Palace is one such driver of imperial heritage, as Viennese coffee houses are for 'savoir-vivre'). In this manner, a sharply circumscribed set of assets is made to permeate all aspects of VTB marketing. Adherence to the manual ensures that the scope and content of the latter celebrates what is different about the city, determining what is marketed (e.g. the Vienna Boys' Choir and the Viennese waltz) and what is excluded (e.g. nightlife and shopping, and heritage, music and food/drink in general). Interviewed for this book, VTB's Head of Brand Communications and International Advertising elaborated upon this approach as follows (Klein, 2013):

> There are coffee shops in Rome, Paris and London, but in Vienna they are special; they have a unique charm and are in a class of their own.

> Most places have pubs and bistros, but only Vienna has heuriger [special taverns open for a limited period in the year and selling only the most recently produced Viennese wines].

> London, Munich have imperial heritage. Just Vienna has the Schonbrunn Palace, so we advertise Schonbrunn – not imperial heritage generally.

> Nightlife is a challenge for us; it's good in Vienna, but it doesn't begin to compare with Berlin, so we don't advertise or talk about it. The same for Christmas. There are markets here, of course, but Christmas is not the essence of Vienna.

> There is only one Vienna Boys' Choir.

With this high level of specificity in respect of content, urban destination marketing VTB-style is undertaken on a grand scale, with great innovation, customer focus and creativity, to the extent that the Board is widely acknowledged as a DMO 'leader of the pack' (see next chapter). In terms of the 'theory of marketing competitive advantage', the fact that few other DMOs use their brand platform in this way (i.e. as a 'sieve' to ensure they rigorously delineate and subsequently 'market the difference') is signal testimony to the prevalence elsewhere in Europe's towns and cities of 'marketing of everything' approaches.

4.5 Theming 'Urban Sameness'

Europe's cities and towns become daily less distinguishable. In Victorian and Edwardian Britain, Manchester was 'King Cotton', Sheffield was 'the name on the knife blade' and Bradford was 'Woolopolis'; 'they made ships' in Glasgow and Newcastle, and cigarettes, cricket bats and bicycles in

Nottingham. Armed with their respective manufacturing capabilities and specialisms, urban places set themselves apart and became 'known'. In today's post-industrial world, towns and cities struggle to etch themselves sharply on the regional and national mind as being 'different', let alone carve out a reputation for themselves upon the world stage. Urban economy is nowadays strongly orientated towards the service sector, associated with which are highly predictable landscapes. Style in architecture has become uniform to the point where so-called iconic buildings are paradoxically international in style. City and town centres major on branded features, so that here in England seemingly everywhere has 'eateries' such as Nando's, Starbucks and Wetherspoons. Belgrade has just opened its 14th McDonald's. Mayors, city managers and town hall spokespersons trot out an identical message: 'we want to be a great place in which to invest, live, and work' and a 'first-choice destination' to visit. The semiotic markers of 21st-century urban life are everywhere the same: 'trendy' cafes, 'upmarket' theatre and opera, 'specialist' shopping, 'boutique' hotels, 'cool' bars, 'animated' public spaces, 'smart' flat and office conversions, 'leading-edge' arenas and sporting stadia, and 'state-of-the-art' public transport systems. Just about every European city boasts an 'extraordinary' gallery of contemporary art. In short, there is almost serial reproduction of urban landscapes, a part of which is standardised tourism products and industry brands. Intuitively, this 'urban sameness' serves to restrict the abilities of urban DMOs to celebrate difference, and it becomes one more reason for their typically adopting unselective 'marketing of everything' approaches.

There is an important sense, therefore, in which DMO 'marketing of everything' reflects and, in turn, contributes to the global and monolithic theming of 'urban sameness' referred to in the paragraph directly above. The author's examination of the promotional videos produced by the destinations listed in Figure 4.2 bears out the observations made by Turkell and Uysal that DMOs deploy remarkably similar imagery. In the case of the videos, it comprises the following: planes landing; trains, trams and subway systems; classical and contemporary art; cafe culture, coffee and cakes; taxis pulling up outside hotels followed by welcome desks and beds; wine in glasses and eating out in upmarket restaurants; clocks, markets, rooftops and skyscrapers; concerts and theatres; parkland and food markets; young people dancing and swimming; stylish women shopping (nearly always as twosomes) and middle-aged men playing golf (nearly always threesomes); the more elderly perusing galleries; couples with young children enjoying museums, and so it goes on. Take away the name of the town and city and its DMO, and the place featured in the 'promo' becomes more or less indistinguishable. In this way, the 'marketing of everything' is a theming of 'urban sameness', complementing and reinforcing the standardised and formulaic urban landscapes which are becoming the hallmark of towns and cities in the 21st century.

Theming 'urban sameness' is the antithesis of DMOs celebrating the ways in which their town or city is special and remarkable. This contradiction is only just beginning to be recognised by DMOs, as is acknowledged in the following comments made by the Acting CEO of *Gothenburg & Co*:

> It's important today to find your own uniqueness and to be authentic; to try and find your own values instead of having aeroplanes flying in, golf courses, happy people etc. We are trying to move away from that glossy, cosmopolitan, much romanticised kind of imagery in which if you close your eyes and put away the city's name, you could be mostly anywhere. We are not Paris and London, and it's a joke to compare ourselves to that. Gothenburg is often grey and wet. We are not the biggest city, nor the best. However, there are quite a few good things about our city, and amongst the best ones are the people. We have never, for instance, used the archipelago and its fishermen as a part of our imagery. (Nymen, 2013)

Arguably, the most critical shortcoming of contemporary urban destination marketing is this 'glossy, cosmopolitan, much romanticised kind of imagery' which could be 'anywhere' and goes 'hand in glove' with globalisation, and the homogeneity and standardisation of landscape and life with which that is associated. In a common-sense fashion and as per the 'theory of marketing competitive advantage', we nearly all of us expect the scope and content of urban destination marketing to highlight and accentuate the differences between urban places, precisely as *Innsbruck Tourism* and VTB in their marketing 'pull out' what makes those places distinctive and special. Unfortunately, in 'celebrating the difference' in this way, these two DMOs turn out be exceptions to the general rule. Content elsewhere is depressingly similar and uniform. It is Turkell's 'United States of Generica', and it is Belgrade's 2014 tourist guide, the Foreword to which by the Acting Director of the city's DMO (the *Belgrade Tourist Organisation*) ends on this note: 'Everything is here in Belgrade, Belgrade is in everything.' It is *Hong Kong Tourist Board* proclaiming it is 'Asia's world city'.

4.6 Conclusions

In practice, we have found in this chapter that the 'theory of marketing competitive advantage' as applied to urban destination marketing is more or less irrelevant in all but a tiny number of cases; for the purposes of this book I have been able only to instance Innsbruck and Vienna. For the most part, towns and cities the length and breadth of Europe do not promote and otherwise celebrate what is different about themselves in their urban destination marketing. The 'theory of marketing competitive advantage' may be seen as 'broken' at each of the 'what', 'how' and 'why' stages shown in

Figure 4.1, inasmuch as it does not accord with much the greater part of practice. Most destinations do not pass the 'Johnson test' and have a stock of USP attractors sufficient to constitute competitive advantage. Nearly all DMOs take an undifferentiated product to market, embodied in a 'marketing of everything' approach which is heavily conditioned by *realpolitik* considerations, especially those of a 'he who pays the piper calls the tune' sort. The outcomes of DMO marketing operations in terms of boosting urban economy and profile are at best of marginal significance. Urban destination marketing in contemporary Europe is explicable more by DMO *realpolitik*, globalisation and 21st-century capitalism than it is by a normative 'theory of marketing competitive advantage' in which a city or town – seemingly in a vacuum – sets out its USP stall, and the customer buys automaton-like its unique and differentiated offers – as if he or she were one of Pavlov's dogs.

Having said that, 'marketing the difference' in some shape or form is important to a handful of DMOs, as noted above in the operations carried out by *Innsbruck Tourism* and VTB. Indeed, the sense in which 'marketing the difference' (as opposed to the 'marketing of everything') is important to success in urban tourism marketing is a theme taken up in the chapter to follow. To this end, we will appraise VTB operations in more detail, along with those of other DMO 'exemplars'. However, it remains the case that 'marketing the difference' as a principle is extremely difficult to translate into a workable *modus operandi*, so much so that it rarely occurs in practice and is perhaps in danger of becoming an endangered species! As we have endeavoured to show in this chapter, 'marketing of everything' rules OK in modern-day Europe, and as a result urban destination marketing is 'much of a muchness', all of which is fundamentally at odds with what one would expect to happen under the 'theory of marketing competitive advantage'. Reflecting their failure to 'market the difference', most DMOs are unable to fulfil their core purpose of 'bringing in the business', a predicament aggravated by the financial and reputational constraints spotlighted in Chapter 2. Of the few that are successful – the DMO 'exemplars' – they are so, precisely because they address these constraints and/or because they succeed in effectively marketing themselves around genuine differences and advantages. It is now time radically to reappraise urban destination marketing theory. At present, the academic and practitioner mind-sets treat the marketing of competitive advantage as a given, whereas in practice the majority of DMO behaviours do not reflect such an approach. The failure to 'tell it like it is' – the yawning gap between theory and practice demonstrated in this chapter – warrants in the author's view a substantial rethinking of the paradigm within which academics and practitioners alike currently seek to explain and otherwise account for urban destination marketing. It is to the hefty task of overhauling the 'theory of marketing competitive advantage' that we devote the next chapter.

5 Towards a New 'Middle-range' Theory: The Dynamics of Urban Destination Marketing

For a long time I believed that there was progress in the history of law, a development towards greater beauty and truth, rationality and humanity, despite terrible setbacks and retreats. Once it became clear to me that this belief was a chimera, I began playing with a different image of the course of legal history. In this one it still has a purpose, but the goal it finally attains ... is the beginning, its own original starting point, which once reached must be set off from again.

Bernhard Schlink (1997) *The Reader*

In this final chapter, I advance a framework of concepts and propositions with which to 'explain' or otherwise account for the practice of urban destination marketing in early 21st-century Europe. This represents a substantial revision and recasting of what we have referred to as the 'theory of marketing competitive advantage'. In terms of Kuhn's *Structure of Scientific Revolutions*, this is less a paradigm revolution in which one paradigm is completely replaced by a new one, and more a paradigm readjustment, necessitated by the 'stubborn refusal' of anomalies to be 'assimilated' (Kuhn, 1970: 97). The adjusted paradigm – which we are calling the *'dynamics of urban destination marketing'* – uses more or less the same data, but places new and existing variables in a different set of relationships to one another. To this new theory we now, without further ado, turn.

5.1 The Dynamics of Urban Destination Marketing

The outputs and outcomes of urban destination marketing may be viewed as an end state which is conditional upon the interplay of four main variables, as summarised in Figure 5.1. The first three variables – an amalgam of political, product and organisational considerations – may be seen as 'building blocks'. Together, they form a foundation or platform upon which

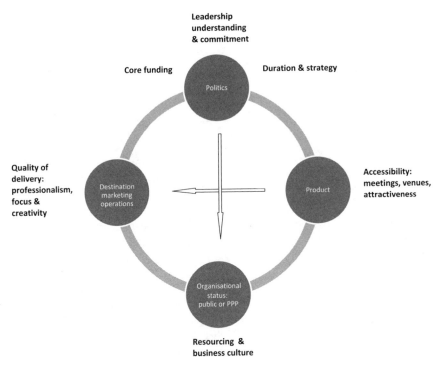

Figure 5.1 The dynamics of urban destination marketing

a fourth variable – destination marketing operations – is undertaken. Crucially, within this model, outputs and outcomes are conditional upon the soundness of the foundation and the effectiveness of marketing operations. Each of the four variables encapsulates a range of factors:

- *Politics* includes leadership understanding and commitment, as this is reflected in levels of DMO core funding, the degree to which support is long term, and strategy.
- *Product* involves criteria of accessibility, venues and urban attractiveness.
- *Organisational status* hinges on a choice between public sector and public–private partnership (PPP) modes of organisation, with the latter affording a further set of advantages in respect of resourcing and business culture which are in practice exploited to a varying degree, especially the extent to which performance management and managerial autonomy obtains.
- *Marketing operations* themselves are undertaken with differing amounts of professionalism, focus and creativity.

In this manner, Figure 5.1 consolidates in a four-variable schema a veritable raft of considerations, all of them conditioning and otherwise shaping the outputs and outcomes of urban destination marketing. In one way or another, all of these factors have been identified and discussed in Chapters 2 and 3, which has established for the reader a factual and empirical basis on which urban destination marketing is currently taking place in contemporary Europe.

As a theory or amended paradigm, the 'dynamics of urban destination marketing' runs along the following lines, as per its constituent four variables summarised in Figure 5.1. First, urban destination marketing occasions a variable degree of political commitment from the leadership of one town or city to the next, and this is especially apparent among senior local government politicians and officers. In turn, this is reflected in differing levels of core funding being made available to support urban destination marketing activities, and in the extent to which there is recognition that strategy for urban destination marketing must perforce have direction and be long term. Secondly, there is the available tourist product, the three main foci of which are accessibility arrangements, venues and urban attractiveness. Product as a variable clearly embraces attributes inclusive of, but going far wider than, the notion of USPs so central to the 'theory of marketing competitive advantage'. This theory prescribes unique strengths or USPs as the only basis on which a DMO can effectively discharge its destination marketing operations. This belies the sense in which tourists are motivated by, for want of a better word, the convenience, price and 'lure' of a place as opposed to specific USP attractors. Intuitively, for instance, it is the lure of Paris – as reflected in its accessibility, venues and urban attractiveness advantages – which precipitates visits to the French capital as opposed to, say, the Eiffel Tower or a Montmartre acting as USPs. Indeed, there are countless examples of successful urban destination marketing taking place in which USPs do not figure at all, as we have seen, for instance, in the 'Stay Play and Explore' campaign referred to in Chapter 3. The latter demonstrates how in urban destination marketing the product offered need only be of a reasonable-to-good standard, as long as it is competitively priced and effectively packaged and distributed. That said, a base of accessibility, venues and attractiveness (as opposed to competitive advantage pure and simple) is clearly an indispensable building block, as per Figure 5.1. Put another way, and not wishing to be unkind to these towns, few tourists are going to make a beeline for the likes of Milton Keynes, Middlesbrough and Motherwell precisely because these places at the present moment in time do not 'have what it takes' in terms of the requisite tourist infrastructure and superstructure afforded by accessibility, venues and urban attractiveness. A third variable is organisational status, which in effect is reducible to adoption of either a city government or PPP mode of organisation, and an exploitation of the potential advantages flowing from the latter. As established in Chapter 2, the PPP model enables a DMO to maximise trading and other 'levered' private sector income streams, and to cultivate an appropriate, results-orientated business culture. Suffice to say, PPP-based

DMOs take advantage of these opportunities to a varying degree. The fourth and final variable is the manner in which the DMO executes its destination marketing operations. In practice, the degree of professionalism, creativity and focus applied varies widely from one DMO to the next, as will be exemplified later in this chapter.

To reiterate, the effectiveness and ultimate impact of urban destination marketing in any one town or city is an outcome of the following: the depth and duration of political commitment and understanding, as this translates itself into resourcing and direction; the 'lure' of the urban destination in respect of accessibility, venues and urban attractiveness; the organisational status of the DMO delivery mechanism, and the extent to which adoption of the PPP model results in the leverage of significant amounts of additional, non-public sector resourcing, as well as the embodiment of a business culture emphasising performance management and managerial autonomy; and, finally, the degree to which the DMO achieves sufficient momentum and quality of service delivery so as to really 'make a difference' in terms of its core marketing and visitor-servicing operations, as these have been appraised in Chapter 3. A basic query now arises: how does urban destination marketing in contemporary Europe fare against the criteria set out in Figure 5.1? The short and rather unpalatable answer to this question is 'not very well', a verdict presaged in Chapter 3 in which I suggested praxis in urban destination marketing in the main represents 'work in progress'. As we shall discover later in this chapter, urban destination marketing in contemporary Europe currently 'shakes down' into a small number of what we term as DMO 'exemplars' who are succeeding in 'making a difference' in terms of outputs and outcomes, and a preponderance of 'others' whose performance against these criteria is unremarkable and 'run-of-the-mill'. Towards the end of this chapter, we return to this basic query. In the meantime, it is important now to elaborate upon each of the four key variables identified in Figure 5.1.

5.2 Politics: Leadership Understanding and Commitment

A prerequisite for success in urban destination marketing is 'top-down' understanding and commitment on the part of the leadership of a town or city, as has been exemplified in Chapter 2. The leadership in question comprises local government politicians and officers, as well as prominent local business persons. The Chief Executive of *Visit Manchester* says:

> The commitment of city leaders is hugely important. We [*Visit Manchester*] need to operate across both civic and business spheres, and retain the credibility of each – we have to understand how each community works. (Simpson, 2014)

Of paramount importance is the support of senior politicians and officers from the local authority, especially the Mayor/Leader of the Council, and the Town Manager/Chief Executive. The CEO of the *Glasgow City Marketing Bureau* (GCMB) puts this with finality: 'You must have the backing of your Council leader and CEO or it won't happen' (Marketing Edinburgh Project Board, 2010: 5).The 'it' in question here is purposeful and effective urban destination marketing.

Understanding on the part of the leadership of town or city is reducible in nearly all cases to an appreciation of the potentially huge economic and commercial potential offered by urban tourism. In this respect, direct economic effects are clearly of great importance, especially turnover/profits and employment/jobs. One of our DMO interviewees reflected on how, over the years, local political administrations had gained a better understanding of the direct economic gains:

> What is interesting is that I never found tourism to be a 'political' issue. So whether it was a Conservative-led authority or a Labour-run one, I think they all in the end understood that tourism could generate economic benefit in the form of spend and jobs. I think in my early days, there was some persuasion to be done about the importance of tourism, because of perceptions that tourism was a 'candyfloss' industry and that the jobs were part-time, seasonal, and low paid. Therefore, tourism was viewed by some politicians as not being about 'real' jobs. I think now, 30 years on, there's been a sea change. (Wilkinson, 2014)

At the time of writing, full-time equivalent jobs and turnover generated by tourism in the city of Gothenburg are estimated at 17,000 and €2 billion, respectively; in York and Berlin, the comparable employment figures are cited as 11,000 and 232,000, respectively. The employment metric has been of critical significance in persuading local government politicians and managers to invest in (and otherwise commit to) urban destination marketing.

Impressive as the figures often are which purport to quantify the outcomes of tourist spending in towns and cities (setting aside their reliability for the moment), of even greater potential significance is the power of tourism to transform urban profile, reputation and image through 'word of mouth' (WOM) recommendation. Through WOM, urban tourism nowadays is arguably the most cost-effective way for a city or town to market itself and become 'known'. As such, it offers a 'best' route-to-market, creating a platform of awareness on which a town or city can go on to attract even more interest and custom from its key external audiences – students, occupiers of property, inward investors and, last but not least, tourists themselves. Whereas the direct employment and other economic gains associated with tourism are nowadays widely understood by the leadership of towns and cities, the WOM effects are arguably much less appreciated, as we shall exemplify later in this section.

Having taken cognizance of the potential benefits, the *logical* outcome in terms of urban destination marketing is that the leadership of towns and cities will commit to it in the form of (a) an agreed, long-term approach (which may or may not be formulated in a documented strategy) and (b) the establishment and resourcing of a focused and independent PPP-based delivery mechanism. As for the shared approach, GCMB's Chief Executive says:

> We now have a city-wide tourism strategy to 2016. All the key stakeholders were involved in putting it together. We all know the roles we each play in its delivery and we all get together monthly to review our progress. It's not rocket science – it just requires coordination. And that's our job. (Marketing Edinburgh Project Board, 2010: 5)

In respect of resourcing, a ground rule to which Chapter 2 amply attests is that local public sector financial support should in the case of PPP-based DMOs be at least sufficient to cover labour and other overhead expenses. For this very reason, this grant is widely referred to as core funding.

In practice, the leadership of many towns and cities don't understand and appreciate the economic significance of tourism (either wholly or in part), and as a result they don't give urban destination marketing their 'full-on' backing in terms of approach, strategy and, crucially, finance. In such circumstances, urban destination marketing starts off 'on the back foot' and any DMO that is established may be viewed as having its 'hands tied behind its back'. A more or less certain indicator of whether or not the leadership have understood the need for urban destination marketing and are giving it fulsome backing is to be found in the composition of DMO governance and the nature of the relationship between that governance and the full-time, professional executive. In terms of composition, are 'top' leaders present or conspicuous by their absence? In Glasgow, for instance, a situation obtains in which there is a longstanding understanding and commitment on the part of the leadership of the city which stretches back to 1983 (Heeley, 2011: 40). In absolute and proportionate terms, core funding provided by Glasgow City Council is generous, as indicated in Table 2.2. As we have also seen in Chapter 2 and as detailed in Figure 2.4, the governance of GCMB is made up of a powerful and influential seven-person board of directors chaired by the Leader of Glasgow City Council (a Labour Party politician), with the Vice-chairmanship taken up by another senior councillor – the leader of the main opposition group on the Council (the Scottish Nationalist Party). The Principal of Glasgow University is another director. Such individuals are 'top' leaders or, as they say in Scotland, 'high heid yins'!

In respect of the nature of the relationship between GCMB's governance and executive, we have demonstrated in Chapter 2 how close and mutually supportive this is. Clearly, political understanding and commitment in the case of Glasgow's urban destination marketing is high, as reflected in the level of core funding made available, the long-term and strategic nature of the approach, a DMO governance populated by politicians and businessmen of stature, and the productive nature of the relationship between executive and governance.

A broadly similar, politically committed situation has obtained in Gothenburg since 1991. Reflecting on the formation in that year of *Gothenburg & Co*, the founder Chief Executive of the company remarks:

> The leading politicians in the city realised that there were too many organisations peripherally involved, with no single structure around with a clear vision and strategy. There was a lot of political will; the politicians wanted to do things and change things, and this was also strongly supported by many industry leaders. In fact, it was the mayor, the leader of the opposition party, and several industry people who approached me and said 'will you come home and do this job for us'? So when I went back, I asked them: 'what is it that you want me to do?' That was my starting point. They had some ideas about branding and the universities, but they didn't really know what they wanted. I talked to maybe a couple of hundred people in the city, and as a result we created a single body to promote Gothenburg (*Gothenburg & Co*). The words we kept repeating were this new organisation should be 'a platform for cooperation' on which we would take a 'holistic view' of the destination and its marketing. While we needed to have the top political leaders serving on the board of directors of *Gothenburg & Co*, I always made it clear it shouldn't be a purely city government organisation because then it would have been totally 'political'. To work, *Gothenburg & Co* had to be a public–private partnership, though such organisations weren't that common then, they really weren't. They didn't exist in any of the big cities in our part of the world. But the top political leaders back in 1991 wanted cooperation with business. So when we eventually formed *Gothenburg & Co* the board had what was then a most unusual structure, made up of top political leaders and the directors of various companies like Volvo. This was a bold step, but it became a good atmosphere and culture of cooperation. There was such a strong commitment and willingness to change. (Bjerkne, 2013)

In Chapter 2, the Acting CEO of *Gothenburg & Co* commented on the high level of political commitment and understanding which continues to characterise urban destination marketing in Sweden's second city – a commitment reflected in strategy and resourcing terms. The company works to a formal three-year business plan (the one operative currently is for 2012–2014), and its 2012 income amounted to some €23 million (Gothenburg & Co, 2013: 52).

The important observation to now make is that few DMOs are anywhere near as fortunate as those of Glasgow and Gothenburg in respect of depth of political understanding and an associated high degree of commitment. The reality for most DMOs, as exemplified in Chapter 2, is that commitment is partial and often fitful, with in many cases core funding in the PPP-based organisations falling well short of covering overhead expenses ('rotten to the core' as practitioners sometimes ruefully remark!). We saw in the Preface how politicians in Bradford have blown 'hot and cold' over urban destination marketing. Similarly, in York, the Labour-controlled city council discontinued encouragement of tourism in favour of policies of containment over a 10-year period, 1985–1995, before adopting the current stance which might best be described as more supportive, but still less than fully committed (Heeley, 2011: 105–107). The former Chief Executive of *Visit York* puts it like this:

> The local politicians don't understand tourism; definitely not. They don't see how marketing tourism impacts on inward investment and students. Destination marketing is not at the forefront of their thinking. They don't see how it all fits together in terms of spending, jobs and profile. The fact that historically the public sector 'walked away' from tourism destination marketing for a long while means that the Council still to this day feels disengaged from decisions as to how the city is promoted. It's getting better, but we haven't quite got the relationship between *Visit York* and the City Council right. It's a relationship which needs to be as tight as possible. A big thing that gets in the way is corporate press and PR. Politicians want to get good publicity for what happens in tourism, but as an 'arms-length' agency we haven't quite found a way of giving the Council what they want. Typically, when the media report on tourism they paint *Visit York* and the attractions and hotels as the 'good guys', and the Council aren't mentioned, or are even the 'bad guy'. You see, *Visit York* is seen by the press as being independent and reasonably objective whereas the local authority isn't. (Cruddas, 2014)

In optimising political understanding and commitment in PPP-based DMOs, a difficult and delicate balance has to be struck between 'arms-length' independence from local government, on the one hand, and stakeholder expectations of 'payback' on the other. Arms-length can so easily 'become off-shore and unloved' (Heeley, 2001: 282), a situation increasingly encountered by DMOs as funding is progressively reduced or withdrawn by the public sector. A DMO Chief Executive bemoans this 'offshore' vulnerability:

> The financial model is now fundamentally broken and flawed, because you've got local authorities reducing their budgets by 20–30% a year. They become hell-bent on self-survival, and the DMO is out on a limb. What they (the local authorities) do is withdraw into themselves. It's a

little bit like a tortoise that goes into its shell; what they do is protect their key services and their own departments, and ultimately their own jobs. So anything that's grant-aided, anything that's given out to external groups to deliver, that's the first thing that gets cut, and it gets cut disproportionately. I've got 20 strategic partners, most of them local authorities, but I've also got three colleges and two universities. All of them are now saying: 'well, money's tight so you're going to have to take a big cut'. The cumulative effect on our finances is quite staggering. It's becoming impossible to bridge the gap. (James, 2013)

So for this CEO, it is less a problem of understanding and more one of commitment, expressed financially:

I would say the councillors and senior officers 'get it'. They appreciate that a marketing campaign is going to make people feel good about a place, bring in visitors, and influence students to choose a particular university and investors to relocate their businesses. They will say: 'that's a great campaign, but don't ask us for another £50,000 because we've got meals on wheels to do', or some such thing. They just throw it back at you on the grounds that destination marketing is not a statutory service. So you have to 'wait in line' with your begging bowl, and are fed the scraps left over from the table. The weakness we have as DMOs is in proving our case. It's not as if you're going into a bank and saying: 'I've got a great business proposition here which will give you a direct return'. Destination marketing doesn't give the local authority investor a direct return, and we struggle to quantify the returns in terms of the wider spending and investment benefits to the community. So DMOs just get looked on as cost. (James, 2013)

The contrast with the Glasgow and Gothenburg situations could not be starker.

5.3 Product: Accessibility, Venues and Urban Attractiveness

It is self-evident that cities and towns can only succeed as urban tourist destinations if they have something in product terms which the customer wishes to experience. As per the preceding chapter, some cities and towns pass the 'Johnson test', being 'naturally' blessed with competitive advantage and other strengths which make them 'worth seeing and worth going to see' e.g. Innsbruck with its wonderful mountain setting and its historic old town. Others endeavour to create such an advantage out of events or iconic 'must-see' constructs; classic instances are the use made of 'mega-festivals' by German cities (e.g. *Kieler Voche*) and the establishment in Bilbao of the iconic Guggenheim Museum. As we demonstrated in Chapter 4, however, most towns and cities don't pass the 'Johnson test' in the sense of possessing competitive advantage compelling enough to be a prime motivator of tourist travel.

Having said that, all towns and cities are accessible, have venues and a varying degree of urban attractiveness. Venues I am here restricting to the purpose-built or other structures used to host the meetings and other business tourism events which are the foci of the DMO convention marketing discussed in Section 3.4 of Chapter 3. Urban attractiveness should be taken as a town or city's stock of cultural, sporting, retailing and entertainment assets, as well as its base of supporting hospitality in the form of accommodation, catering and other outlets. On the basis of accessibility arrangements, venues and urban attractiveness being more or less fit for purpose, there is therefore some validity in a town or city attempting to be an urban tourism player, irrespective of whether or not they possess a genuine and singular degree of competitive advantage. As we established in the last chapter, the resultant DMO marketing operations will invariably embody a 'marketing of everything' approach. A further illustration of such an approach, the Chief Executive of *Visit Manchester* says this about the 'what' of his organisation's destination marketing operations:

> There is the strength of Manchester Airport on which we can capitalise, and there is the compactness of the city with a clustering of hotels, conference venues, food and drink outlets and visitor attractions, all of them within a short space of each other. Clearly, Manchester United, as one of the world's strongest sporting brands, is also important. We have a targeted approach in the sense of the market we are trying to attract. Obviously, *we want to include everything that is pleasant – all our events and assets* [author's italics]. Our role as *Visit Manchester* is to create opportunities for visitors to explore them in ways which are otherwise not readily available. (Simpson, 2014)

As we have discovered in the last two chapters, DMO executives typically label this 'broad-brush' and inclusive approach as a 'themed' one. A further example is evidenced here:

> I think in my early days here in Scarborough it was very much about a product-led approach. As our marketing got more refined, we then started to introduce a more thematic approach. The holiday guide was still the prime means of attracting visitors to the area, and I shifted it towards four themes – coast, countryside, culture and cuisine. I think that worked. Later on, when I was head of the *Lancashire and Blackpool Tourist Board*, we developed a thematic approach based on six themes. (Wilkinson, 2014)

Two additional examples of so-called 'themed' approaches may conveniently be cited here. The Chief Executive of *Marketing Cheshire* describes the content of the urban destination marketing her organisation undertakes for the city of Chester as embodying two broad themes:

> You need to have something stuck in your head about Chester that makes you want to desire it. We want people to know two things; that there is two thousand years of history here, so you are walking in the footsteps of the Romans and the Tudors or whoever; and that there is a very 'buzzy' and contemporary shopping, eating out and drinking scene. That's the two ingredients that people want for the perfect weekend away. (Michel, 2014b)

Similarly, the Chief Executive responsible for Derbyshire as a tourism destination, including the city of Derby and several other smaller towns, points to the impracticability of promoting competitive advantage:

> Being honest, the way we operate is thematic, so that our customers want either a city break or a countryside break. If you actually break it down, there is only one thing that's totally unique about Derbyshire, and that is well-dressing. Does that motivate people to visit us? No, it sends most people to sleep. Of course, people still come in their busloads to take photographs of the villages that have done some dressing, but that's not something we can market. The great strength we have in Derbyshire is that we actually border four big cities. It's prime real estate in your back garden. You can be there in half an hour to an hour and a half, and that's great if you don't have too much money to spend. So we call our country breaks 'The Great Escape'. Tourists can come here and relax, chill out, and get away from it all. We try and capture that, but clearly it isn't unique. But looked at as a Brummie [colloquial term for a resident of Birmingham], 90 minutes to Derby is a distinct advantage. So we capitalise on accessibility, and our destination marketing is an 'anywhereshire' – the opposite, if you like, of competitive advantage. (James, 2013)

Such 'marketing of everything' and associated thematic approaches are self-evidently at odds with the 'theory of marketing competitive advantage', where more or less unique selling points are the indispensable and exclusive foundation upon which urban destination marketing takes place, forming the content or thrust of that marketing. In contrast, 'marketing of everything' approaches are entirely consistent within the theory I am calling the 'dynamics of urban destination marketing' (as summarised in Figure 5.1), as are the minority of instances in which competitive advantage is the embodiment of urban destination marketing; reference the cases of *Innsbruck Tourism* and the *Vienna Tourist Board* (VTB) exemplified in Section 4.4 of the preceding chapter.

5.4 DMO Organisational Status: Resourcing and Business Culture

Referencing my practitioner experience and the numerous comments to this effect made in Chapter 2 by our interviewees, effective urban destination marketing operations are invariably associated with PPPs as opposed to the city government mode of organisation. To reiterate, the main reasons for this are twofold. First, DMOs organised as PPPs tend to be better resourced than their city government based counterparts because – as we have demonstrated in Chapter 2 – they are able to access private sector and trading income streams on a significant scale. As the Commercial Director of *Marketing Birmingham* succinctly states: 'If you want to leverage money from the private sector, you have to have a vehicle which the private sector trusts' (Marketing Edinburgh Project Board, 2010: 5). Suffice to say, the DMO vehicle in question is that of PPP. The 'levered', non-public sector monies referred to above typically provide the basis for much the greater part of DMO operating income, as we demonstrated in Chapter 2 where reference was made specifically to GCMB and its 2012/2013 budget totalling £5.9 million. This indicated that the lion's share of the Bureau's operating cash or working capital (67%) derived from earned and private sector income streams more or less wholly facilitated by the Bureau being constituted as a PPP. Secondly, and as again demonstrated in Chapter 2, the 'volunteer' governances and 'professional' executive teams recruited to PPP-based DMOs permit a business culture to obtain which routinely emphasises performance management, managerial autonomy and operating efficiency. On the one hand, performance management means that the operations of the CEO and senior directors are monitored by governance in a results-orientated and accountable manner, typically through key performance indicators. On the other hand, managerial autonomy allows DMO marketing professionals fully to express their skills, experience, knowledge, energies, innovation, commerciality and creativity. Managerial efficiency, in the words of the CEO of *Visit Manchester*, translates into 'greater flexibility, ability to connect more effectively with the private sector, and speed of response' (Simpson, 2014).

The sense in which operating efficiency flows from PPP status is captured in the following remarks made by the Chief Executive of *Leicester Shire Promotions*:

There is a grey area as to whether local authorities by law can do some of the activities that a DMO needs to do. Particularly when it comes to trading; to selling and promoting city breaks, retailing goods and services in tourist information centres, and that sort of thing. So there are possible legal constraints to consider. But setting that aside, there is simply no way that a department of a local authority can operate effectively as a DMO and relate well to the private sector. Hotels, in particular, need to know that you're talking their language, and understand how their businesses are working. You can never have relationships like that working from within a local authority, even with the most supportive of commercial partners. There is always the view that 'we pay business rates to the local authority, so why should we stump up any extra money for you'. Things take too long in the public sector; local authorities are not responsive; they cannot react quickly enough. There are quite a few places in England where the DMO is part of local government, but I don't think you have to scratch too far beneath the surface to realise such arrangements are not as effective as the public–private partnership mode of delivery. (Peters, 2014)

The Chief Executive of *Bath Tourism Plus* comments on the advantages of PPP as follows, while highlighting some of the delicate balancing acts involved:

By being a public–private partnership, we can own the mantle of 'official'. This sets us apart from the local authority and from purely commercial organisations such as hotels, advertising and design agencies, and publishers of local magazines. Consequently, we are seen as impartial and trusted by consumers, and this is important. However, many businesses still think that we are part of the local authority, and therefore bureaucratic, slow-to-act, distanced from commercial reality, and all the rest of it. They sometimes even expect us to do things 'for free' because they mistakenly think we are civil servants and part of the council. The reality nowadays is that we have to be largely self-funding. This tightrope of doing things for the greater good, balanced with doing things that are commercial for our own sustainability, is a tricky one. (Brook-Sykes, 2014)

PPP in urban destination marketing is therefore a fundamental organising principle. It is about running the DMO as a business, creating a regime which will maximise income, embody results-orientation, and release staff energies and talents. The other side of the coin is that DMOs organised as departments of city government are more or less unable to take advantage of the enhanced resourcing and business culture associated with PPP. In short, PPP affords great potential to get both a 'bigger buck', and a 'bigger bang from each and every buck'! Having said that, the extent to which these potential gains and advantages are realised is itself a major variable, to which Brook-Sykes's 'tightrope' and associated balancing act bears witness.

5.5 Marketing Operations: Quality of Delivery

The three previous subsections have discussed the 'building blocks' which provide the foundation upon which urban destination marketing operations take place. The extent to which this foundation is fit for purpose differs markedly from one DMO to the next. Critically, the robustness or otherwise of the foundation conditions the amount of resourcing becoming available to the DMO, as well as the business culture within which it is expended. Also exerting a profound influence on the outputs and outcomes of DMO marketing operations is the quality dimension, that is, the degree to which urban destination marketing is discharged effectively or otherwise which, in turn, is a function of professionalism, focus and creativity. Self-evidently, the quality dimension is a difficult one to convey to the reader because it hinges ultimately on the attitudes and abilities of the individuals that populate a DMO and, in particular, its full-time professional staff led by the CEO. As much is suggested in the following comments by the chief executive of a small, but dynamic and much respected Polish convention bureau:

> We are good at what we do for a number of reasons – it's a combination of things. Of course my team is very good. And it's not just me saying that; people come up to me and say 'listen, your girls are great'. And we get lots of written references, too. I think our secret is that we love what we do. I love what I do. I am very lucky to have this job because I really love it. And my colleagues also love doing their work, and it shows. We have the best smartphone application of any convention bureau in Poland, and I think it is fair to say that we generate more profile than the others. Last year we won the ICCA best marketing award for what we did during EIBTM [European Incentive and Business Travel and Meetings Exhibition] when it was held in Barcelona in November 2012. As it was nearing Christmas, we organised our stand presence at EIBTM so that any caller could paint a bauble and then leave it with us – together with any 'freebie' items they cared to donate like pens, memory sticks, badges, stickers, calendars, postcards, sweeties etc. People really took to the idea of painting a bauble and leaving us a gift bound for a charity. You see, after the show, we gave all the stuff we had collected to a foster home in Barcelona, and this got our Bureau a lot of publicity. We just created something out of nothing, and it worked so well and was so popular that we won the ICCA award. To win this, we had to compile a written report and make a 15-minute presentation on our EIBTM experience. The other contenders as convention bureaux were big and sophisticated by our standards – Melbourne, Denmark and Montreux. But we won the award because what we did was simple, attention-grabbing and appealing. It created a warm glow, if you like, and our presentation was outstanding. (Górska, 2014)

In order to crystallise in the reader's mind the nature of quality service delivery and its essentially attitudinal and professional underpinnings, the next two sections present concrete examples of best practice in urban destination marketing. In this respect, peer group opinion, together with awards and other accolades, point unequivocally towards VTB and GCMB as being current embodiments of DMO best practice. The quest for excellence running through both organisations is reflected in the following comments, although the approach adopted is a contrasting one. VTB's Head of Strategic Destination Development remarks:

> So right now we are looking outside of Europe and evaluating ourselves on a global scale. We are starting from a blank sheet, and are benchmarking with the world's best DMOs in order to find out what we can do differently and what we can make better. The working title is *The DMO of the 21st Century*. That's the sort of vision that we are going to have for the future. At the moment we're doing quite well in Europe; we're doing quite well I think. (Penz, 2013)

The Chief Executive of GCMB is minded to say:

> We don't benchmark against anybody. I don't actually follow any convention bureau. We are inventing, developing and creating; if we weren't doing that, then perhaps we would be benchmarking against somebody else. (Taylor, 2013)

As we have said already, it is important for the reader to appreciate the extent and manner in which the operational delivery of DMO 'leaders of the pack' outdistances the rest. The sheer magnitude of this gulf is quite striking, as we will now exemplify by examining how in 2013 the DMOs for Vienna and Glasgow were seeking to attract leisure and business tourism, respectively.

5.6 The *Vienna Tourist Board*: Attracting Leisure Tourism

In respect of leisure tourism marketing, VTB stands out as a titan among European DMOs, and for that reason alone merits serious attention. VTB was formed in 1955 under the Vienna Tourism Act which constituted it as a PPP. Its PPP status at that time marked an 'almost revolutionary ... separation of tourism from the administration of the city' (VTB, 2006: 3). The passing of this legislation, and the arms-length principle it enshrined, reflected commitment on behalf of Vienna's senior politicians, and in the intervening 59 years VTB has become a byword for 'stability, reliability and trust' (VTB, 2006: 4–7). The Board's growth and rise to prominence and then pre-eminence among Europe's DMOs has been chronicled elsewhere (Heeley, 2011: 9–10,

71–75). In this section we review how this DMO conducts its innovative, impactful and otherwise outstanding leisure tourism marketing, as these operations were being undertaken in April 2013.

The starting point for such a review must perforce be the 'Vienna: Now or Never' brand framework which became operative in October 2009, replacing the former destination brand which carried with it a 'Vienna Waits for You' strapline. Interestingly, the latter by 2009 was being viewed as carrying with it a negative connotation of 'one-day-sometime, but perhaps never' (Heeley, 2011: 71–72). The brand which replaced it in 2009 hones in on five 'brand modules' or competitive strengths, of which 'imperial heritage', 'music and culture' and 'savoir-vivre' (especially food and drink) are uppermost (Heintschel, 2011). Extensive research was undertaken to arrive at these five modules; interviews took place with no less than 1200 potential consumers and 550 industry partners, and 25 discussion groups were convened. Linked to each of the five strengths are specific 'brand drivers' relevant to Vienna and Vienna alone, and (as we showed in the last chapter) these are used in a systematic fashion to delineate and specify marketing content, e.g. St Stephen's Cathedral is a brand driver for 'imperial heritage', Viennese coffee houses are likewise a brand driver for 'savoir-vivre', as is Viennese opera for 'music and culture'. The favoured design solution for all the Board's advertising and promotional activity is a 'communication square' within which messages are inserted enticing the visitor to commit to visiting the city, always against a striking signature shot emphasising one of the five modular strengths and a particular brand driver (Heintschel, 2011). In one image, for instance, an historic and elegant Viennese coffee shop is shown whose customers are at leisure reading their newspapers and sipping coffee: the caption in the box says: 'At this very moment someone is reading the latest headlines surrounded by Old Masters. Where are you reading your paper?'

The 'Vienna: Now or Never' brand architecture – strapline, modules, drivers and 'communication square' design solution – are utilised in all VTB leisure tourism marketing activities, achieved through strict adherence to a brand manual. As we showed in Chapter 4, the brand platform is as important operationally for what it excludes as it is for its concentration on selected and specific Viennese attributes. Various dimensions of Vienna life and commerce, which most other DMOs would consider to be well worth promoting and which would almost certainly figure prominently were a 'marketing of everything' approach to be followed, are invisible (or at most hardly figure) in VTB leisure tourism marketing, e.g. nightlife, retail, sport and shopping. The Board's Head of Brand Communications and International Adverting says:

'Vienna: now or never' does not stand for shopping. It is good in Vienna, but it's not a competitive advantage. It's not London, it's not Paris, and it's not Berlin. So by exclusion we are saying 'don't come to Vienna for shopping'. We don't have shopping as a module, so we don't have brand drivers and signature shots with which to promote shopping. We exclude many other things in this way. For example, there is Christmas. I mean Christmas is not the essence of Vienna. Christmas is Christmas. Nightlife is another example. We did develop one signature shot showing this, because we needed an image, but in general we don't promote nightlife. So by promoting some things and excluding others, this is how we market Vienna in an authentically Viennese way. 'Vienna: now or never' means this is life in Vienna and it is different to life in Berlin or London or wherever. At this moment something is happening in Vienna which is different and worth seeing. So come to Vienna – this is our thinking. (Klein, 2013)

In this way, and more or less uniquely among urban DMOs in Europe (see Section 4.4 of the previous chapter), VTB consciously and meticulously emphasises competitive advantage in its leisure tourism marketing, in stark contrast to the mainstream practice in which 'marketing of everything' approaches are adopted. With reference to Figures 2.3 and 3.1, it may be seen that four departments of VTB are central to its leisure tourism marketing – Market and Media Management (for media and travel trade relations), Brand Communications and International Advertising (advertising and promotional campaigns), Content Management and Production (print and web/digital) and Visitor Services (tourist information and other services).

In April 2013, the *media relations and travel trade liaison* activities were discharged through VTB's Market and Media Management Department; this department comprised no less than 25 communications professionals headed by its Director, Gudrun Engl. Each year, her department is involved in organising upwards of 1000 press trips, as well as assisting in familiarisation visits for over 3000 representatives of tour operators, airlines and travel companies. In addition, approximately 50 major press conferences are staged each year, and over 100 trade shows are attended (VTB, 2013a). Flowing from the media relations work is sustained destination publicity and profile; journalists, bloggers, photographers and camera crews are invited to Vienna on hosted trips in which they follow set itineraries designed by the Board to highlight the city's competitive advantages as per the brand framework to which reference was made above, and utilising the 'show, wine and dine' formula with which we are already familiar from Chapter 3. For instance, journalists will 'take in' the annual Fête Impériale event (showcasing 'imperial heritage') or be taught how to make Viennese cookies (showcasing 'savoir vivre'). The Director of Market and Media Management describes her departmental modus operandi in respect of media relations as follows:

The goal is to do strategic, targeted media work. We don't just sit here and wait until a journalist writes an email. We have a very pro-active approach, and for the most part it is targeted. Different countries are receptive to different themes. Each year we have a list of media that we actively work on. So for each country market we have a list of let's say 10–15 media. By media, I mean of course all sorts of media – not just print, but TV, radio, bloggers, etc. So each media manager has a budget that he/she works to. Sometimes we pay for the air fare and the hotel, in other instances we don't. Quite often Austrian Airways take care of the fare. It all depends on the media and how much we want them. Media in Arabic countries or in Russia are not the same as in Germany. We have to use different approaches to take into account different circumstances, and that is what makes us strong. There's no such thing as standard procedure here. I'm against that. (Engl, 2013)

Engl emphasises the skills and capabilities of her media managers:

They (the media managers) are each responsible for a handful of countries, and they have to think creatively about how they are going to engage with journalists in those places, so as to get us some coverage on Vienna. My managers are highly educated; they have great insight into how the media operates in their respective countries. They build up a special knowledge relevant to their specific countries. They occupy highly quali- fied management positions. I think it is really important to have strong people. I need people who are confident and can go out there and present Vienna as the exceptional place it is. Either you have the personality with which to do this as a person – you have a passion for it – or you're no good at it. At the end of the day, of course, we assess the managers on what they do; we look at the outcomes of their work, and we evaluate whether or not they have been successful. (Engl, 2013)

The 'best' from the resultant prodigious output of press and other media coverage – upwards of 3000 Vienna reports per year in print, online, radio and TV formats (VTB, 2013a) – is impressively documented in a weighty annual review (VTB, 2013e). Reports from UK titles in the edition for the 2012 year contain headlines such as 'Good Night Vienna' (*The Sun*), '36 Hours in Vienna' (*The Daily Telegraph*) and 'Vienna Goes Crazy for Poster Boy Klimt' (*The Times*). This annual publication is arguably a far more impressive and meaningful statement of outcome than is the advertising equivalence and 'opportunities- to-see' metrics rolled out by other DMOs (see Chapter 3), as both of these present potentially misleading indications of effectiveness in this field. Gudrun Engl, unsurprisingly, speaks highly of the annual review document:

When we do this book at the end of the year, I ask all the managers to bring me what they think is their best coverage. So on my desk there is this tremendous pile of clippings from which I select the ones to figure in the book. I think we can be proud of the result. For years it's been the same. I have books from the last 15 years, before I myself even started. I think VTB has always been strong on the media side; we very much emphasise it. It is a real strength of our organisation. It's a very limited budget from which we chalk up great results. (Engl, 2013)

Limited, that is, in finite terms; the operating budget available for VTB media management activities (€0.9 million in the 2012 year) is well in excess of DMO spending elsewhere on this activity.

In addition to hosted media visits, VTB's Market and Media Management Department from time to time initiates special projects designed to garner appropriate media coverage and other benefits. In 2012, for instance, a year-long competition entitled *European Home Run* was organised in which leading designers in six European countries took part in an invitation-only competition to devise innovative, contemporary and authentically themed and produced Viennese souvenirs. The various proposals were judged by the public and by an international panel of design experts. Three pop-up miniature models of Vienna landmarks attracted 34,000 votes on VTB's website to win the public award, while playing cards with a Viennese design theme gained the jury's top prize (VTB, 2013d: 21). Throughout, press and PR coverage was systematically garnered, with 175 press clippings subsequently being recorded (VTB, 2013f). Both of the winning souvenirs are now being retailed in the city.

Using the same 'show, wine and dine' formula as it does for the media, familiarisation visits organised for the travel trade aim to persuade operators to include Viennese products in their itineraries. A key reference point here is the Vienna Experts Club International which, via a dedicated website and other means, networks in the region of 12,000 staff working in airlines, travel agencies and tour operators in 37 countries, updating them on new 'things to see and do' in the city and encouraging them to visit with special offers and discounts. Hotels offer a range of attractive prices to all club members, and entry to attractions and opera and usage of public transport are all free. No other DMOs offer such a service, and Engl views the Club as one of her finest achievements, setting a new standard in DMO B2B communications:

We started the Vienna Experts Club International in 2006; initially in Germany and then in Switzerland, Italy, the Netherlands, Spain and Romania, and every year we add more countries, so that now we can claim it is more or less a worldwide scheme. The point to bear in mind is that bringing the travel trade here on familiarisation trips to show them Vienna is generally a one-off business and, of course, it is very time consuming. If you do it on the scale we do it, then it also begins to cost quite a lot of money. We wanted to provide a way of keeping in touch with travel agents, airlines and tour operators so that we didn't lose the connection and rapport we had built with them. In particular, we wanted to communicate what's happening which is new in Vienna. So the Experts Club is really about relationship marketing with the travel trade. Like all good ideas, it seems such an obvious and easy thing to do, but in practice it takes a long time to nurture. So now we have this Club, it's on the web, and it's easy for us to communicate with the travel trade on an ongoing basis in the 37 countries. So this is the big challenge for me personally – the big thing is to keep the scheme lively so people don't just register and then become dormant. We don't just send out two newsletters a year; we offer club members all sorts of encouragement and incentives to come to Vienna, though they fly at their own expense and that helps to keep costs down. It's a club with all sorts of perks, and the goodies on offer are also valid for a friend – a partner or a spouse, so it's available for two people and this is really an incentive that works for us. So we have hundreds of agents coming to Vienna at their own volition, more or less, and at little or no cost to ourselves and our resident tourist businesses. When we started doing this, I did a lot of research to find out if other tourist boards had membership clubs of this sort. We didn't find any, and I don't know of any other cities who have copied our scheme. We had a student working on some benchmark research a while ago, and we could not find any other tourist board with a worldwide club like ours. (Engl, 2013)

Over the recent past, VTB's travel trade relations activity has come to major on the Experts Club. To be sure, the 3000 or so visits by travel trade representatives cited above include many in which VTB is proactively organising and funding (wholly or in part) familiarisation trips by the travel trade, whereas others are arranged essentially by airlines and incoming travel agencies and tour operators, with the Board playing a supportive role. The sense in which the Experts Club breaks new ground lies in it seeking to motivate trade representatives to come to Vienna voluntarily, in their own leisure time and at their own expense.

The simple, comparative point to stress in respect of VTB media relations and travel trade liaison activities is that in terms of scale and quality of delivery they dwarf other DMOs in Europe. Finance is the crucial enabler:

Honestly, even when I started here at the VTB in 1999 as a market manager, there was always this feeling in our organisation that we were doing things right somehow. We even then had a lot of recognition in Vienna; from the hotels, the incoming agencies, all those people who are involved with tourism, so out there in the marketplaces we were being repeatedly told that we were doing a good job. Since I was promoted to head of department in 2004, I've always tried to keep a close look at what other tourist boards are doing. One of the DMOs we benchmark ourselves against is *Visit Berlin*. But the thing that makes us different – and we are privileged in this respect – is that we have good budgets with which we can work. It's not a case of every year there is a threat of cuts and reductions. We have always had solid budgets to work with. I very much appreciate that, and sometimes if my people get a little frustrated or whatever, I cite other tourist boards and the problems they are having with their budgets, and the stop-gap way in which they can't really go ahead with planning anything. We can think big here, and do things with flair; it's become our trademark, and we can act in this way because we have the money and we are removed from politics. I have a certain amount of budget, I have my people, I have my markets, and then we go ahead. I know how other tourist board middle managers need constantly to write reports in order to justify this, that, and the other. It's great here. I don't think many other city tourist boards have such a good situation. (Engl, 2013)

Thinking 'big' and acting with flair is also evident in respect of the innovative and distinctive *advertising and promotions* work of VTB, the centrepiece of which in the 2012 year was a programme of high impact 'in your face' events conducted in 16 European cities at a cost of some €4.8 million, consuming the lion's share (88%) of the Board's €5.4 million advertising and promotions budget (Klein, 2013). The events themselves were cleverly conceived, sometimes with an almost breath-taking degree of creativity and imagination. All were executed with great attention to detail, interactivity with the public, and visual imagery. For example, for a two-week period a giant poster in a Paris underground station displayed eight Vienna choirboys who passers-by were able to make sing by means of pressing notes on a giant keyboard. For a week on the beach at Barcelona, people could sit on deckchairs by the side of an orchestra sculptured out of 200 tons of sand, borrowing headphones to listen to celebrated Viennese musical scores. In Trafalgar Square, a spectacular, gravity-defying horizontal waltz was performed over a two-day period on a 69-foot vertical stage. All 16 events in the 2012 year attracted large audiences who were enjoined to visit Vienna, and press and PR coverage was assiduously cultivated. As the Head of VTB's Brand Communications and International Advertising, Bernard Klein, opined in April 2013: 'The people like it, the press come, and then it goes viral' (Klein, 2013). He went on to say:

It was my idea to change our approach and switch from traditional DMO newspaper and magazine advertising to a programme of events of this kind. The concepts for each event are dreamed up from within my team, or else they come from our agencies. Impact comes from how many people you reach. There were 3000–4000 in Trafalgar Square for each live performance of the waltz. Newspapers and radio came, and also *Strictly Come*

Dancing (a prime-time Saturday evening TV programme), so we hooked the BBC. That was amazing. We monitor each event so that we know, for instance, that 'Sound in the Sand' in Barcelona was remembered by 20% of all the city's residents. The comparable figure was 17% for an event we did in Hamburg. We have that kind of impact – far more than would have been the case with press advertisements. No other city in Europe is following our lead and is promoting itself in this way. (Klein, 2013)

Similarly, VTB's *web, print and visitor-servicing* operations are executed on a heroic scale relative to other urban DMOs, with customary innovation, customer focus and creativity. With regard to print, the headline annual statistics are the production of 200 brochures/leaflets/posters in 17 different languages, which is equivalent to 220 tons of material shipped around the globe (VTB, 2013a). Within the city, approximately 4 million copies of the Board's self-financing visitor map and mini-guide are distributed (VTB, 2013a). The website www.wien.info offers great functionality – including online hotel booking and an events database updated daily. It is available in no less than 13 different languages, and during the 2012 year it registered 5.5 million unique visitors, 476,000 of whom downloaded a mobile version of the site (VTB, 2013d). VTB's social media presence is aggregated on a bespoke website, www.socialmedia.wien.info. In the 2012 year, 65 internet advertising campaigns were launched, as well as search engine optimisation and other initiatives in 23 countries (VTB, 2013d). Visitor-servicing arrangements revolve around two units open 365 days a year: a city centre tourist information centre (TIC) with a visitor throughput in 2012 totalling 465,000; and a call centre dealing with electronic and postal enquiries (mainly accommodation booking requests), of which 35,000 were processed in 2012 (VTB, 2013d). In the same year, the Vienna visitor card, offering discounts and 'free' public transport, achieved record sales of just over 343,000, winning first place in the independent ADAC (German Automobile Association) 'mystery shopping' test carried out in 16 leading European cities (VTB, 2013d).

5.7 *Glasgow City Marketing Bureau*: Winning Conferences

As with its counterpart in Vienna, the operations of GCMB enjoy the benefit of sustained political support going back in its case to 1983 (Heeley, 2011: 39–44). During the intervening period to the time of writing, the DMO has pursued an event-led tourism strategy. Its prowess in attracting events of a sporting and cultural kind is indicated in the city's hosting of the Commonwealth Games in 2014. As we have already considered this aspect of GCMB's work in Chapter 3, we restrict ourselves in this section to an appraisal of the Bureau's business tourism marketing which, as at January 2013, was being discharged by the company's 18-strong convention department (see Figure 2.4).

The work of GCMB's convention department hinges on systematically exploiting four factors: (1) accessibility, especially Glasgow International Airport boasting circa 90 direct flight connections and situated just 20 minutes' drive from the city centre; (2) the quality of the various conference venues within the city, notably the Scottish Exhibition and Conference Centre which is Scotland's premier convention facility, its centrepiece being the architecturally striking Clyde Auditorium which has a capacity of 3000 seats and which can draw upon 5600 easily accessible hotel rooms located within a 5-mile radius of the complex; (3) the corporate strength of the academic, scientific and professional communities existing within the city, as networked by the Bureau in its pioneering and much-copied conference ambassador scheme – this boasts 1700 active members and is serviced by no less than three Bureau staff dedicated full-time to this purpose; and (4) the ability of the Bureau's convention department to provide event organisers with subsidy or 'subvention'. In respect of the latter, GCMB has introduced its so-called 'Glasgow Model' in which 'clients, venue and city are active stakeholders in the success of a conference' (Taylor, 2011).

As far as the ambassador programme is concerned, the Head of Conventions has this to say:

> Our ambassador programme is really critical to our international association success in Glasgow. It represents over £40 million worth of economic impact in the city last year, so that's roughly 30–40% of the conference business we convert. It is all about galvanising support from academic or medical professionals: we help them lobby to bring their conference to our city. We have one of the largest ambassador programmes in the world, as I understand it, and we like to think we pioneered it here in Glasgow. Certainly, it has been running for 23 years this year, and it is really fundamental to the business we bring in to the city. The professionals concerned (the academics and others networked by the scheme) are really quite easy to get in touch with because they nearly always have a biography and profile on the university website. Our ambassador team at the Bureau are essentially researchers, and they look for any links there might be between the ambassadors and the specific events we want to attract and its related conference subject matter. We can then use the ambassador to approach the association's headquarters, and in that way we proactively encourage the conference to come to our city. (Crawford, 2013)

During the 2011/2012 year, GCMB's convention department secured 409 meetings worth an estimated £155 million (Crawford, 2013). There is some ambiguity as to how much of this £155 million is wholly attributable to the Bureau, as Crawford herself recognises:

> It is important to say first of all what is meant by conferences secured by the Bureau and its partners. We never say that all conference business is brought in purely by GCMB. It is brought in by the teams that work at the Bureau, the venue and the universities. We measure the conferences that we have worked on. They are predominantly association meetings. If any of our member venues and hotels let us know about other conferences that come to the city, which they are very good at doing, then we have the opportunity to work with the organiser, offering all the support that we can. In those cases, the conferences concerned would go through the GCMB figures. And if there is business that we know comes to the city that we haven't been able to offer support to, we don't put that through our figures. But we do keep it as a separate total. (Crawford, 2013)

Nonetheless, even allowing for conferences only indirectly assisted as opposed to directly secured, the order of magnitude of Bureau outputs and impacts is well in excess of that achieved by convention departments in the vast bulk of other towns and cities. In addition to conference bidding, it should be noted that GCMB's convention department also offers a comprehensive and bespoke 'You 1st' event support package designed to facilitate the smooth running of meetings as they are being hosted, helping organisers, venues and other partners to maximise PR and other opportunities.

As we have discovered already in Chapter 3, the 'lead times' involved in business tourism marketing may be as long as the process is exacting, and Crawford cites as an example the 2018 World Federation of Haemophilia (WFH) international conference which will lead to an estimated 4000 delegates visiting the city with an associated economic impact of £8 million. She summarises the timeline involved in securing this event:

> It all started late in 2001 when we began to research the event. We studied the criteria against which we could make a bid, and in 2003 eventually contacted the UK Haemophilia Society, but the message we got was that they were not interested in making a bid to host the event in the UK – it wasn't our time! Nevertheless, we maintained contact with the Haemophilia Society, and we kept our local ambassador in the picture. Then in 2011 all the parts of the jigsaw began to come together. In 2011 we made a presentation to the Society jointly with our local ambassador, with a view to Glasgow hosting the 2018 international WFH conference. That led to a bid document being put together in 2012 which was followed by a site inspection and then – at the Federation's meeting

in Paris in 2012 – we bid against Guadalajara and we won! So WFH is a very good example of how long it can take to win an international conference, and how relationships have to be nurtured. All your energies have to go into showing that you're the right destination for the client. (Crawford, 2013)

Within such a process, success or failure in bidding becomes a continuous learning process, underpinned by patience and persistence:

It's obviously incredibly disappointing to lose a bid, especially when the relationship with the client has been built up over a long period of time. Anyone with experience of working with international associations knows that it can take years to bring a bid to fruition, during which you build up a great rapport with your local ambassador and with your clients, and you want success for them as well as for the city. So it's really disappointing on lots of different levels. You feel you've let down your ambassador, and you hope they're not too upset. You realise the event could have come to the city, and now it isn't, and that a loss of prestige for the city, as well as being disappointing for the venue, hotels, taxi drivers, restaurants and all those who would have benefited directly or indirectly. You have to analyse what went wrong. You can't let it hold you back, however, you have to go and try again and sometimes – after we've lost a bid – we have reapplied and been successful on the second or third attempt. Really, you have to learn from every bid, absorb what it is telling you, and then make an even better bid next time around. (Crawford, 2013)

The watchwords in respect of GCMB convention marketing are, in the words of the Bureau's Head of Conventions: 'excellent database and research skills'; 'an experienced and consistent team who understand the requirements'; 'client focus'; 'coordinating an exceptional city offering for the client and delegate experience'; and a 'team approach across all the city partners – universities, venues, hotels and service providers' (Crawford, 2013). Significantly, in terms of scale, GCMB's convention department in January 2013 had a staffing compliment of 18 which to the best of the author's knowledge made it the largest convention bureau in Europe. Staff complements in two of Europe's top-performing bureaux – those for Copenhagen and Vienna – stood at 15 and 10, respectively. Tellingly, and by way of comparison, the bureaux for Stockholm, Belfast, Salzburg, Liverpool and Sheffield had staffing levels of eight, six, four, three and one, respectively. In February 2014, at an awards ceremony organised by an influential trade magazine (*Meetings and Incentive Travel*), GCMB's convention department was awarded the accolade of the UK's best convention bureau – for the eighth year in a row!

5.8 Classifying Urban Destination Marketing by Scale and Quality

Combining scale and quality dimensions, it is possible to classify DMOs and the urban destination marketing they undertake into five 'ideal types', as shown in Table 5.1. The 'ideal type' is a mode of classification deriving from the German sociologist, Max Weber, in which 'patterned orientations of meaningful action' are established whose aim is neither to 'provide an exhaustive description of empirical reality nor to introduce general laws or theories' (Kalberg, 1994: 84). As such, ideal type classifications are heuristic; they assist analysis and understanding, as opposed to replicating reality accurately (Kalberg, 1994: 85):

> Instead of 'capturing reality', the ideal type, as a logical construct that documents patterned action, establishes clear points of reference and orientational guidelines against which a given slice of reality can be compared and measured. (Kalberg, 1994: 87)

Our particular 'slice of reality' is the world of urban DMOs, and the schema in Table 5.1 is introduced to enable what are huge variations in scale and quality to be chartered and contextualised, so that operations 'large' and 'small', and 'exemplary' and 'average' may be compared and contrasted against each other. The term 'exemplary' is being used here to denote a paragon – an 'outstanding' example as opposed to an 'average'/'typical'/'run-of-the-mill'/'routine' one. As such, the 'exemplars' cited in Table 5.1 act as role models, setting standards for other DMOs to attain. Using boxing terminology, DMOs are then classified in Table 5.1 either as 'large' ('heavy-weights', 'light heavy-weights' and 'middle-weights') or 'small' ('feather-weights' and 'fly-weights'). On a UK basis, only about one in 20 urban DMOs would be classified as 'large' under this schema, and all of these would fall within the middle-weight ranking, having annual budgets towards the lower end of the £4 million to less than £8 million band, e.g. *Visit Belfast, Marketing Manchester* and GCMB. On a pan-European basis, annual budgets of the 'large' grouping may be seen to range from £4 million to £15 million and above. For instance, *Visit Berlin* and VTB registered budgets in 2013 of £15 million and £21 million, respectively. The consumer-facing websites of middle-weights typically attract between 2–3 million unique visitors a year, while the comparable ranges for the light heavy-weights and heavy-weights are between 3–4 million and upwards of 6 million, respectively. Between 500 and 1500 press visits per year are typically hosted each year by 'large' DMOs, e.g. *Visit Berlin* last year showed 1200 journalists around the city. Through the quality as well as scale of their marketing delivery, 'exemplars' among the 'large' DMOs are able to generate 'significant' to 'high' amounts of destination profile from press visits and other media

Table 5.1 Ideal type classification of DMOs by scale and exemplars

Scale	Ideal type classification	As a percentage of DMOs	DMO exemplars	Annual budget (£ million)	Unique visitors to consumer website (million)	Bednights generated	Profile generated
Large	'Heavy-weight'	1%	Vienna Tourist Board Gothenburg & Co	>15	>4–6	Significant	High
	'Light heavy-weight'	4%	Wonderful Copenhagen	8–15	3–4	Significant	Appreciable
	'Middle-weight'	5%	Glasgow City Marketing Bureau	4–<8	2–<3	Significant	Significant
Small	'Feather-weight'	40%	Visit York Leicester Shire Promotions	1–<4	0.5–<2	Marginal	Some
	'Fly-weight'	50%	Gdansk Tourism Organisation	<1	<0.5	More or less zero	Some

relations activities, as well as to create 'significant' levels of value in terms of bednights and overnight stays generated. The latter may be 'proven' to be forthcoming less from advertising and promotional campaigns aimed at leisure tourism audiences, not least because of the imponderable of estimating 'market share', and more from convention marketing activities which (as we have seen in Chapter 3) lend themselves to more rigorous assessment and evaluation in terms of conversion and outcomes. For the 'large' and 'exemplary' DMOs, the volume of conference business won annually will typically range from 300,000 to 600,000 bednights.

Numbered among the heavy-weights and light heavy-weights are: *Gothenburg & Co, Wonderful Copenhagen, Visit Berlin, Visit Brussels, Innsbruck Tourism* and VTB. Under the schema in Table 5.1, GCMB is a middle-weight, although in terms of the scale and quality of its delivery it might be regarded as 'punching above its weight'. Other middle-weights are *Amsterdam Tourism and Conventions* (now part of *Amsterdam Marketing*) and *Barcelona Tourism*. As evidenced by informal peer group ratings and by industry awards and other accolades, a few of the 'large' DMOs cited directly above may be ranked as 'exemplars'. As such, they are 'leaders of the pack' in respect of selected aspects of DMO operations, e.g. VTB's destination branding and its leisure tourism marketing, GCMB's attraction of business and events tourism, *Wonderful Copenhagen*'s convention marketing, *Gothenburg and Co*'s governance arrangements and partnership working, *Barcelona Tourism*'s exploitation of trading income streams, and the visitor servicing undertaken by *Amsterdam Tourism and Conventions*. It is worth noting how these DMO 'exemplars' score highly against each of the four key variables contained in Figure 5.1: there is long-term political commitment manifesting itself in strategy and core funding, alongside a strong product base in respect of accessibility, venues and urban attractiveness; the DMO is organised on PPP lines, and exploits the gains which flow from this in terms of leverage and business culture, majoring on performance management, managerial autonomy and operating efficiency; and finally, DMO marketing operations are executed with a momentum and quality sufficient to contribute significantly to the net local economic benefit of tourism. In turn, this serves to indicate the predictive capacity of the 'dynamics of urban destination marketing' as a theory.

Turning now to the feather-weight and fly-weight categories shown in Table 5.1, the simple yet important point to stress here is that these 'small' DMOs predominate numerically, to the point where the author estimates they account for approximately 90% of the European DMO universe. By dint of opportunism, professionalism and creativity, a handful of DMOs in the feather-weight category may be regarded as 'exemplars' and, as such, are able to generate valuable but ultimately relatively modest outcomes across bednights and profile. Inevitably, the feather-weights are greatly constrained in what they can achieve by their limited resourcing (i.e. annual budgets of £1 million–£4 million). Even the best performing will typically have consumer websites attracting less than two million unique visitors per annum, and they will only be able to register upwards of 100 press visits hosted annually. 'Exemplars' within the feather-weight category are *Visit York* and *Leicester Shire Promotions*, as we have evidenced in Chapter 3.

The smallest of the DMOs (the fly-weights in Table 5.1) are usually (but not always) constituted as a part of local government. Their role is less proactively to attract visitors, but rather to service them through guides, TICs and information-based websites. As a rule, their activities have little or no effect in terms of creating visitors and generating urban profile. In the case of *Visit Bradford* , for instance, there is a budget overall of £530,000 which is devoted to the provision of literature and visitor servicing (refer to the Preface for more detail); media relations, short-break packages, and the 'wooing' of 'footloose' conferences or other events are activities conspicuous by their absence. Occasionally, fly-weights are able through exceptional leadership and creative endeavour to go beyond visitor servicing and influence destination profile. In this way they, too, become 'exemplars', with the *Gdansk Tourism Organisation* (GTO) being a good case in point. Although nominally constituted as a PPP, 90% of its current year budget of £490,000 is sourced from the local authority, and its Chairman is the city's Deputy Mayor. As noted already in Section 5.5 of this chapter, GTO excels among Polish DMOs, maintaining a high profile for the destination through media visits and attendance at exhibitions and industry events, even winning coveted awards such as the ICCA one mentioned above. In this manner, GTO is able to raise awareness of the city as a business and leisure tourism destination, although the organisation's CEO concedes that tactical, targeted sales activities are rendered problematic by the relatively small size of her executive team and by the onerous and often conflicting demands placed on them. Of her convention marketing activities, the CEO says:

> We do a lot of awareness-raising, but not much actual bidding. We don't have time. Bidding occupies less than 10% of our time as a convention bureau. I tell my staff we need to do it more and more, but we just don't have time. So I need to change the proportion of time we devote to bidding for conferences, and this is something our commercial members want us to do – they say we don't bring in enough conferences, and they want us to act more as a sales office. However, the city council want us to do more and more on the awareness and profile side; they are very demanding, too, and at the end of the day they provide us with 90% of our budget. I think getting the right balance between bidding and sales, on the one hand, and awareness and profile, on the other, is a problem for most convention bureaux. (Górska, 2014)

To reiterate, in urban destination marketing 'small' DMOs predominate over 'large' ones. For instance, in my home county of Yorkshire, there are just nine 'small' urban destination marketing organisations. There are no 'big' players with annual budgets in excess of £4 million per annum, as per the schema in Table 5.1. The nine urban DMOs divide into four feather-weights (*Visit Hull and East Yorkshire, Visit Leeds, Visit Harrogate* and *Visit York*) and five fly-weights (*Visit Bradford, Visit Doncaster, Marketing Sheffield, Experience Wakefield,* and a DMO called *Discover Yorkshire Coast* which is made up essentially of the seaside towns of Scarborough, Whitby and Filey). With the exception of the Hull and East Yorkshire arrangements, the featherweights are PPP-based organisations, whereas the fly-weights are local government structures. Of the nine, only *Visit York* arguably justifies being ranked as 'exemplary', as evidenced by outputs from its energetic media relations activities (Heeley, 2011: 113–114) and the bednights generated from the various campaigns it mounts; as we have seen, one such campaign (instanced in Section 3.3 of Chapter 3) generated a total of 7000 bednights. *Visit York* may also be seen as an 'exemplar' by reference to its leverage of trading and private sector revenues, the vitality of its commercial membership scheme, the 1.7 million unique visitors per year to its website, and the excellence of its visitor-servicing arrangements (Visit York, 2012). For the most part, the five fly-weight local government based DMOs eke out existences on annual budgets of considerably less than £1 million, and are essentially 'routine' visitor-servicing operations, as we have previously exemplified by reference to *Visit Bradford.* Although their names and public relations activities suggest otherwise, these fly-weight DMOs should be seen as per Table 5.1 as having little or no impact in terms of generating tourist traffic and raising destination profile, as is confirmed by the paucity of the annual operating budgets available to them; in the cases, for instance, of *Marketing Sheffield* and *Discover Yorkshire Coast,* the figure for each organisation currently stands at just £60,000.

So it is that in the world of urban destination marketing a *Marketing Sheffield* and a *Vienna Tourist Board* are located at the opposite ends of the DMO spectrum, the latter with an operating budget at the time of writing some 271 times greater than the former, enabling it demonstrably to 'market the difference' and 'make a difference' (as we saw in Chapter 4 and Section 5.6 above). *Marketing Sheffield*, on the other hand, is restricted to visitor servicing, with a more or less tokenistic encouragement of business and leisure tourism. The important point to remember, however, is that for every heavy-weight VTB there are 50 or so fly-weights like *Marketing Sheffield*. Inasmuch as small and often run-of-the mill DMOs predominate, the perhaps rather surprising (and indeed worrying) diagnosis is that much the greater part of urban tourism marketing is failing to deliver to anything like its full potential.

5.9 Interpretations and Observations

In the previous chapter, I suggested the 'theory of marketing competitive advantage' was simplistic, idealised and normative and, as such, is fundamentally unrealistic and unworkable. Specifically, it fails to account for the greater part of DMO praxis (especially the pointed anomaly of 'marketing of everything' approaches and the associated failure to register substantial outcomes). Overwhelmingly, urban destinations do not market competitive advantage or otherwise 'market the difference', while at the same time prospective tourists are influenced to visit places by a multitude of factors other than DMO marketing materials and initiatives. In place of the 'theory of marketing competitive advantage', I have in this chapter set out an alternative, four-variable model entitled the 'dynamics of urban destination marketing'. Within the latter theory, imperfect praxis and 'run-of-the-mill' outcomes co-exist alongside more impactful marketing operations, as illustrated above by VTB and GCMB as DMO 'leaders of the pack', and by GTO as a fly-weight 'exemplar'. In addition, the new theory accommodates a mainstream approach to DMO operations which I have characterised as 'the marketing of everything', something which the 'theory of competitive advantage' is manifestly unable to do. The new theory also takes on board those much rarer instances in which a DMO does 'market the difference', as with the leisure tourism marketing of *Innsbruck Tourism* and VTB. The commentary in this chapter, supported by Figure 5.1 and Table 5.1, hopefully gives the reader a better understanding of why, in such a potentially important field of human endeavour as urban destination marketing, effectiveness is so problematic. Hopefully, too, academics and students alike will have gained an understanding of the 'real' world of urban destination marketing. The intent throughout has been to 'tell it like it is' in a conceptually robust and empirically valid manner.

Although the paradigm adjustment I have put forward in this chapter uses more or less the same data as obtains within the 'theory of marketing competitive advantage', it places old and new concepts in a different set of relationships, so as to accommodate the various anomalies and counter-instances. A note of caution may be introduced here. The reader should regard this as a rough 'first-cut' of a proposed new theory, hence the 'towards' in the title to this chapter. As such, the theory requires further testing, development and refinement, and it invites discussion and debate in academe and practice. As far as the former is concerned, it is an open question as to how far the 'dynamics of urban destination marketing' as a theory will be deemed correct and acceptable. Kuhn counsels us that paradigm change – even when it is adjustment as opposed to outright replacement – is nearly always resisted, irrespective of whether it is 'right' or 'wrong' (Kuhn, 1970: 64, 151). Indeed, a vigorous defence of the 'theory of marketing competitive advantage' may be sparked off by this text, and as a result the theory I am proposing may be rejected. Another scenario is that inertia will prevail, and the envisaged discussion and debate will fail to occur. As I write these concluding remarks, I guess that 'only time will tell' whether or not deliberations within academe will take place and, if so, what the outcomes will be. Whatever the case, hopefully into the future theorising about urban destination marketing will become more authoritative and credible than it is at present.

For practitioners, the adjusted paradigm advanced in this chapter raises important issues, as well as a perhaps welcome adumbration of the 'big picture' which the daily discharging of workload can so effectively camouflage. For planners and policy makers, the new theory focuses attention on the question of how in the future there might be more 'winners' and fewer 'losers', so that increasing numbers of towns and cities can elect to maximise the impact locally of the world's largest industry and, at the same time, become 'known'. In a profound and some would say more pessimistic vein, the headline conclusion to be drawn from this new paradigm is that much the greater part of urban destination marketing is currently 'run-of-the mill' stuff, lacking in substantive economic impact. Moreover, the content of DMO marketing in terms of imagery and message represents a theming of 'urban sameness' which may be seen as contributing to globalisation, and the monolithic and uniform standardisation of 'place' with which it is associated. There is no gainsaying that conclusions such as these are harsh and damning ones, but what must be borne in mind here is that under the 'theory of marketing competitive advantage' (which as a paradigm, remember, is shared by practice as well as academe), stakeholder and public expectations have centred on DMOs delivering major outcomes and on 'marketing the difference'. The failure of urban destination marketing to by and large deliver against these two prime criteria is deeply worrying, and prompts an obvious question: why bother setting up a DMO and undertaking urban destination marketing in the first place?

In the author's view, the root problem currently facing urban destination marketing and its bespoke DMO delivery mechanisms lies in the expectations which surround them, as embodied in the core purpose the DMO is designed to fulfil. Such expectations are, of course, grounded in the perspective I have labelled the 'theory of marketing competitive advantage'. DMOs, as such, have been 'nailed to a cross' of generating overnights and bednights. As we established in Chapter 2, the core purpose underpinning contemporary urban destination marketing is 'bringing in the business'. Such a purpose or mission is the only one conceivable in a paradigm where towns and cities identify USPs, take them to market through the DMO, and then as a community rake in the spoils in terms of turnover, income and employment. 'Bringing in the business' forms the collective mindset of DMO governances and their various stakeholders, as one of our DMO interviewees so lucidly described it:

We have a board of directors with nine members, three of which are from the city. The head of the board is the deputy mayor of the city. If he tells me to do something, then I do it! He is my boss. He signs my vacation slips. That's how it is. But I also report to the other members of the

Board, who mostly represent our commercial membership. As far as my Board and the commercial membership are concerned, then the main purpose of Gdansk Tourism Organisation is simply to bring more visitors to the city. (Górska, 2014)

In Chapter 3, we suggested 'bringing in the business' as a core purpose was unrealistic. In terms of resourcing, the ideal-type classification in Table 5.1 suggests that upwards of 90% of DMOs will at best have only a marginal impact in terms of the generation of overnight stays. Moreover, even where significant bednight generation is a possibility (i.e. in the remaining 10% of DMOs that have annual budgets in excess of £4 million), there remains the DMO 'Achilles' heel' we identified in that same chapter, viz. an inability rigorously and persuasively to measure the direct returns from marketing activities, and to compute a 'share' of key industry outcomes, notably the overall volume and value of visitor expenditure and the associated level of tourism-related employment. A core purpose of 'bringing in the business' also means that internally DMOs lack unity of purpose, bearing in mind that swathes of their operational activities are about raising destination profile and servicing visitors, as opposed directly to attracting them via 'tactical' leisure tourism campaigns and convention marketing and sales. In these circumstances, externally and among its own stakeholders, DMOs can easily be 'picked off' as 'woolly' marketing organisations, an accusation not without foundation precisely because DMOs are hitched to a core purpose of 'bringing in the business'. Reinforcing such scepticism is the perception and likelihood that DMO marketing influences are generally incidental to customers choosing a particular destination. In short, the existing core purpose creates expectations which go unfulfilled, opening up a credibility gap which DMOs are by and large unable to close. One of the practitioners interviewed in this book summed up this gap by suggesting that critics and detractors of DMOs viewed urban destination marketing as a 'pretend industry'.

   In the author's view, it is now time to dispense with the existing unmeasurable and, for the most part, unrealisable core purpose of 'bringing in the business', derived as it is from a flawed 'theory of marketing competitive advantage'. Instead, a related and more meaningful core purpose with which to underpin urban destination marketing is that of raising the internal and external profile of the city or town in question. In line with this, I would go as far as saying that DMOs should rename themselves as DCOs (destination communication organisations). My reasoning is as follows. All aspects of the current DMO marketing template in Figure 3.1 fall within such a purpose, as even 'tactical' promotions and sales activities may be viewed as delivering their most important 'payback' through profile, i.e. post-visit, word-of-mouth recommendation – WOM as we termed it in Chapter 3. In any case, we have noted already that the bulk of DMO marketing campaign activity is centred on generic awareness-raising, as opposed to 'tactical' sales and promotions. Moreover, the destination 'narratives' or 'storylines' that urban DMOs are tasked with promoting are ultimately reducible to the residents of that town or city and their achievements, be those past, present and future. The grand aim of such 'storylines' is surely that of raising the profile of the city or town in question. To be sure, bednights or overnights may be generated as a consequence, and in 'tactical' sales and promotion activity that goal would remain uppermost, but the overriding ambition would be to raise profile. As far as the author is concerned, DMO core purpose should major on the enhancement of urban profile: profile first and bednights second, and not vice-versa, as is currently the case. In short, the dependent variable in respect of understanding and assessing DMO performance should in future be safeguarding and enhancing urban profile.

In line with this change of emphasis, the foci of urban destination marketing would be as much about addressing internal residents and businesses as it would external audiences across business, events and leisure tourism audiences. A 'bringing in the business' core purpose eschews the internal in favour of the external, yet strong evidence exists to support the view that the most cost-effective way to market a destination is by looking inwards so as to: (a) galvanise the people of a town and a city to act as its 'front-line' ambassadors; and (b) attend to the myriad planning and development issues which optimise the visitor welcome and engender repeat visitation, as per Stage 4 ('the visitor experience') of Mandy Lane's 'Visitor Journey' (Lane, 2007). In relation to 'front-line' ambassadorial initiatives, it is worth emphasising that the advice of friends and relatives is far more important as a travel motivator and 'influencer' than are DMO campaigns and marketing materials. Equipping residents and companies to 'sell on' their town or city to its various external audiences is – at least intuitively – a more direct and valid route to market than the current DMO practice of concentrating more or less exclusively on external markets, with what in most cases are 'hit and miss' forays into social media, advertising, exhibitions, sales missions, and the like. In the above respects, the work of *Berlin Partners* (as highlighted in Section 1.5 of Chapter 1) is arguably indicative of a 'way forward'. With its huge ambassador network and its ubiquitous Berlin Box, *Berlin Partners* conduct a local 'hearts and minds' Berliner campaign as the foundation stone on which national and international initiatives can then be mounted. Surely, too, Amsterdam and Glasgow, the two cities that introduced city branding to Europe and that remain to this day its acknowledged, leading exponents (Heeley, 2011: Chapters 7 and 8), are also moving in this direction with their 'I Amsterdam' and 'People Make Glasgow' city brand platforms, whose brand 'essences' are reducible to Amsterdamers and Glaswegians, respectively.

In proposing a core purpose centred upon the raising of urban profile across internal as well as external audiences, I am aware that this amounts to a radical change of emphasis and direction. It will be viewed by some as 'naive' and 'unrealistic', and by others (less critically) as possibly ushering in a more prosaic and mundane future for DMOs. In prioritising profile over 'bringing in the business', the argument will be made that the already tenuous commitment of some politicians and business leaders to urban destination marketing will be weakened further. On the other hand (and precisely because the 'theory of marketing competitive advantage' is an unworkable and broken paradigm), a few DMO chiefs are already recognising the need fundamentally to rethink the rationale for their organisations' existence. One of our DMO respondents remarks:

> The world has changed significantly of late, especially in terms of technology, and the DMOs of old simply will not survive. They need to take on a much broader agenda and ensure relevance within their destination. (Simpson, 2014)

Interestingly, a LinkedIn practitioner group has recently been established dedicated to the task of finding a new model for destination marketing in a world dominated by commercial, online intermediaries whose existence is premised on overnight stay generation. For instance, the 5 million plus unique visitors to VTB's destination website, commendable as it is as an annual total, pales into insignificance when set against the comparable 260 million a month registered by TripAdvisor (Egan, 2014). In today's electronically interconnected world, there is a strong sense in which marketing in its traditional and highly visible form – 'top-down' branding, advertising and promotions – is now outmoded, mistrusted and 'dying', giving way to 'bottom-up' communications in which public and private organisations must above all else be transparently legitimate, authentic and reputable (Gregory, 2014).

In today's world – Marshall McLuhan's (1964) 'global village' in which the 'medium is the message' – DMO or DCO core purpose *must* be real and achievable, meaningful and valid. To cite Lincoln as we did at the start of Chapter 2, without 'public sentiment' nothing can succeed. In 'putting profile first', DMOs or DCOs are armed with a valid and realisable core purpose around which they can begin to mould stakeholder and public opinion. In so doing, they will be able to nurture a reputation for themselves as valued and credible organisations. Moreover, in 'putting profile first', it must be emphasised that the generation of overnight stays will still have its place, albeit a more circumscribed one. Historically, 'putting profile first' marks a return to first principles; from Beau Nash in the early part of the 18th century onwards to the late 1980s, safeguarding reputation and promoting image was to the forefront of day-to-day urban destination marketing activities, as these were conducted by resort publicity departments and their public relations officers (see Section 2.2 of Chapter 2). A preoccupation with 'bringing in the business' and the associated generation of bednights or overnights began to take hold only in the 1980s. One reason for this was that old and newly established DMOs in Europe started to ape their North American visitor and convention bureaux counterparts. In America and Canada, accommodation taxes finance bureaux, so that bednight generation and the marketing and sales activities with which it is associated inevitably becomes the overriding mission. Another, more important reason was to be found in so-called 'new ways of working' in local government, an important element of which was assessing managerial performance. With that came the cult of the key performance indicator, as discussed in Chapter 3, and here the bednight was an unambiguous and readily available KPI metric with which to monitor the effectiveness of DMO marketing. In this way, the bednight came to occupy a central position within the 'theory of marketing competitive advantage', whose Stage 3 is overnight stay generation, as shown in Figure 4.1.

'Putting profile first', therefore, may be seen historically as getting 'back to basics'; a reaffirmation of a core purpose stretching back to Georgian times and Beau Nash. As for marketing content – which the profile-raising should centre upon – I suggest we take our lead here from the 18th-century quote with which we began Chapter 3 of this book. In it, Samuel Johnson muses at the 'wonderful', 'minute diversities' of urban landscape and life which serve to differentiate towns and cities from the 'sameness' which otherwise besets them. In the author's opinion, the content of urban destination marketing *should* celebrate these 'diversities', 'marketing the difference' in a way that is relevant both to the people of the town or city in question, and to its visitors. In this respect, there need be no fundamental disconnect between the requirements of internal as opposed to external audiences. The 'difference' itself may include a USP or competitive advantage such as a Leaning Tower of Pisa, a Charles Bridge or a Statue of David, but 'difference' in the sense I am using it here is a much wider concept, comprising the myriad aspects of custom, economy, cuisine, environment and lifestyle which together serve to make every place special and ultimately unique. My home city, Sheffield, can offer no USPs in the conventional sense of the word, but it nonetheless has a quite distinctive urban 'narrative' based upon aspects of its geography, history, and contemporary economy, society and culture. This, in turn, has the potential to be developed, packaged and promoted so as to offer a contrasting 'destination experience' to that of, say, York, Manchester and New York.

In raising awareness of Johnson's 'minute diversities [that] in everything are wonderful', there lies a truly meaningful and enduring rationale for urban destination marketing and its DMO or DCO delivery mechanisms. Suffice to say, its outcome would be diametrically opposite to the mainstream 'marketing of everything' and associated theming of 'urban sameness' which obtains today. Surely it is time to put such approaches to bed, and with it what one of our DMO respondents referred to in the last chapter as 'that glossy, cosmopolitan, much romanticised kind of imagery in which if you close your eyes and put away the city's name, you could be almost anywhere'

(Nymen, 2013). Moreover, as we have seen in this chapter, a role model for the effective implementation of 'marketing the difference' is available courtesy of VTB and the manner in which it deploys its 'Vienna: Now or Never' brand. So, in putting profile first, let us at the same time dispense with 'marketing of everything' approaches and the 'almost anywhere' with which it is associated.

In conclusion, I have sought in this book to question an orthodoxy I have chosen to style the 'theory of marketing competitive advantage', seeking to adjust and reformulate it as a paradigm I am calling the 'dynamics of urban destination marketing'. If the latter becomes a shared outlook – and this is a big 'if' as explained above – then into the future we might well see reinvented DCOs ('new wine in old bottles') whose overriding core purpose would be raising urban profile across local as well as external fronts, with a view to celebrating and 'marketing the difference'. As such, DCOs would be the official custodians of urban image and brand, and their lifeblood would be the people of the city or town which they at one and the same time would be promoting and serving. In getting 'back to basics' in this way, the DCO and its urban destination marketing will have arrived – as in the title quote to this chapter – at its 'own original starting point' from which it must once again 'set off'. On that journey, the residents, businesses and institutions of the town or city in question will be the DCO's cardinal reference point. As much is alluded to in this closing remark by the former Chief Executive of *Gothenburg & Co*: 'Looking back over my long years as CEO of *Gothenburg & Co*, I would say the best thing we ever had was very good support from the people of Göteborg' (Bjerkne, 2013).

Epilogue: Coventry, Millennium Eve, 1999

> *It is quite true what philosophy says; that life must be understood backwards. But then one forgets the other principle: that it must be lived forwards.*
>
> Søren Kierkegaard (1843)

On the last day of 1999, as the world was about to rejoice at the dawn of a new millennium, I found myself in the rather unfashionable Midlands city of Coventry. As Chief Executive of *Coventry and Warwickshire Promotions* (CWP), I had been hard at work over the previous three years marketing the destination, seeking to exploit its accessibility and its rich historical associations – the Godiva legend, birthplace of the British motor car industry and evocative symbol of peace and reconciliation, to name but a few. Our aim at CWP was simply to put Coventry 'on the map' by attracting tourists and raising city profile. In respect of the latter, CWP had been asked by the local authority – Coventry City Council – to orchestrate an annual programme of festivities. I recruited a small team of specialists, and we developed a jazz event (sadly now defunct) and each June we staged a Godiva procession and music festival, happily still going strong. As a 'one-off', CWP was tasked on Millennium Eve with delivering a night-long festival of fun and entertainment, the high point of which was to be a French tightrope walker making his way across a thin steel rope suspended between the spires of Holy Trinity Church and the old cathedral (Heeley, 2011: 85–86). My Head of Cultural Events, Rae Hoole, had dreamed up this breathtaking idea, and as you would expect she and her team were busy that night attending to all manner of last minute exigencies. My Head of Press and PR, Peter Walters, was naturally milking the event for all it was worth in terms of the not inconsiderable media attention the high-wire stunt was attracting. As CEO, I had piloted the evening's cultural programming through a political minefield, in particular assuaging the fears of local politicians and clergy, a number of whom considered the high-wire act to be simply too spectacular (for humdrum, provincial Coventry) and too risky in terms of possible weather and safety scenarios. Initial opposition from these quarters in the early days of the project had left me with little option other than to take the high-wire proposal to the local newspaper, the *Coventry Evening Telegraph*, which conducted a poll of its readers. Suffice to say, CWP and the high-wire proposal won hands down. Self-evidently this had been a high-risk strategy. As a result, CWP and its CEO in particular were now walking another sort of line: success on the night would bring out a thousand fathers, doubtless among them the very politicians and church leaders who had been steadfast in their antipathy; failure would have left CWP orphaned (Heeley, 2011).

Let's now pick up on what the local media were calling the city's 'party of a lifetime' half-way through that festive night:

> Just before 8.30 p.m. on Millennium Eve (31 December 1999) a wheel fell off a camera trolley in the studios where the BBC was filming that momentous night's National Lottery draw. The draw was live, part of the special rolling coverage of Millennium Eve, and just up ahead was (the Coventry tight-rope act followed by) the moment when the Queen arrived at the Embankment to see the fireworks and, later on, link arms with Prime Minister Tony Blair in an awkward climax to the celebrations. Technicians needed more time to fix the wheel and the decision was taken to stay with the lottery, scrap the next item in the schedule and then go straight to the Embankment. And so Coventry's astonishing tightrope walk between two medieval towers, surely the most visually arresting image of the night in Britain, never got the national audience. By the time it was screened in the early hours, all but insomniacs had gone to bed. To the 100-strong BBC team who had hired Britain's tallest crane to film tightrope walker Ramon Kelvink as he teetered in a white suit between the parapets of Holy Trinity and the ruined cathedral, it was a disaster that induced tears and apoplexy in roughly equal measure. A prime slot in an historic television event watched by millions had been dashed from their hands. (Walters, 2013: 231)

This prime-time slot was to have lasted four minutes. After live transmission on the BBC, there was to be onward distribution to ITV, Sky and four foreign TV companies. A senior BBC producer had suggested the global reach would lie between a low of 1 billion people and a high of 2. The freakish loss of this destination profile momentarily left me stunned and incredulous, reminding me yet again of the equivocation by Bob Dylan with which I closed the Preface to this book: 'there's no success like failure, and failure's no success at all'.

On the failure side of the equation, Peter, Rae and I had worked so hard to get that BBC coverage, and I felt quite devastated by the fact that due to a quirk of fate we had missed out on an audience of between 1–2 billion. Rae and Peter were altogether more sanguine, but for a seasoned urban tourism practitioner like myself this was literally a once in a lifetime opportunity that had gone begging. The formidable brief I had given my Head of Events was to work within a relatively small £250,000 budget, but nonetheless come up with cultural programming that would set Coventry apart from 'the rest' in terms of media profile, on a night when our competition would be just about every other town or city on the planet – from neighbouring Birmingham through to London, Moscow and Sydney. Had the planned-for BBC slot gone ahead as anticipated, then seemingly against all the odds that original brief would have been handsomely met.

As for success, a crowd of around 30,000 had turned up in the city centre that night, watching in awe and admiration as Kelvink completed his stunning act. The next day came, and the night's celebrations and the high-wire walk in particular were universally and unambiguously praised. There was a front-page picture of the wire act in the *Sunday Times*, with *The Mail on Sunday* carrying a report on the 'amazing 260ft tightrope walk'. One and a half years later, a leader column in the *Coventry Evening Telegraph*, reviewing my tenure as the city's tourism chief and announcing my imminent departure to head up Birmingham's urban destination marketing activities, went as far as saying: 'The Millennium night celebrations in Broadgate quite simply knocked every other UK city's celebrations into a cocked hat' (Coventry Evening Telegraph, 2001).

Back to the night itself, my mixed emotions were a function of knowing I had done a really good job professionally, to the utmost of my abilities, alongside an overwhelming sense of failure. Because that darn wheel had stuck, the massive profile I had sought in setting Rae her original (and incredibly challenging) brief had eluded me. In attempting to understand Millennium Eve backwards, in true Kierkegaardian style, arguably the main lesson to be learned is that any quest for the holy grail of what makes for success is a transitory and malleable one (and perhaps that is the real meaning behind Dylan's equivocation). As success or failure happens at a certain point in time, in this case the staging of Coventry's Millennium Eve festivities, we can never 'properly' take stock of that situation as it happens or in its immediate aftermath, although this is exactly what we attempt to do – in our minds and/or more formally in the sort of performance-planning exercises and KPI indicators we examined as part of Chapter 2. Over time, any contemporaneous notions or evaluations we might have held of success or failure are then subject to change – hence the principle of understanding life backwards. In this way, I now regard Coventry's Millennium Eve festivities as an outstanding success in which I played no small part. An unfortunate and very heavy loss of external profile attributable to a wheel falling off now appears regrettable, but far from catastrophic. Far more important was the staging of an awesome spire-to-spire act which royally celebrated a place, bringing together its people across class, creed, age and gender for a 'party of a lifetime'.

Rather than seeking out what makes for success in the 'here and now' of today, with all the judgemental, rudimentary and often spurious performance management and appraisal arrangements which lie at back of our formal attempts to make such evaluations, we should arguably take a more existential, as well as Kierkegaardian stance. In *La Peste* by Albert Camus, an allegorical novel in which medical workers find meaning in life through their labour, the narrator exclaims at one point:

> There lay certitude; there in the daily round. All the rest hung on mere threads and trivial contingencies; you couldn't waste your time on it. The thing was to do your job as it should be done. (Camus, 1967: 37)

I knew in my heart and mind that I had done a really good job of work on Millennium Eve (the existential thing that should have really mattered to me), but at the same time I suffered acute emotions of failure which with hindsight now appear time-bound and superficial to the point almost of irrelevance. As people near the end of their lives, the final paradigm shift this nearly always occasions often renders meaningless any notions whatsoever of success and failure, as in John Williams' *Stoner*:

> A kind of joy came upon him, as if borne in on a summer breeze. He dimly recalled that he had been thinking of failure – as if it mattered. It seemed to him now that such thoughts were mean, unworthy of what his life had been. (Williams, 2012: 277)

Rather than crucifying ourselves to the cross of achieving some or other ill-defined and hollow criterion of success, I leave you with the thought that a more valid and meaningful approach is as follows: live life forwards by immersing yourself in it and doing it to the utmost of your abilities, while reconciling yourself to the fact that you will only properly understand it (and its associated and probably more or less meaningless successes and failures) backwards. As the man said: 'there's no success like failure, and failure's no success at all'.

References

Aitken, J.S. (2013) Interview with the Head of Events, Glasgow City Marketing Bureau, 9 January.

Anholt, S. (2007) *Competitive Identity – The New Brand Management for Nations, Cities and Regions*. Basingstoke: Palgrave Macmillan.

Ashworth, G. (2011) Should we brand places? *Journal of Town and City Management* 1 (3), 248–253.

Ashworth, G. and Goodall, B. (1990) *Marketing Tourism Places*. London: Routledge.

Ashworth, G. and Page, S.J. (2011) Urban tourism research: Recent progress and current paradoxes. *Tourism Management* 32 (1), 1–15.

Belfast Visitor and Convention Bureau (2011) *BVCB Board of Directors 2013*. Belfast: Belfast Visitor and Convention Bureau.

Birks, S. (2013) Interview with Visitor Services Development Manager, Derby City Council, 22 August.

Bjerkne, C. (2013) Interview with the former CEO of Gothenburg & Co, 15 October.

Bontink, P. (2011) How we are now integrating our activity areas. Presentation by the Chief Executive of Visit Brussels. *Annual Meeting of the Chief Executives of Capital and Major Cities*, Vienna, 12 December. Dijon: European Cities Marketing.

Bornhorst, T., Ritchie, J.R.B. and Sheehan, L. (2010) Determinants of tourism success for DMOs and destinations: An empirical examination of stakeholders' perspectives. *Tourism Management* 31 (5), 572–589.

Boswell, J. (2008) *The Life of Samuel Johnson*. Harmondsworth: Penguin.

Bradford Telegraph (2011a) Tributes are paid to £100,000-plus officer who acted as an 'ambassador' for city. *Bradford Telegraph and Argus*, 13 January.

Bradford Telegraph (2011b) Why tourism is on the increase in the Bradford district. *Bradford Telegraph and Argus*, 5 July.

Bramwell, B. and Rawding, L. (1996) Tourism marketing images of industrial cities. *Annals of Tourism Research* 23 (1), 201–221.

Brook-Sykes, N. (2014) Bath Tourism Plus. Presentation. *Destination Marketing Symposium*, Sheffield Hallam University, 5 February.

Bryson, B. (1997) *Notes from a Small Island*. London: Doubleday.

Buckley, P. and Witt, S. (1985) Tourism in difficult areas: Case studies of Bradford, Bristol, Glasgow and Hamm. *Tourism Management* 6 (3), 205–213.

Buhalis, D. (2000) Marketing the competitive destination of the future. *Tourism Management* 21 (1), 97–116.

Camus, A. (1967) *La Peste*. Harmondsworth: Penguin.

Clarke, A. (2012) A review of 'Inside City Tourism: A European Perspective'. *Tourism Geographies* 15 (2), 366–368.

Coles, T., Dinan, C. and Hutchison, F. (2012) May we live in less interesting times? Changing public sector support for tourism in England during the sovereign debt crisis. *Journal of Destination Marketing and Management* 1, 4–7.

Cooper, C. and Hall, C.M. (2013) *Contemporary Tourism: An International Approach*. Oxford: Butterworth-Heinemann.

Cooper, C., Fletcher, J., Fyall, A., Gilbert, D. and Wanhill, S. (eds) (2008) *Tourism: Principles and Practice*. Harlow: Pearson Education.

Coventry Evening Telegraph (2001) The man who put Coventry on the tourist map. *Coventry Evening Telegraph*, 11 May.

Cox, C. and Wray, M. (2011) Best practice marketing for regional tourism destinations. *Journal of Travel and Tourism Marketing* 25 (5), 524–540.

Crawford, A. (2013) Interview with the Head of Conventions, Glasgow City Marketing Bureau, 9 January.

Crouch, G.I. (2012) Managing destination competitiveness: The state of research. Paper delivered at the inaugural *Advances in Destination Management Conference*, University of St Gallen, 5–8 June.

Cruddas, G. (2014) Interview with former Chief Executive, Visit York, 21 January.

Daily Telegraph (2010) Bradford: Britain's worst tourism city: 'Dangerous, ugly and boring'. *The Daily Telegraph*, 19 January.

Destination Marketing Association International (2013) *DMO Advocacy*. Promotional video, published 26th August, accessed at: http://www.youtube.com/watch?v=gTbgfDUOx0o (accessed 7 November 2014).

Diender, S. (2011) City tourism or city marketing – the integrated approach. Presentation by the Chief Executive of Amsterdam Tourism and Conventions. *Annual Meeting of the Chief Executives of Capital and Major Cities*, Vienna, 12 December. Dijon: European Cities Marketing.

DMO World (2005) *DMO World Newsletter*, March.

Dyer, M. (2013) Email communication, Senior Marketing and Communications Manager, Glasgow City Marketing Bureau, 6 February.

ECM (2011) *ECM Member Finance Survey: Report of ECM's Interim Chief Executive Officer*. Dijon: European Cities Marketing.

Egan, H. (2014) Email communication, Head of Destination Marketing Sales, Europe, Middle East, Africa and Asia, *TripAdvisor*, 23 April.

Elliott, J. (1997) *Tourism: Politics and Public Sector Management*. London: Routledge.

Engl, G. (2013) Interview with the Director of Market and Media Management, Vienna Tourist Board, 23 April.

Fenn, E. (1988) Tourism in difficult areas: The Bradford case study. Paper delivered at the *Planning for Tourism and Leisure Conference*, University of Ulster, May 1986 (pp. 59–69).

Friel, E.J. (1989) Convention market. In S. Witt and L. Moutinho (eds) *Tourism Marketing and Management Handbook* (pp. 75–77). London: Prentice Hall.

Friel, E.J. (2011) City tourist offices and convention bureaux – who really needs them? Keynote address. *European Cities Marketing Spring Meeting*, Sofia, March.

Fyall, A. and Garrod, B. (2012) Editorial. *Journal of Destination Marketing and Management* 1, 1–3.

GCMB (2011) *Glasgow Tourism Strategy to 2016*. Glasgow: Glasgow City Marketing Bureau.

GCMB (2012) *Publication Scheme* (pp. 1–11). Glasgow: Glasgow City Marketing Bureau.

Getz, D., Anderson, D. and Sheehan, L. (1998) Roles, issues, and strategies for convention and visitors' bureaux in destination planning and product development: A survey of Canadian bureaux. *Tourism Management* 19 (4), 331–340.

Gilbert, D. (1990) Strategic marketing planning for national tourism organisations. *Tourist Review* 1, 8–27.

Glasgow City Council (2009) *Glasgow Strategic Major Events Forum: Strategy and Business Plan to 2016*. Glasgow: Glasgow City Council.

Godfrey, K.B. (2001) Urban tourism: An 'overview' perspective. *International Journal of Tourism Research* 3, 77–79.

Goodwin, D.K. (2013) *Team of Rivals: The Political Genius of Abraham Lincoln*. Harmondsworth: Penguin.

Górska, A. (2013) Email communication, Chief Executive Officer, Gdansk Tourism Organisation, 4 March.

Górska, A. (2014) Interview with the Chief Executive Officer, Gdansk Tourism Organisation, 17 March.

Gothenburg & Co (2013) *Annual Report 2012*. Gothenburg: Gothenburg & Co.

Gregory, A. (2014) Building trust from the inside – the role of public relations in 'authentic' tourist organisations. Paper delivered at the Belgrade International Tourism Conference, *Thematic Tourism in a Global Environment: Advantages, Challenges and Future Developments*, Belgrade, 27–29 March (pp. 71–76).

Grupp, J. (2010) The Berlin Partner Organisation and the 'Be Berlin' city marketing campaign. Powerpoint presentation. *European Cities Marketing Autumn Meeting*, Uppsala, October.

Hankinson, G. (2009) Managing destination brands: Establishing a theoretical foundation. *Journal of Marketing Management* 25 (1–2), 97–115.

Heeley, J. (1980) The definition of tourism in Great Britain: Does terminological confusion have to rule? *Tourist Review* 2, 11–13.

Heeley, J. (1981) Planning for tourism: An historical perspective. *Town Planning Review* 52 (1), 61–79.

Heeley, J. (1982) Whither the study of tourism in Britain? *Tourism Management* 3 (2), 120–121.

Heeley, J. (1987) The problematics of urban resort development. *Journal of the Scottish Association of Geography Teachers* 16, 45–50.

Heeley, J. (1988) Planning for tourism: What should be the role of the local authorities? Paper delivered at the *Planning for Tourism and Leisure Conference*, University of Ulster, May 1986 (pp. 7–17).

Heeley, J. (2001) Public-private partnerships in tourism. In A. Lockwood and S. Medlik (eds) *Tourism and Hospitality in the 21st Century* (pp. 273–283). Oxford: Butterworth-Heinemann.

Heeley, J. (2011) *Inside City Tourism: A European Perspective*. Bristol: Channel View Publications.

Heeley, J. (2012a) *BVCB Business Plan 2012–2013: Consultative Document*. Belfast: Belfast Visitor and Convention Bureau.

Heeley, J. (2012b) *Membership Strategic Development: Report to BVCB by Best Destination Marketing*. Belfast: Belfast Visitor and Convention Bureau.

Heeley, J. (2012c) *Strategic Review of BVCB Visitor Servicing: An Independent Report by Best Destination Marketing*. Belfast: Belfast Visitor and Convention Bureau.

Heintschel, K. (2011) Vienna: destination branding and communication. PowerPoint presentation. *European Cities Marketing Networking Meeting*, Bilbao, November.

Hope, C.A. and Klemm, M.S. (2001) Tourism in difficult areas revisited: The case of Bradford. *Tourism Management* 22 (6), 629–635.

IACVB (2005) *Fundamentals of Destination Management and Marketing*. Washington, DC: International Association of Convention and Visitor Bureaux.

Innsbruck Tourism (2013) Official guest magazine, Innsbruck Tourism. *Hallo Innsbruck*, Spring.

Jakobsen, S. (2012) Email communication, Director of Conventions, Wonderful Copenhagen Convention Bureau, 27 November.

James, D. (2013) Interview with the Chief Executive, Visit Peak District and Derbyshire, 20 August.

Judd, D.R. (1995) Promoting tourism in US cities. *Tourism Management* 16 (3), 175–187.

Kalberg, S. (1994) *Max Weber's Comparative Historical Sociology*. Cambridge: Polity Press.

Kant, A. (2009) *Branding India: An Incredible Story*. London: Collins Business.

Kavaratzis, M. and Ashworth, G.J. (2005) City branding: An effective assertion of identity or a transitory marketing trick? *Tijdschrift voor Economische en Sociale Geografie* 96 (5), 506–514.

Klein, B. (2013) Interview with the Director of Brand Communications and International Advertising, Vienna Tourist Board, 23 April.

Kolb, B.M. (2006) *Tourism Marketing for Cities and Towns: Using Branding and Events to Attract Tourists*. Oxford: Butterworth-Heinemann.

Kotler, P. (1997) *Marketing Management*. Upper Saddle River, NJ: Prentice-Hall.

Kotler, P., Rein, I.J. and Haider, D. (1993) *Marketing Places: Attracting Investment, Industry, and Tourism to Cities, States and Nations*. New York: Free Press.

Kraft, F. (2013) *Interview with the Director, Innsbruck Tourism*, 25 April.

Kuhn, T.S. (1962) *The Structure of Scientific Revolutions* (1st edn). London: University of Chicago Press.

Kuhn, T.S. (1970) *The Structure of Scientific Revolutions*. London: University of Chicago Press.

Lane, M. (2007) *The Visitor Journey*: The new road to success. *International Journal of Contemporary Hospitality Management* 19, 3.

Law, C.M. (1992) Urban tourism and its contribution to economic regeneration. *Urban Studies* 29 (3–4), 599–618.

Law, C.M. (2002) *Urban Tourism: The Visitor Economy and the Growth of Large Cities*. London: Continuum.

Laws, E. (1995) *Tourist Destination Management: Issues, Analysis and Policies*. London: Routledge.

Lickorish, L.J. and Jenkins, C.L. (1997) *An Introduction to Tourism*. Oxford: Butterworth-Heinemann.

Maitland, R. and Ritchie, B.W. (2009) *City Tourism: National Capital Perspectives*. Wallingford: CABI.

Marketing Cheshire (2012) *Destination Management Plan 2013–2018*. Chester: Marketing Cheshire.

Marketing Cheshire (2013) Chester ad Brief. Powerpoint presentation (supplied to the author as an email attachment).

Marketing Edinburgh Project Board (2010) *Marketing Edinburgh: Business Case*. Edinburgh: Marketing Edinburgh Project Board.

McKenna, K. (2013) A slogan for Glasgow? I have a few choice words. *The Observer*, 29 June.

McLuhan, M. (1964) *Understanding Media – The Extension of Man*. London: Routledge and Kegan Paul.

McMullan, A. (2013) Backin' Belfast Campaign. PowerPoint presentation, 11 February (supplied to the author as an email attachment).

McMullen, K. (2014) Interview with the Head of Visit York, 21 January.

Melbourne Convention Bureau (2013) *2012/13 Annual Report*. Melbourne: Melbourne Convention Bureau.

Merton, R.K. (1949) *Social Theory and Social Structure*. New York: Free Press.

Michel, K. (2014a) Marketing Cheshire. Presentation. *Destination Marketing Symposium*, Sheffield Hallam University, 5 February.

Michel, K. (2014b) Interview with the Chief Executive Officer, Marketing Cheshire, 14 February.

Middleton, V.T.C. (1989) Tourist product. In S. Witt and L. Moutinho (eds) *Tourism Marketing and Management Handbook* (pp. 573–576). London: Prentice Hall.

Morgan, N., Pritchard, A. and Pride, R. (2008) *Destination Branding: Creating the Unique Destination Proposition*. Oxford: Butterworth-Heinemann.

Morrison, A.M. (2013) *Marketing and Managing Tourism Destinations*. London: Routledge.

MPI (2013) *The Economic Impact of the UK Meetings and Event Industry*. London: Meeting Professionals International Foundation.

Mutschlechner, C. (2013) Interview with the Director of the Vienna Convention Bureau, Vienna Tourist Board, 23 April.

Mutschlechner, C. (2014) Vienna Convention Bureau. PowerPoint presentation. *Poland Meetings Destination Symposium*, National Stadium, Warsaw, 17 March.

Nottingham Evening Post (2003) On the up! Think big! New chief's pledge to transform Nottingham's tourism into £600 million industry. *Nottingham Evening Post*, 11 October.

Nymen, C. (2013) Interview with the Acting CEO, Gothenburg & Co, 15 October.

Ogilvy, D. (1973) *British Travel News*, No. 43, 1973, p. 13.

Omberg, K. (2012) Attachment to email communication, Administrative Consultant, Visit Oslo, 29 November.

Page, S. (1995) *Urban Tourism*. London: Routledge.

Paskaleva-Shapira, K.A. (2007) New paradigms in city tourism management: Redefining tourism promotion. *Journal of Travel Research* 46 (1), 108–114.

Pearce, P.L. (2005) *Tourist Behaviour: Themes and Conceptual Schemes*. Clevedon: Channel View Publications.

Pearlman, M. (1989) Appraising tourism potential. In S. Witt and L. Moutinho (eds) *Tourism Marketing and Management Handbook* (pp. 9–14). London: Prentice Hall.

Penz, M. (2013) Interview with the Head of Strategic Destination Development, Vienna Tourist Board, 23 April.

Peters, M. (2014) Interview with the Chief Executive, Leicester Shire Promotions, 24 February.

Pike, S. (2008) *Destination Marketing: An Integrated Marketing Communications Approach*. Oxford: Butterworth-Heinemann.

Pike, S. (2013) A review of 'Destination Marketing and Management – Theories and Applications'. *Tourism Management* 34, 247–248.

Pike, S. and Page, S.J. (2014) Destination marketing organisations and destination marketing: A narrative analysis of the literature. *Tourism Management* 41, 202–227.

Pike, S. and Schultz, D.E. (2009) Tourism research – how is it relevant? *Tourism Recreation Research* 34 (3), 326–328.

Pimlott, J.A.R. (1947) *The Englishman's Holiday: A Social History*. London: Faber & Faber.

Pirnar, I. (2012) A review of 'Inside City Tourism: A European Perspective'. *Tourism Planning and Development* 2 (2), 211–212.

Plaza, B. (2006) The return on investment of the Guggenheim Museum Bilbao. *International Journal of Urban and Regional Research* 30 (2), 452–467.

Rice, T. (2013) Interview with the Head of Communications and Marketing, Glasgow City Marketing Bureau, 9 January.

Richards, G. and Palmer, R. (2010) *Eventful Cities: Cultural Management and Urban Revitalisation*. Oxford: Butterworth-Heinemann.

Ritchie, J.R.B. and Crouch, G.I. (2003) *The Competitive Destination: A Sustainable Tourism Perspective*. Wallingford: CABI.

Robertson, J. (2013) *The Professor of Truth*. Harmondsworth: Penguin.

Robles, A.A. (2013) The successful reconversion of an industrialised metropolis and the challenges of its current urban projects. Presentation. *Place Marketing Forum*, Aix-en-Provence, 14–15 October.

Rodgers, T. (2013) *Conferences and Conventions: A Global Industry*. Oxford: Butterworth-Heinemann.

Rodven, A.W. (2012) Models for structuring city convention bureaux and other marketing organisations. Presentation. *51st ICCA Congress*, Puerto Rico, 23 October.

Santamaria, G.C. (ed.) (2013) *Urban Megaprojects: A Worldwide View*. Bingley: Emerald Group Publishing.

Schlink, B. (1997) *The Reader*. London, Phoenix, 1998.

Selby, M. (2004) *Understanding Urban Tourism*. London: I.B. Taurus.

Shaw, G., Williams, A. and Bailey, A. (2011) Aspects of service-dominant logic and its implications for tourism management: Examples from the hotel industry. *Tourism Management* 32 (2), 207–214.

Simpson, P. (2014) Marketing Manchester. Presentation. *Destination Marketing Symposium*, Sheffield Hallam University, 5 February.

Steden, P. and Holtgrewe, S. (2013) Berlin Partner GmbH and business development in the Capital region. Presentation. *UBC Business Commission*, 22 May.

Stockholm Business Region (2013) *Annual Report 2012*. Stockholm: Stockholm Business Region.

Swarbrooke, J. (2000) Tourism, economic development and urban regeneration: A critical evaluation. In M. Robinson, R. Sharpely, N. Evans, P. Long and J. Swarbrooke (eds) *Developments in Urban and Rural Tourism* (pp. 269–285). Sunderland: Centre for Travel and Tourism.

Sweeney, N. (1988) International tourism marketing. Paper delivered at the *Planning for Tourism and Leisure Conference*, University of Ulster, May 1986 (pp. 37–49).

Tames, R. and Tames, S. (2009) *A Traveller's History of Bath*. Moreton-in-March: Chastleton Travel.

Taylor, S. (2011) The Glasgow model. PowerPoint presentation. *European Cities Marketing Networking Meeting*, Bilbao, November.

Taylor, S. (2013) Interview with the Chief Executive, Glasgow City Marketing Bureau, 9 January.

The Times (2006) *Quotations*. London: Times Books.

Thomas, R. (2011) Academics as policy-makers: (Not)researching tourism and events policy formation from the inside. *Current Issues in Tourism* 14 (6), 493–506.

Tillotson, P. (2014) Interview with the Tourism Manager, Bradford Metropolitan District Council, 11 March.

Turkell, B. (2012) Untitled address to North American visitor and convention bureaux. *Annual Convention of the Destination Marketing International Association*, Seattle, 16–18 July.

Urry, J. (1990) *The Tourist Gaze*. London: Sage.

Uysal, U.E. (2013) Urban tourism promotion: What makes the difference? *Current Research Journal of Social Sciences* 5 (1), 17–27.

Vargo, S.L. and Lusch, R.F. (2004) Evolving to a new dominant logic for marketing. *Journal of Marketing* 68 (1), 1–18.

VTB (2006) *50 Years and the Future, 1955–2005*. Vienna: Vienna Tourist Board.

VTB (2009) *Tourism Concept 2015 – Executive Summary*. Vienna: Vienna Tourist Board.

VTB (2012) Congress success: ESTRO 2014 and EMTC 2016 to be held in Vienna. Press release, 21 August. Vienna: Vienna Tourist Board.

VTB (2013a) *The Vienna Tourist Board: PR and Marketing for Vienna's Tourist Industry*. Vienna: Vienna Tourist Board.

VTB (2013b) Gastroenterology Congress: 2014–2019 in Vienna and Barcelona. Press release, 31 October. Vienna: Vienna Tourist Board.

VTB (2013c) *Vienna Meetings Industry Report 2012*. Vienna: Vienna Tourist Board.

VTB (2013d) *2010–2012 Review*. Vienna: Vienna Tourist Board.

VTB (2013e) *1,000 Reasons for Vienna: International Media Coverage of Vienna in 2012*. Vienna: Vienna Tourist Board.

VTB (2013f) *European Home Run: Six Thoughts for Contemporary Souvenirs from Vienna*. Vienna: Vienna Tourist Board.

Visit York (2012) *Annual Report and Financial Statement 2011/12*. York: Visit York.

Visit York (2013) Company profile. See www.visityork.org/members/about/company-profile.aspx (accessed September 2013).

Visit York (2014) *York Visitor Survey 2012–13: Executive Summary*. York: Visit York.

Walters, P. (2013) *The Story of Coventry*. Stroud: History Press.

Walton, J.K. (1983) *The English Seaside Resort: A Social History*. Leicester: Leicester University Press.

Wang, Y. (2008) Collaborative destination marketing: Roles and strategies of convention and visitors bureaux. *Journal of Vacation Marketing* 14 (3), 191–209.

Weiss, B. (2009) The Vienna Tourist Board. PowerPoint presentation. *1st Win with the Lion Tourism Conference,* Lviv, Ukraine, October.

Wilkinson, M. (2014) Interview with the former chief executive of DMOs covering Hull, Scarborough and Blackpool, 6 March.

Williams, J. (2012) *Stoner*. London: Vintage Books.

Witt, S. and Moutinho, L. (eds) (1989) *Tourism Marketing and Management Handbook*. London: Prentice Hall.

WTO/ETC (2009) *Handbook on Tourism Destination Branding*. Madrid: World Tourism Organisation and European Travel Commission.

Wright Mills, C. (1959) *The Sociological Imagination*. Oxford: Oxford University Press.

Yates, N. (1988) Selling the seaside. *History Today* 38 (8), 20–27.

Young, G. (1973) *Tourism: Blessing or Blight?* Harmondsworth: Penguin.

Index